Professional Results

Crystal Reports®

George Peck,
The ABLAZE Group

McGraw-Hill Osborne

New York Chicago San Francisco Lisbon
London Madrid Mexico City Milan New Delhi
San Juan Seoul Singapore Sydney Toronto

The McGraw·Hill Companies

McGraw-Hill/Osborne
2100 Powell Street, Floor 10
Emeryville, California 94608
U.S.A.

To arrange bulk purchase discounts for sales promotions, premiums, or fund-raisers, please contact **McGraw-Hill**/Osborne at the above address. For information on translations or book distributors outside the U.S.A., please see the International Contact Information page immediately following the index of this book.

Crystal Reports® Professional Results

1234567890 CUS CUS 019876543

ISBN 0-07-222951-9

Publisher:	Brandon A. Nordin
Vice President &	
Associate Publisher	Scott Rogers
Acquisitions Editor:	Nancy Maragioglio
Project Editor:	Carolyn Welch
Acquisitions Coordinator:	Athena Honore
Technical Editor:	Julia Hennelly
Copy Editor:	Bob Campbell
Proofreader:	Claire Splan
Indexer:	Claire Splan
Computer Designer:	George T. Charbak
Illustrators:	Kathleen Fay Edwards, Lyssa Wald
Series Design:	Mickey Galicia
Cover Series Design:	Jeff Weeks

This book was composed with Corel VENTURA™ Publisher.

For Denise
My Partner in Business and Life

About the Author

After more than 10 years as an internal consultant and trainer in a large corporation, George founded his own consulting and training firm, The Ablaze Group, in 1994 (www.AblazeGroup.com). He has trained, consulted, and developed custom software for large and small organizations throughout the United States, Canada, the United Kingdom, and Puerto Rico.

George works as both a trainer and consultant exclusively with Crystal Reports, Crystal Enterprise, and Seagate Info. He serves on the Executive Committee of the Crystal Decisions User Group of North America, and has authored four other titles in the *Crystal Reports: The Complete Reference* series, best-sellers also published by McGraw-Hill/Osborne.

Prior to his computer career, George was a broadcaster. His voice may still be heard in various national radio and TV commercial and promotional campaigns.

Contents

Acknowledgments

Let me begin by thanking my colleagues and friends Jen Boyle, Julia Hennelly, Lauren O'Malley, and Brian Norris. You provide me with support, friendship, and some good tips! Capable editors Bob Campbell and Julia Hennelly deserve recognition for keeping the sentences together and making sure things are technically accurate.

Special thanks go to folks from McGraw Hill/Osborne. In particular, Nancy Maragioglio (Nancy, I'm glad we mostly communicated via e-mail—I didn't have to perfect pronouncing your name!), Carolyn Welch, and Wendy Rinaldi have been so helpful in bringing this project to completion.

And Dad, you continue to be an inspiration for me. Thanks so much.

Contribute to the Next Edition!

Do you know a shortcut to make report design easier? Have you found a workaround to a common problem? Do you know an easier way to accomplish something already in this book?

Share it with us. Your contributions will make the next edition of *Crystal Reports Professional Results* possible. If we use your submission, you'll get printed credit, as well as a free copy of the next edition!

Submit your ideas online at www.CrystalBook.com.

Introduction

Over the past few years, I've found myself presenting Crystal Reports breakout sessions and seminars to user groups over much of the United States. Inevitably, these revolved around a "Tips 'n Tricks" theme, with me rattling off different ways of accomplishing things in Crystal Reports.

I was often a little worried that I'd be showing the group something they already knew and that I'd be rewarded with lots of heads on hands and bored looks. On the contrary, most of the time I was rewarded with lots of frantic note taking and reactions like "Wow, I didn't know it could do this!" or "I always wanted to know if there was an easier way to do that."

As a result, I started thinking about a book that would be a radical departure from my "textual" (some might say verbose) *Crystal Reports: The Complete Reference* series. Instead, this new book would be concise and to the point with no more than one or two pages devoted to each "tip or trick." Furthermore, I'd invite readers to submit their own techniques for future editions. I decided to pitch it to Wendy Rinaldi, my long-time friend at McGraw-Hill/Osborne.

Coincidently, Wendy called me before I could call her, saying "I've got some vague thoughts on a project you might want to think about." I replied, "Great, I actually have an idea to run by you, too." She said in a reserved tone not typical for Wendy, "OK… but you need to know that we're a little picky these days about new titles—we just aren't being as adventurous as we might have been in the past."

I began talking about my idea for the new book anyway, describing it as a vast departure from the 800-plus page "door stops" that I'd developed in the past. After the initial description, Wendy was courteous, but not bowled over by any stretch of the imagination. I continued. This new book would offer concise, quick step-by-step material that would be very specific in nature. The techniques would range from simpler things that applied to beginning report designers, as well as more advanced techniques that someone using the tool for years would benefit from. All the examples in the book would be downloadable from a web site. People would be encouraged to submit their own experiences for future editions.

As I described each additional idea I had about the book, Wendy became more and more animated. By the time I was finished, she was her old self again, reminding me more of the talent agent I'd had in Hollywood in an earlier part of my life, than an editorial director at a computer book publishing house.

She agreed to accept the book. I then casually asked her, "What other project did you want to chat with me about?" After a slight pause came a simple "Never mind."

One of the early tasks was deciding on a title for the book. Because this book was a new entry in the Osborne line-up, there wasn't a simple "Complete Reference" or other similar series to plug into. Trite terms like "tips," "tricks," "techniques," "how-to's," "shortcuts," and the like were thrown around. Then the word "professional" came up. I'd always hated that word when I was in the corporate world—it seemed to have no meaning. Well, you now know which word won out!

So, here is the end result. You'll find concise, tips, tricks, techniques, how-to's— whatever you want to call them—organized by functional area. You'll find ways to improve the speed of your reports. You'll learn how to use formatting techniques and features you probably didn't know existed. You'll see how to make charts and graphs with all kinds of new visual effects. You'll get examples of how to prompt report viewers for values and then use the results throughout all aspects of your reports. You'll find great uses for new formula techniques you probably hadn't thought of before. You'll learn some new routines that make cross-tabs and subreports more useful. And, unlike other books out there (including mine), you'll find all this in a simple step-by-step fashion. You can download almost every sample report illustrated in the book from CrystalBook.com or Osborne.com.

Unless you've had very little time with Crystal Reports, you'll probably already know some of the material here. However, even if you've worked with the tool every day for years and years, I'll bet you don't know all the material here. If my user group presentations are any indication, you'll get lots of really good "Wow, I didn't know that" value out of this title. Also, the often-requested Formula Language Reference has finally appeared (see the appendix in the back of the book). Keep it handy for reference when you're in the middle of creating a formula and can't quite remember the proper syntax for a function or operator, or if you want fresh thoughts on how a function can be used or need some good formula examples.

And, since the "user group" theme inspired this book, I'm continuing the concept toward the next edition. Unlike a version-specific book that can always be revised when "version x" ships, this book will only grow with more ideas. I'd like them to come from you, the "user." If you know a neat way to accomplish something with Crystal Reports, if you've found a hidden feature that may help others, or if you know of a better way to accomplish something that's already here, please let me know. If I use your tip in the next edition, you'll get printed credit and a free copy of the book!

I hope you find this new book helpful. It's a culmination of my years and years of experience with this powerful business tool. Hopefully, you'll be able to use the power in this book to make your reports look and work better.

George Peck, June 2003
author@CrystalBook.com
www.CrystalBook.com

Chapter 1

Report Formatting and Appearance

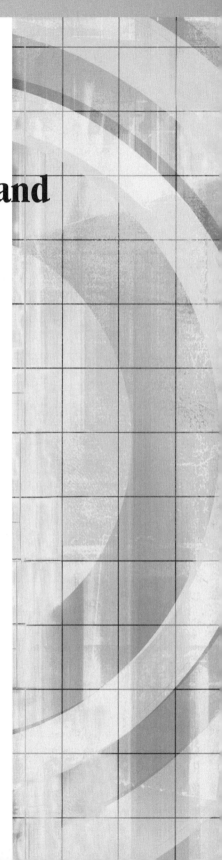

Crystal Reports, being a Windows-based report writer, provides all the tools you need for creating presentation-quality reports. While you may think you need to use a word processor or a desktop publishing tool to get real presentation quality output, you can often get exactly what you need with Crystal Reports directly. This chapter shows you how to make innovative use of some of Crystal Reports' formatting options.

Create a Watermark

A *watermark* is a graphical or textual element that is placed behind the rest of your report. Examples of useful watermarks are your company logo, the word "Draft," or other items that you may want to appear right behind the rest of the elements of your report.

AZ			
Bicycle Races	Mr. Seth Smithers	Tempe	$659.70
Biking and Hiking	Mr. Ukariah Jonstone	Phoenix	$65.70
CA			
Changing Gears	Mr. David Baker	Irvine	$26,705.65
Rowdy Rims Company	Dr. Anthony Shoemaker	Newbury Park	$30,131.46
Off the Mountaing Biking	Ms. Laurie Lee-Johnson	Irvine	$25,000.00
Sporting Wheels Inc.	Mr. Patrick Reyess	San Diego	$85,642.56
Tyred Out	Mr. Donald Edwards	Santa Ana	$18,126.33
Bike Shop from Mars	Mr. John MacCloud	Newbury Park	$25,873.25
CO			
Fred's Bikes	Mr. Fred Danforth	Denver	$7,874.25
CT			
Phil's Bikes	Mr. Phil Franklyn	Concord	$27.00
DC			
Colin's Bikes	Mr. Colin White	Washington	$40.50
DE			
Barry's Bikes	Mr. Barry Wilcox	Dover	$33.90
FL			
Wheels and Stuff	Mr. Dan Simpson	Clearwater	$25,556.11
Extreme Cycling	Mr. Zach Fabro	Clearwater	$69,819.10
GA			
Tony's Better Bikes	Mr. Anthony Weatherhead	Atlanta	$2,735.25

 *Watermark.rpt from CrystalBook.com*

1. Open the report you wish to add the watermark to. Ensure that the Design tab is selected.

2. Position your mouse over the gray Page Header section name. Right-click.

3. Choose Insert Section Below from the pop-up menu. This will insert a second page header section (you'll now see Page Header a and Page Header b).

4. Insert the graphic or text you want to appear behind the rest of the report into Page Header b (it's helpful if the graphic has been lightened with a graphic editing program, or if the text is formatted with a light shade of font color).

5. If you want the watermark to appear more toward the vertical center of the page, make Page Header b taller and move the graphic or text farther down in the section.

6. If you want to repeat the watermark more than once on a page, insert it into Page Header b several times, or copy and paste the original item several times in Page Header b.

7. Position your mouse over the gray Page Header b section name. Right-click.

8. Choose Format Section from the pop-up menu in Crystal Reports 8.5, or Section Expert from the pop-up menu in Crystal Reports 9. This will display the Section Expert.

9. Choose the Underlay Following Sections check box for Page Header b in the Section Expert. Click OK to close the Section Expert.

10. If you wish to underlay items in the existing Page Header a section (field titles, the report title, and so forth), swap Page Header b and Page Header a by holding your mouse button down on either gray Page Header section name. When the mouse cursor changes to the hand icon, drag and drop the page header on top of the other page header. The sections will swap.

Change Graphics According to a Condition

Crystal Reports features the capability to format report objects (database fields, formulas, text objects, and so forth) *conditionally,* depending on the contents of a field, formula, or other condition. However, you may wish to actually insert several different graphic or picture files on your report and display them only when a certain condition occurs.

Contact	City	Last Year's Sales	
Mr. Jerry Esler	Tualatin	$41,954.72	
Mr. Will Castillo	Tualatin	$68,000.00	
Miss Elizabeth Kawa	Philadelphia	$301,568.22	
Mr. Bill Carter	Conshohocken	$23,789.25	
Mr. Joe Lee	Philadelphia	$25,162.05	

DOWNLOAD *Conditional Graphics.rpt from CrystalBook.com*

1. Open or create the report that you wish to add multiple conditional graphics to.

2. Add as many graphics to the report as are required. For example, if you want to display "thumbs up" and "thumbs down" graphics, add both graphic files to the report.

3. Place the graphics side by side, so that you may select each graphic individually.

4. Select the first graphic by clicking on it. Right-click. From the pop-up menu, select Format Graphic. The Format Editor will appear.

5. Select the Common tab. Next to the Suppress check box, click the Conditional Formula button. The Format Formula Editor will appear.

6. Add a Boolean formula to conditionally suppress the graphic. For example, to suppress the graphic if Last Year's Sales is less than $50,000, enter a formula similar to this:

```
{Customer.Last Year's Sales} < 50000
```

7. Click the Save button to close the Format Formula Editor. Click OK to close the Format Editor.

8. Repeat steps 4–7 for the remaining graphics, using "mutually exclusive" condition formulas, so that only one graphic at a time will display. For example, to suppress another graphic if Last Year's Sales is greater than or equal to $50,000, enter a formula similar to this:

```
{Customer.Last Year's Sales} >= 50000
```

9. Select each graphic and place it on top of the others, so that all graphics are placed in the same position. Because of the "mutually exclusive" conditional formatting, only one will appear at a time when the report is displayed.

Use WingDings and Other Symbol Fonts

By default, Crystal Reports uses a particular font face and size for report objects. While you can change the default font choices in the File | Options dialog box, you can also choose font face and size for individual report objects. You are not limited to standard letter-oriented fonts—you may choose symbol fonts such as Wingdings and Webdings as easily as you can choose letter-oriented fonts.

☺ $50,000 or greater in sales

☹ less than $50,000 in sales

Contact	City	Last Year's Sales	
Mr. Jerry Esler	Tualatin	$41,954.72	☹
Mr. Will Castillo	Tualatin	$68,000.00	☺
Miss Elizabeth Kawa	Philadelphia	$301,568.22	☺
Mr. Bill Carter	Conshohocken	$23,789.25	☹
Mr. Joe Lee	Philadelphia	$25,162.05	☹

DOWNLOAD *Symbol Fonts.rpt from CrystalBook.com*

1. Add a database field, text object, formula, or other textual element that you wish to display as a symbol to the report.

2. Ensure that the object returns a character value that will "map" to the proper symbol. For example, to display a smile or frown with the Wingdings font, you might create a formula similar to this:

```
If {Customer.Last Year's Sales} < 50000 Then
     "L"
Else
     "J"
```

3. Select the object you wish to format with a symbol font.

4. Either using the Formatting toolbar or the Format Editor, select the symbol font (such as Wingdings or Webdings) that you'd like to use.

TIP *To determine what the proper character value is for the desired symbol, make use of the Windows Character Map. You may choose the symbol font and character you'd like to use and copy the character to the clipboard. Then, when you paste the character into a Crystal Reports formula or text object, the proper symbol will appear when you format the object with the symbol font. The Character Map is available from the System Tools submenu of the Accessories menu from the Start button Programs list.*

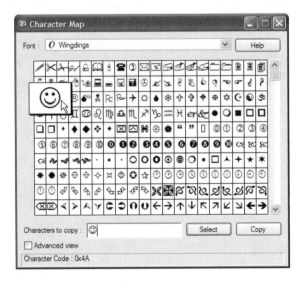

Print Bar Codes

Crystal Reports opens up a wealth of possibilities for inventory, sales, and manufacturing reporting. A common requirement is printing bar codes for labeling, mailing, manufacturing, tracking, or a multitude of similar applications.

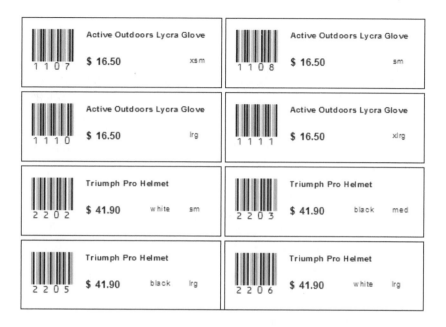

DOWNLOAD *Bar Code.rpt from CrystalBook.com*

1. Add the object (database field, formula, and so forth) that you wish to display as a bar code to your report.

2. If necessary, create a formula using the StringToCode39, StringToPostnet, NumberToCode39 or NumberToPostnet functions from the Additional Functions category of the Formula Editor. These functions are provided by the U2LBAR.DLL User Function Library (available for download from support.crystaldecisions.com).

3. Using the Formatting toolbar or the Format Editor, format the object using the proper bar code font face and size.

NOTE   *You'll need to obtain and install your own bar code fonts. Crystal Reports doesn't include any bar code fonts with the product.*

Eliminate Blank Address Lines

Crystal Reports is often used for form letters, envelopes, or other mailing applications. In many cases, there is a need to eliminate blank address or "suite number" lines in an address for certain addresses. This can be accomplished in two ways: by embedding multiple address lines in a *text object,* or by using *multiple report sections.*

The text object method, while simpler in approach, will not automatically adjust vertical placement of objects that follow on the report. For example, if the address contains four lines in one form letter and three lines in the next, the remainder of the form letter below the text object will not move up or down automatically depending on the vertical size of the text object. For situations that require automatic vertical adjustment of text that follows the address, you'll need to use multiple report sections.

March 6, 2003

Rowdy Rims Company
Dr. Anthony Shoemaker, Sales Agent
4861 Second Road
Newbury Park, CA 91341

Dear Dr. Shoemaker,

Thanks for purchasing $30,131.46 in merchandise last year.
- -
March 6, 2003

Rowdy Rims Company
Dr. Anthony Shoemaker, Sales Agent
4861 Second Road
Newbury Park, CA 91341

Dear Dr. Shoemaker,

Thanks for purchasing $30,131.46 in merchandise last year.

 *No Blank Address Lines.rpt from CrystalBook.com*

Text Object

To eliminate blank lines using a text object, follow these steps:

1. Add a text object to your report. You will combine several database fields inside this text object.

2. Display the Field Explorer. Drag desired fields into the text object, separating database fields with necessary characters, such as commas and spaces. In particular, drag the first address line (that might contain the street number) into the text object. Press ENTER to add a carriage return. Then, drag the

second address line that will not always contain data (this might contain the suite number) into the text object. Press ENTER again. Then, drag in City, State, and Zip Code.

3. End editing by clicking anywhere outside the text object.

4. Select the text object you just created. Right-click and choose Format Text from the pop-up menu. The Format Editor will appear.

5. On the Common tab, click the Suppress Embedded Field Blank Lines option. This will suppress any lines in the text object that contain no data.

Multiple Report Sections

To eliminate blank lines using multiple report sections, follow these steps:

1. Add fields up to and including the first address line into an existing report section.

2. Reduce the vertical size of the existing section so that its bottom border is even with the bottom of the first address line. If you choose, you may right-click the existing gray section name and choose Fit Section from the pop-up menu.

3. Insert an additional section (such as Details b) below the existing section. Right-click the gray section name of the existing section. From the pop-up menu, choose Insert Section Below. An additional section (such as Details b) will appear.

4. Place the second address line that will not always contain data (this might contain the suite number) into the new section. Reduce the vertical size of the second section so that its bottom border is even with the second address line.

5. Insert a third section using the same right-click, Insert Section Below sequence. A third section (such as Details c) will appear.

6. Add the remainder of the fields, such as City, State, and Zip Code into the third section.

7. Right-click the gray section name of the second section containing the second address field. Choose Format Section from the pop-up menu in Crystal Reports 8.5 or Section Expert from the pop-up menu in Crystal Reports 9. The Section Expert will appear.

Eliminate Blank Address Lines

8. Choose the Suppress Blank Section option for the section containing the second address line. Click OK to close the Section Expert.

9. When the report displays, the section containing the second address line will be suppressed if the address field is empty. The remainder of the material on the report will "flow up" vertically, with no extra vertical space left over.

Print Page Continuation Messages

Although Crystal Reports features the Repeat Group Header On Each Page option to display a group header at the top of each page where the group appears, there's no built-in capability to print a similar message at the bottom of the page. Also, if your report is just sorted and not grouped, the Repeat Group Header On Each Page option is not available.

By creating simple formulas, you may indicate if the field that a report is sorted or grouped on continues on the next page or is continued from the previous page. The formulas use the Next and Previous functions to determine if the database value on the next or previous record is the same as the current record.

2,819	64.84	3/14/1998 12:00:00AM	3/14/1998 12:00:00AM	Purolator
2,394	1,619.55	11/21/1997 12:00:00AM	11/25/1997 12:00:00AM	Loomis
1,010	14,872.30	12/3/1996 12:00:00AM	12/3/1996 12:00:00AM	UPS

Dag City Cycle

3,144	863.74	6/20/1997 12:00:00AM	6/21/1997 12:00:00AM	Parcel Post

Deals on Wheels

1,738	1,030.08	6/19/1997 12:00:00AM	6/28/1997 12:00:00AM	Pickup
2,099	59.70	9/14/1997 12:00:00AM	9/14/1997 12:00:00AM	Pickup
1,002	5,060.28	12/2/1996 12:00:00AM	12/2/1996 12:00:00AM	Pickup
2,841	659.70	3/21/1998 12:00:00AM	3/23/1998 12:00:00AM	Purolator
1,469	587.65	3/30/1997 12:00:00AM	4/2/1997 12:00:00AM	Pickup
1,438	3,065.55	3/20/1997 12:00:00AM	3/22/1997 12:00:00AM	Parcel Post
2,321	1,084.48	11/3/1997 12:00:00AM	11/6/1997 12:00:00AM	UPS
2,387	16.50	11/19/1997 12:00:00AM	11/19/1997 12:00:00AM	Parcel Post
2,459	43.50	12/7/1997 12:00:00AM	12/11/1997 12:00:00AM	Loomis
2,026	43.50	8/26/1997 12:00:00AM	8/28/1997 12:00:00AM	Parcel Post
2,566	40.50	1/4/1998 12:00:00AM	1/14/1998 12:00:00AM	Purolator

Deals on Wheels continues on next page

Next Page Previous Page Message.rpt from CrystalBook.com

1. Ensure that the report you wish to add a "continues on next page" or "continued from previous page" to is sorted or grouped by the desired field.

2. To display a "continues on next page" message, create a formula similar to this:

```
If {Customer.Customer Name} = Next({Customer.Customer Name}) Then
    {Customer.Customer Name} & " continues on next page"
```

3. Place the formula in the page footer of the report.

4. To display a "continued from previous page" message, create a formula similar to this:

```
If {Customer.Customer Name} = Previous({Customer.Customer Name}) Then
    {Customer.Customer Name} & " continued from previous page"
```

5. Place the formula in the page header of the report.

CAUTION *If you use these techniques with a report containing groups and group summaries, you may occasionally find a "widow" or "orphan" situation where this technique will not work properly. For example, if a group's last details section appears at the bottom of a page and the associated group footer appears at the top of the next page, the "continues on next page" message won't appear. This is because the Next function will determine that a mismatched record appears as the first record on the next page. Should this occur, you may see improved results by using the Keep Group Together option when creating the group. Or, you may develop a set of more sophisticated formulas using variables that determine if a group has changed when a new page appears.*

Shade Every Other Report Line

Although most companies have replaced mainframe "green-bar" or "blue-bar" reports with laser-printed output, there's still a benefit to shaded sections when heavy textual information is being viewed. Shading lines in alternate colors or shades makes it easier for the eye to follow the line across the page. Crystal Reports enables this technique to be easily used for reports that may be printed on paper or viewed online.

Shade Every Other Report Line

By using the Mod function (which performs *modulus arithmetic*—returning the remainder of a division operation instead of the quotient), combined with the RecordNumber function (which simply numbers each report record sequentially), you may produce creative banded reports.

Customer Listing			
Customer Name	City	Region	Country
7 Bikes For 7 Brothers	Las Vegas	NV	USA
Against The Wind Bikes	Rome	NY	USA
AIC Childrens	Hong Kong	Hong Kong	China
Alley Cat Cycles	Concord	MA	USA
Ankara Bicycle Company	Ankara	Ankara	Turkey
Arsenault et Maurier	Clermont-Ferrand	Auvergne	France
Aruba Sport	Oranjestad	St. George	Aruba
Athens Bicycle Co.	Athens	Evia Evvoia	Greece
Auvergne Bicross	Vichy	Auvergne	France
Backpedal Cycle Shop	Philadelphia	PA	USA

DOWNLOAD   *Banded Shading.rpt from CrystalBook.com*

1. Point to the gray Details section name in the Design tab, or the gray D section name in the Preview tab. Right-click.

2. Choose Format Section from the pop-up menu in Crystal Reports 8.5 or Section Expert from the pop-up menu in Crystal Reports 9. The Section Expert will appear.

3. Ensure that the Details section is selected in the Section Expert. Click the Color tab.

4. Click the Conditional Formatting button. The Format Formula Editor will appear.

5. Enter a formula similar to the following (you may change the formatting color to your desired color):

```
If RecordNumber Mod 2 = 0 Then crSilver Else crNoColor
```

6. You may alter the frequency of the banding if you desire. For example, to shade every two lines, you can modify the formula as follows:

```
If RecordNumber Mod 4 In 1 To 2 Then crSilver Else crNoColor
```

TIP   *Use of the crNoColor color constant instead of crWhite will show the alternating report sections with a certain degree of transparency. This may be helpful for certain reporting situations where you wish background information (such as a watermark) to appear behind the sections.*

Choose from Thousands of Colors

As with most Windows-oriented design tools, Crystal Reports allows very flexible choices of colors when formatting report objects and report sections. By using the Format Editor or Section Expert, you may choose from a standard set of colors, such as red, green, blue, and cyan. However, most recently acquired video and printing hardware support a much broader set of color choices. Crystal Reports allows you to choose from a much larger set of colors, such as pastels and subtle shades, as well.

DOWNLOAD   *Thousands Of Colors.rpt from CrystalBook.com*

1. Select the object you wish to format with a unique color.

2. Using the Format Editor (from pull-down or pop-up menus, or the toolbar button), choose the color property you want to set. You may choose any color property, such as a font color, background color, or border color.

3. Choose Custom from the color choice list in Crystal Reports 8.5, or More from the color choice list in Crystal Reports 9. The Windows Color dialog box will appear.

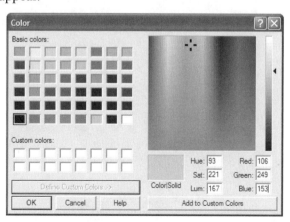

4. Choose from the expanded set of basic colors, or click the Define Custom Colors button to choose from a broad array of available colors. (The Color dialog box is already expanded to show the broad array of colors in Crystal Reports 9.)

5. If you want to use a custom color in conditional formatting, choose the color you wish to use in the Custom Color dialog box. Make note of the Red, Green, and Blue numeric values for your custom color.

6. Click OK to close the Color dialog box. The color you chose will appear in the Format Editor. Click OK to close the Format Editor.

7. If you wish to apply the custom color conditionally, use the Red, Green, and Blue values you noted earlier with the Color function in the conditional formula, as in the following example:

```
If RecordNumber Mod 4 In 1 to 2 Then Color (106,249,153) Else crNoColor
```

Chapter 2

Database Interaction

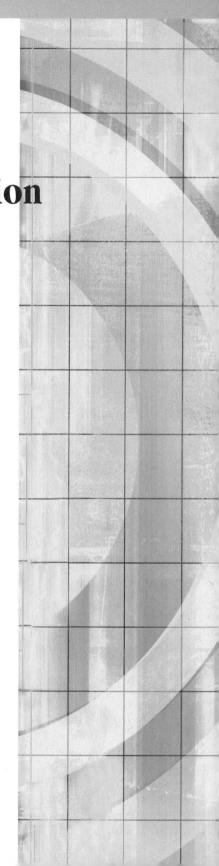

As Crystal Reports is a *database report writer,* one of the first requirements for designing a report is connecting to a database. While Crystal Reports supports a wide array of database types (including proprietary data sources, such as a hard disk drive directory or Microsoft Outlook folders), many companies and organizations need to generate reports from industry-standard databases: Microsoft SQL Server, Oracle, Informix, and others.

The way Crystal Reports interacts with these databases can sometimes cause undesirable or unexplainable behavior. By learning more about the way Crystal Reports interacts with your database, you can often gain significant report performance or create more sophisticated reports.

See What Is Sent to the Database

Most common corporate-oriented databases (SQL Server, Oracle, Informix, and many others) are based on Structured Query Language, or *SQL.* Crystal Reports actually generates a SQL (often pronounced *Sequel*) query based on the way you design your report: the tables and fields you add, the record selection criteria you specify, and sorting and grouping.

Although you don't have to be familiar with SQL in order to design a Crystal report, you may find it helpful to see what SQL query Crystal Reports sends to the database when you run the report. And, when you need to troubleshoot a slow report (see "Troubleshoot Database Performance Problems" later in this chapter), often the first place you'll turn to is the SQL query generated by Crystal Reports.

Viewing the SQL Query

Crystal Reports provides a menu option to view what is being sent to the database. Follow these steps to use this option.

1. Open or create a report based on a SQL database, ODBC data source, or OLE DB data source (you can't see a SQL query for other types of reports).

2. Choose Database | Show SQL Query from the pull-down menus. You may be asked to log on to the database or respond to parameter field prompts. Do so if prompted.

3. The SQL query will appear in its own dialog box. If you need to discuss the query with your database administrator (perhaps he or she wishes to work with the query in the database's query tool), you may copy and paste the SQL query from this dialog box to another application.

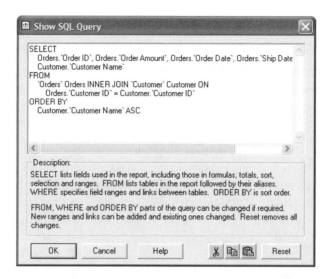

See What Is Sent to the Database

> **NOTE**
>
> *SQL syntax in the Show SQL Query dialog box may differ from that of your "native" database. This is often because you are accessing the database via ODBC or the particular database "driver" being used by Crystal Reports makes some subtle changes to the SQL between the time Crystal Reports generates it and it reaches the server. While this won't affect the way Crystal Reports works with your database, it will come into play if you try to edit the SQL query manually (as discussed later in this chapter).*

Modifying the SQL Query

If you are familiar with SQL, or your database administrator asks you to make modifications to the SQL query, you may perform some modifications to what Crystal Reports creates. Perhaps you would like to add some sort of SQL function to the WHERE clause, or use a "subselect" to run one query based on another query.

> **NOTE**
>
> *While Crystal Reports 8.5 and earlier versions allow modification of the SQL query, Crystal Reports 9 only allows the SQL query to be viewed. If you need to customize SQL sent to the database with Crystal Reports 9, create a SQL Command and base your report on it.*

1. Click inside the Show SQL Query box and edit the query as desired.

2. Remember that you cannot edit the SELECT clause, as Crystal Reports requires that this portion of the query must remain as originally created. Even if you make changes to the SELECT clause, they won't "stick" when you refresh the report—the SELECT clause will be returned to its original state.

3. As at least part of the WHERE clause is generated by the record selection you choose when designing the report, changes you make to the WHERE clause may remove your previous record selection criteria. If this happens, you'll notice that any tabs you'd set up previously in the Select Expert will be gone.

4. If your edits to the SQL query result in database errors or erratic behavior, you can return to the default Crystal-generated SQL by redisplaying the Show SQL Query dialog box and clicking the Reset button (you may need to re-add the record selection you added earlier if it was removed by previous edits to the WHERE clause).

Add More Than One Database Type to a Report

In many cases, all the data you need for your report can be found in a single database. However, there are times where it's convenient, if not absolutely necessary, to include data from more than one physical database in your report.

For example, you may want to include one table from Microsoft SQL Server and another from Microsoft Access in the same report. Or, you may have several Oracle tables in your report, but you want to add a Microsoft Excel spreadsheet as an additional lookup table (see "Link Your Database Table to an Excel Spreadsheet" later in this chapter). Crystal Reports can accomplish both of these tasks, as well as other situations where multiple database types need to reside in one report.

DOWNLOAD *Multiple Database Types.rpt from CrystalBook.com*

■ If you are creating a new report from scratch, use the Data Explorer (version 8.5 or earlier) or the Database Expert (version 9) to add any necessary tables from the first database.

■ Choose the additional database from an alternate folder in the Data Explorer or Database Expert. Add the desired table from the different database type.

■ When you click OK, the Visual Linking Expert or Links tab will appear. Drag and drop the appropriate links from the first database type to the second database type.

TIP

You may receive a message indicating that the data field types don't match. Double-check the data types for both fields—even though you receive this message, you still may be linking on the proper types (for example, a number field to another number field). This message may result because of subtle differences in database drivers or data types. Even if you see this warning message, the report may run properly.

■ When you click OK to close the Visual Linking Expert or Database Expert, you'll receive a message indicating that you are using multiple database types. You won't be able to use certain "homogenous database type" features, such as SQL Expressions.

There are several caveats you should be aware of when using multiple database types in the same report with Crystal Reports 8.5 and earlier:

■ Even though Equal Join appears when you point your mouse to the link line or display the Link Options dialog box, a left outer join is typically used. You cannot change this default join type when linking disparate database types.

■ Due to differences in database drivers, data types in different databases, and other factors, you may not always be able to correctly link tables from disparate databases. If you encounter a situation where proper linking is not possible in the Visual Linking Expert, you'll want to consider using a linked subreport to accomplish your reporting needs.

■ You are limited to using a single SQL stored procedure in a report. Once you've based a report on a stored procedure, you can't add any additional tables, other stored procedures, or views from other databases. If you need to add additional data to a report based on a stored procedure, you'll need to use subreports.

NOTE

Most of these limitations are eliminated with Crystal Reports 9's new query engine. With version 9, you can, for example, add multiple stored procedures and other tables to a single report, as well as choosing from a limited set of join and link types when linking disparate database types.

Use Indexed Fields for Faster Report Performance

Most common industry-standard databases feature a technique known as indexing. *Indexing* refers to the process that generally "presorts" data in a table on an *indexed field*. By using this presorted index, the database can evaluate queries based on an indexed field much faster. Accordingly, you may find that your reports run faster if you use one or more indexed fields in record selection or if you link to an indexed field when linking tables. In fact, when designing reports based on some PC-style databases, such as Microsoft Access, xBase, and Paradox, you are required to link to an indexed field.

1. Display the Visual Linking Expert or Links tab of the Database Expert using Database pull-down menu items or the appropriate toolbar button.

2. Look for colored arrows next to certain fields. A colored arrow indicates that the field is indexed (as a general rule, the colors of the arrows are unimportant—that a field has an arrow next to it is).

3. If a report is running slowly, make an effort to use indexed fields in record selection.

4. If a report is based on a PC-style database, such as xBase or Paradox, you'll be required to link *to* an indexed field (you don't have to link from an indexed field). If you try to link to a nonindexed field, an error message will appear in the Visual Linking Expert.

NOTE   *The requirement to link on an indexed field with a PC-style database has been eliminated in Crystal Reports 9.*

In Crystal Reports 8.5 and earlier, only PC-style databases will show colored arrows next to indexed fields. Most other database drivers, such as direct drivers for SQL databases, and ODBC databases, won't show arrows next to indexed fields. While SQL databases and ODBC-based databases have no requirement that you link to an indexed field or use an indexed field in record selection, you may enjoy performance improvements if you do. In these cases, contact your database administrator to find out what fields are indexed in the database tables you are using in your report. You may also ask the database administrator to add indexes on fields you frequently use in record selection to potentially improve report performance.

If you are using a PC-style database and can't link tables properly because there's no index on the proper field, modify the database yourself (if you know how) or contact a database designer to add an index to the necessary field. If, for some reason, this can't be done, you'll need to use a linked subreport to get data from the "unlinkable" table.

Link Your Database Table to an Excel Spreadsheet

In many cases, it's difficult, if not impossible, to add your own particular set of data to a large corporate database. However, it's often handy to be able to add your own particular set of data to a report for your individual reporting needs.

For example, you may wish to categorize customers into specific geographical areas, even though the main database doesn't contain such categorizations. While it may not be practical or possible to add a new table to the main company database to do this, it's probably fairly easy to create an Excel spreadsheet that places each customer in the desired geographic area. You can then link the spreadsheet to the main database to categorize your customers.

Customer Name	City	Region	Last Ye:
Midwest			
City Cyclists	Sterling Heights	MI	
Pathfinders	DeKalb	IL	
Bike-A-Holics Anonymous	Blacklick	OH	
Poser Cycles	Eden Prairie	MN	
Spokes 'N Wheels Ltd.	Des Moines	IA	
Trail Blazer's Place	Madison	WI	1
Clean Air Transportation Co.	Conshohocken	PA	
Hooked on Helmets	Eden Prairie	MN	
Hercules Mountain Bikes	DeKalb	IL	
Bikes and Trikes	Sterling Heights	MI	
Uni-Cycle	Blacklick	OH	
Crank Components	Champaign	IL	
Corporate Cycle	Des Moines	IA	
Blazing Saddles	Brown Deer	WI	
Pedals Inc.	Madison	WI	
Blazing Bikes	Eden Prairie	MN	
Spokes	DeKalb	IL	
Wheels Inc.	Des Moines	IA	
Cyclist's Trail Co.	Sterling Heights	MI	
Deals on Wheels	DeKalb	IL	
Insane Cycle	Conshohocken	PA	
Our Wheels Follow Us Everywhere	DeKalb	IL	
Backpedal Cycle Shop	Philadelphia	PA	
Karma Bikes	Blacklick	OH	
Rocky Roadsters	Conshohocken	PA	
Bikes, Bikes, and More Bikes	Des Moines	IA	

 *Linked To Excel.rpt from CrystalBook.com*

There are two general steps required to use an Excel spreadsheet in your report: prepare the spreadsheet, and add the spreadsheet to the report. Steps to prepare the spreadsheet are the same regardless of the version of Crystal Reports that you are using. However, steps to add the spreadsheet to your report differ depending on whether you're using Crystal Reports 8.5 or earlier, or Crystal Reports 9.

Preparing the Spreadsheet

You must perform a few steps to make your spreadsheet ready to act as a Crystal Reports table:

1. Open the Excel spreadsheet that contains the data you'd like to include in the report.

2. Ensure that the data is organized in a "table" fashion. That is, ensure that the block of data in the spreadsheet that you'll use is consistent from row to row and column to column—these will act as the fields and records for your database table.

3. Add a field "name" to the top of each column. These may already exist in the spreadsheet as normal column headings. If not, add them, as Crystal Reports will always consider the first row of the spreadsheet to contain field names.

4. Highlight the range of cells that makes up your "database table," including the top row containing field names.

5. Choose Insert | Name | Define from the Excel pull-down menus. The value of the first field name will appear by default.

6. Type the name you wish the range of cells you just highlighted to show when you add the table to Crystal Reports. Click OK.

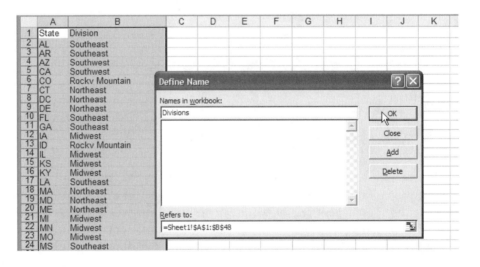

7. Save the spreadsheet.

Adding the Spreadsheet to the Report

Crystal Reports 9 adds a direct data connection to Microsoft Excel that isn't available in earlier versions of Crystal Reports—you can add and reference a spreadsheet right from the Database Expert. Crystal Reports 8.5 and earlier requires the use of an ODBC data source name to reference an Excel Spreadsheet.

Crystal Reports 9

1. Display the Database Expert by choosing Database | Database Expert or clicking the Database Expert button in the Expert Tools toolbar.

2. Click the plus sign next to Create New Connection.

3. Click the plus sign next to Access/Excel (DAO).

4. Type in the filename, or click the ellipses button to choose the filename of the Excel spreadsheet you wish to add. In the Database Type drop-down list, choose the appropriate version of Excel that you used to create the spreadsheet.

5. Click Finish. The list of "tables" (made up of the range name or names you saved in the spreadsheet) will appear below the spreadsheet name in the Available Data Sources list.

6. Choose the desired table and add it to your report with the right arrow.

7. If you need to add any additional tables, choose them from the Available Data Source list.

8. When finished choosing tables, click the Links tab to link them as you normally would.

Crystal Reports 8.5 and Earlier

1. Create an ODBC data source name for the spreadsheet you have prepared. Begin by launching the Windows Control Panel.

2. In the Windows Control Panel, double-click the Data Sources (ODBC) icon. If you are using Windows 2000 or XP, you'll need to open the Administrative Tools folder to find the Data Sources (ODBC) icon. The ODBC Data Source Administrator dialog box will appear.

3. Click the System DSN tab. A list of existing data source names will appear (the System tab will allow you to create a data source name that will be available to all user IDs that log on to your computer).

4. Click the Add button. The Create New Data Source dialog box will appear, showing all ODBC drivers that have been installed on your computer.

5. Scroll through the list of drivers until you find the Microsoft Excel Driver. Choose it and click Finish. The ODBC Microsoft Excel Setup dialog box will appear.

6. Choose a meaningful data source name and type it in the Data Source Name text box. You may type an optional comment in the Description box as well.

7. In the Version drop-down list, choose the appropriate version of Excel that you used to create the spreadsheet.

8. Click the Select Workbook button and navigate to the spreadsheet you wish to use in your report.

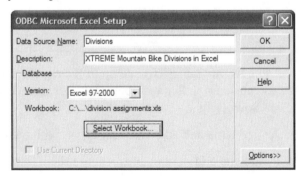

9. Click OK to add the data source name and close the ODBC Microsoft Excel Setup dialog box. Click OK to close the ODBC Data Source Administrator.

10. Open the report that you wish to add the Excel spreadsheet to.

11. Display the Data Explorer by choosing Database | Add Database To Report from the pull-down menus.

12. Click the plus sign next to the ODBC category. Find the ODBC data source name you just created.

13. Click the plus sign next to the proper ODBC data source name. The list of "tables" (made up of the range name or names you saved in the spreadsheet) will appear below the data source name.

14. Choose the desired table and click the Add button.

15. When finished choosing tables, close the Data Explorer. The Visual Linking Expert will appear.

16. Link the spreadsheet table to another table as you would a regular database table.

Change a Report from Test to Production

Oftentimes, you may need to change a report from one database to another. Perhaps you have multiple databases in your organization for different divisions. Although they are organized the same, with the same set of tables and fields, they are contained in different database files on the same server, or are on different database servers entirely. Or, you may have a test database you use to design a report initially and the report needs to be "moved to production."

1. Open the report that you wish to point to a different database.

2. Choose Database | Set Location from the pull-down menus. The Set Location dialog box will appear.

3. Choose the first table (if there is more than one) that you wish to point to the new database location. Click the Set Location button. The Data Explorer will appear.

4. Choose the appropriate category and database that you wish to connect to. Log on to the database if necessary. The list of tables in the new database will appear in the Data Explorer.

5. Choose the matching table in the new database for the table that you originally chose in the Set Location dialog box. Click the Set button. The Set Location dialog box will reappear with the new connection information for the table appearing at the bottom.

6. You may be asked if you wish to propagate changes to other tables with the same original source. Click Yes if you wish to have Crystal Reports set a new location for additional tables in the same original database.

7. If necessary, choose other tables in the Set Location dialog box and click the Set Location button to redirect them.

8. When finished redirecting all tables, click Done to close the Set Location dialog box.

> **NOTE** *The Set Location dialog box behaves differently in Crystal Reports 9 than it does in Crystal Report 8.5 and earlier. In particular, Crystal Reports 9 allows you to choose the database entry in the top and bottom portions of the dialog box, rather than individual tables. This allows a quicker way of pointing the report to an entirely new database, rather than requiring each table to be redirected.*

9. If field names differ in the new database, you'll be presented with the Map Fields dialog box.

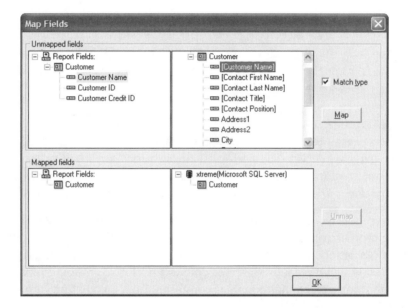

10. Click the first unmapped field in the left top of the dialog box. Choose the matching field name from the new database on the right side. Click the Map button.

11. Repeat step 10 as many times as necessary to remap all fields. Click OK when finished.

Troubleshoot Database Performance Problems

Larger corporations and organizations are moving mainframe systems to SQL database-based systems on a regular basis. As such, industry-standard databases, such as Microsoft SQL Server and Oracle, are being used to host larger and larger sets of data. It's not uncommon to find databases that contain multimillion-record tables.

With these increasingly large databases comes the potential for slower reports. Common sense dictates that the larger the amount of data that must be selected, formatted, calculated, and so on, the longer the period of time required to run the report. When reports run slowly, there are some simple steps you can take to determine where the performance bottleneck is. And, depending on where the bottleneck is, there are some steps (sometimes simple, sometimes not) that can be taken to improve performance.

Determine Where the Problem Exists

The first step in evaluating a slow report is determining where the performance problem comes from. The Crystal Reports processing model can be broken down into two very high-level steps: the *database query step* and the *report processing step.*

- ■ **The database query step**   This is the part of the overall report process when Crystal Reports sends a SQL query to the database for processing. The database server then performs various processes, such as optimizing the query, running it against its local database, and returning the resulting set of data back to Crystal Reports.

- ■ **The report processing step**   Once the set of data (known as a *result set*) begins to arrive from the database server, Crystal Reports must conduct its own set of report processes. These can include running secondary record selection that the database server couldn't perform, grouping records, performing object and report section formatting, calculating formulas and totals, and so on.

Determining which of these steps is slowing the overall report process down is fairly straightforward:

1. Refresh the report with the Report | Refresh Report Data option, or the Refresh toolbar button.

2. Watch the status bar at the bottom of the Crystal Reports screen. You'll initially see a message indicating "Accessing Database."

3. As long as the Accessing Database message appears in the status bar, Crystal Reports is waiting for a result set to be returned from the database. This is the database query step.

4. Once the database server begins to deliver the result set to Crystal Reports, the Crystal Reports status bar will change. Messages may include "Reading Records," "Calculating Summaries," "Processing Subreports," and so forth. You'll also notice record counts and percentages appearing on the right side of the status bar. This is the report processing step.

5. By seeing how long each of the two major steps takes, you can narrow down which step is causing the performance problem.

Solve the Problem

Once you've determined which of the major steps is slowing your report down, you may begin the process of solving that particular problem.

Database Performance Problem

If your report appears to be slowed down by a database performance problem (the Accessing Database message appears for an inordinate amount of time), you may need to work with your database administrator to improve the performance of the supplied SQL query.

1. Choose Database | Show SQL Query from the Crystal Reports pull-down menus. This will show the actual SQL query that's being sent to the database server by Crystal Reports.

2. Look for the WHERE clause in the SQL query. This portion of the query should closely match the record selection you've set up in your report.

3. You may wish to copy the contents of the SQL query to the Windows clipboard. You may then paste it into an e-mail message, a text editor such as Notepad, or a database query tool such as Microsoft Query Analyzer.

4. Double-check with your database administrator to see if the fields contained in the WHERE clause are indexed on the database server. You may find a substantial improvement in query speed if indexes are added for some or all of these fields.

NOTE *If you base your report on a stored procedure, the Show SQL Query dialog box won't be available. You'll need to consult with your database administrator about the performance issue with the stored procedure.*

Troubleshoot Database Performance Problems

Report Performance Problem

If your report appears to be slowed down by a report performance problem (the Accessing Database message appears only for an instant, but other status bar messages, record counts, and percentage increments take an inordinate amount of time), there are several immediate steps you can take:

1. Choose Database | Show SQL Query from the Crystal Reports pull-down menus. This will show the actual SQL query that's being sent to the database server by Crystal Reports.

2. Look for the WHERE clause in the SQL query. If you don't see a WHERE clause, or the WHERE clause contains few, if any, of the fields you included in the report's record selection, you are not making the best use of the database server—Crystal Reports itself is performing most or all of the record selection.

3. If you determine that record selection is being performed "locally" by Crystal Reports, there are several steps you can take to add fields back into the WHERE clause to have the database server perform record selection. Look in Chapter 5 of this book under "Improve Performance with the Select Expert" or "Speed Up Your Report with SQL Expressions."

4. If subreport processing is taking a long time, there are several steps you can take to improve performance:

    ■ Edit the offending subreport so that it appears in its own separate Design tab.

    ■ Preview just the subreport in its Design tab. Supply sample values to any parameter prompts if the subreport is a linked subreport.

    ■ Perform similar analysis on the subreport as described earlier in this chapter. Take steps to improve the subreport's performance.

    ■ Determine if subreports are really required for this reporting situation. In some cases, other steps (more innovative linking, using a stored procedure or view, and so forth) can be used to reduce the need for subreports.

Chapter 3

Formulas

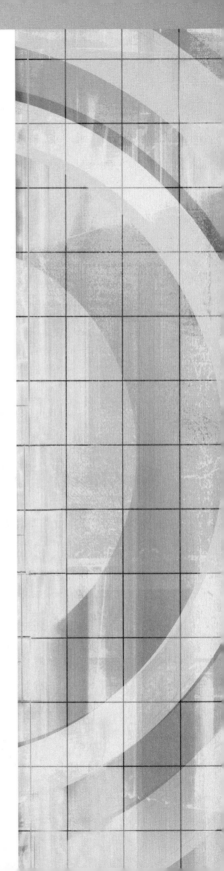

Crystal Reports, by its nature, requires some sort of database connection to be useful—it's a database report writer. Because the database itself often doesn't contain all the data you need for your reports, or contains data in an undesired form, you will quickly hit a brick wall if you limit your reports solely to the actual fields contained in the database. By use of Crystal Reports formulas, you have extremely flexible control over how you can customize reports to your particular requirements.

The Crystal Reports formula language consists of many functions, statements, and operators—its more complex portions closely resemble a programming language. And, as with many things, increased complexity comes with increased flexibility. The techniques that follow will help you overcome that complexity and make better use of Crystal Reports formulas.

NOTE   *Crystal Reports 8 and later features two formula languages or syntaxes: Crystal Syntax and Basic Syntax.* Crystal Syntax *is the original formula language of Crystal Reports.* Basic Syntax *is designed for those who are already familiar with a Basic programming language (such as Microsoft Visual Basic for Applications). As the Basic language is already a standard tool that is well documented, this chapter will present examples in Crystal Syntax.*

Simplify If-Then-Else with Select Case

More complex formulas are often based on If-Then-Else logic. In some cases, these If-Then-Else formulas can contain large amounts of *nesting*—where the result of a Then or Else clause is another If-Then-Else statement. This level of nesting can sometimes become difficult to follow if there are many conditions that need to be tested. Using Select Case logic is often easier to understand and maintain. Select Case logic is specifically designed to present a "list" of choices and results, often making a formula easier to understand and maintain.

DOWNLOAD   *Formula Examples.rpt from CrystalBook.com*

1. Choose an existing formula that contains multiple nested If-Then-Else statements. Or, when initially creating a formula, consider Select Case logic instead of multiple If-Then-Else statements.

2. Consider the following example of a nested If-Then-Else formula:

```
If {Customer.Region} In
    ["WA","ID","OR"] Then
    "Northwest"
```

```
Else If {Customer.Region} In
    ["CA","TX","NV","AZ","NM"] Then
    "Southwest"
Else If {Customer.Region} In
    ["AL","AR","LA","MS","TN","VA","WV",
     "FL","NC","SC","GA"] Then
    "Southeast"
Else If {Customer.Region} In
    ["CT","DC","DE","MD","NJ","ME","NH",
     "NY","MA","PA","RI","VT"] Then
    "Northeast"
Else If {Customer.Region} In
    ["UT","CO","WY","NE","MT"] Then
    "Rocky Mountain"
Else
    "Midwest"
```

3. Replace the If-Then-Else logic with Select Case logic, such as the following:

```
Select {Customer.Region}
    Case "WA","ID","OR":
        "Northwest"
    Case "CA","TX","NV","AZ","NM":
        "Southwest"
    Case "AL","AR","LA","MS","TN","VA",
         "WV","FL","NC","SC","GA":
        "Southeast"
    Case "CT","DC","DE","MD","NJ","ME",
         "NH","NY","MA","PA","RI","VT":
        "Northeast"
    Case "UT","CO","WY","NE","MT":
        "Rocky Mountain"
Default:
    "Midwest"
```

4. Begin the formula with the word **Select**, followed by the field or other formula that you wish to test.

5. Begin the first condition that you want to test for with the word **Case**, followed by the value or values you want to test for. You can use more than one value with each separated by a comma, or beginning and ending range values separated with the word "To".

6. Make sure to end each case statement with a colon—a syntax error will result if you don't.

7. Following the colon, place the value you want the formula to return if the case statement is true. Surround string values by quotation marks or apostrophes.

8. Add additional case statements, colons, and values for each additional condition you want to test for. Note that every value you follow the case statement with must be the same data type. You can't, for example, have some case statements return numeric values while others return strings.

9. Although not required, you can place a default statement as the last part of your Select Case logic. The default statement is a "catch-all," returning a value if all the other case statements are false.

10. Begin with the word **Default**, followed by a colon.

11. Then, place the value you want the formula to return if all the previous case statements are false. As with all the other values following the case statements, the value following the default statement must be the same data type.

Automatically Complete Parts of Your Formula

One of the features of some programming environments is automatic completion of programming statements as typing occurs. These environments attempt to anticipate what the programmer is typing and either automatically complete portions of the programming statement or present a set of choices that can be easily chosen without typing the entire programming statement character by character.

Crystal Reports 9 has added this feature to the Formula Editor. Now, when you press a special key combination when editing a formula, Crystal Reports will present you with a logical set of choices. By making a choice from a list, you can reduce the amount of manual typing or double-clicking in the Function or Operator tree.

NOTE   *This feature is available only in Crystal Reports 9 and later.*

1. Begin typing your formula.

2. At any time, you may get a list of "probable" functions or operators that you may use by pressing CTRL-SPACE.

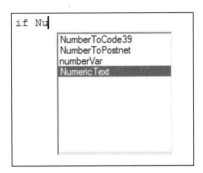

3. The list that appears is based on what you've typed already. If you press CTRL-SPACE before typing anything, or after a space in a formula statement, every possible formula keyword appears in the list.

4. If you've typed a few characters before pressing CTRL-SPACE, the list of available keywords that matches the letters you've already typed appears in the list.

5. You may choose one of the choices from the list in several ways:

   ■ Double-click the choice with your mouse.

   ■ Use cursor keys to choose the desired choice. Then, press TAB, SPACE, or ENTER.

   ■ Continue typing characters with the list visible. When you've typed enough unique characters to narrow down to one choice in the list, that keyword will be autotyped for you.

6. Continue creating your formula as you normally would—either by choosing options from the Formula Editor trees, or typing. You may press CTRL-SPACE at any time to present another list of possible keywords.

Troubleshoot a Runtime Formula Error

As you develop more sophisticated formulas, you will probably encounter a runtime formula error. A *runtime formula error* occurs when the actual data value of some portion of your formula causes an error when the report is running. This is the only time you'll encounter the error—the Formula Editor indicates that there are no errors with the formula when it is initially created.

This is frustrating, as a formula that you checked only a few seconds ago and appeared to be correct suddenly results in an error message. And, it's often challenging to determine what part of the formula or what record on the report is causing the error. If you click the Check button in the Formula Editor after the error occurs, the "No Errors Found" message will gleefully reappear.

Crystal Reports 9 introduces the call stack, which appears in the Formula Workshop when a runtime formula error occurs. The *call stack* is a list of individual formula parts (other formulas, database fields, and so forth) that make up the offending formula. The call stack shows the current values of the formula parts, allowing you to more clearly determine what portion of the formula, and what record in the report, is responsible for the error.

> **NOTE**   *This feature is available only in Crystal Reports 9 and later.*

1. A runtime formula error will occur when the report encounters a particular data value that cannot be properly evaluated in the formula. An error message will appear only when the report runs, not when you check the formula.

2. Click OK on the error message dialog box.

3. The Formula Workshop and Formula Editor will appear with the offending formula displayed inside. The call stack will appear in the left "tree" of the Formula Workshop.

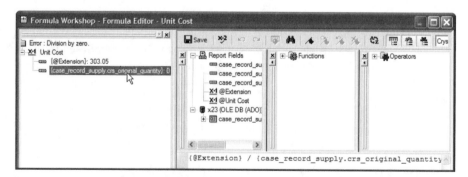

4. Examine the entries and their current values in the call stack. Oftentimes, you'll be able to determine the cause of the error by looking at these items.

5. If your formula contains a custom function that may be causing the error, click the name of the function in the call stack. It will appear in the Formula Editor, where you may examine its elements as well.

6. Make corrections to the formula as necessary, such as checking for a zero value before performing division (see "Avoid Divide by Zero Errors" later in the chapter).

7. Either click the Design tab, then the Preview tab again, or refresh the report to rerun the corrected formula.

Share Formulas with Others in Your Organization

A larger organization may employ many report designers. In many cases, specific report formulas that pertain to your organization's individual business rules or calculations need to be shared among all the report designers. This avoids "reinvention of the wheel." There are several ways to accomplish this, depending on which version of Crystal Reports you are using and on the particular reporting environment in your company.

Storing Formulas in a Common Text Document

With Crystal Reports versions prior to 9, there is no "built-in" Crystal Reports capability for sharing of formulas for formula logic. As such, a simple text document (word processing or plain text file) can be used to share and store common formulas in a shared network location.

1. Copy individual formulas that you wish to share to the clipboard. Do this by highlighting the formula in the Formula Editor and pressing CTRL-C.

2. Open or create a new word processing or text file. Paste the formula into the document by pressing CTRL-V (or by using the particular word processing or text editor Paste command).

3. Organize the shared document in a logical fashion. Perhaps categorize shared formulas by type, department, or business unit.

4. Use your own particular network security capabilities to limit who can change or update the shared file, and who can merely read it.

Once you've created a document containing shared formulas, using one of the common formulas in a report is a straightforward process:

1. Open the shared document in your word processor or text editor.

2. Locate the shared formula you wish to use in your report. Highlight it and copy it to the clipboard (CTRL-C is typically used to copy to the clipboard).

3. Navigate back to Crystal Reports. Create a new formula or open an existing formula that you wish to use the shared formula in.

4. Press CTRL-V to paste the copied formula into the Formula Editor. If necessary, make any manual changes to the copied formula.

5. Check for proper formula syntax with the Check button. Save the formula.

CAUTION   *There are several considerations when sharing formulas this way. First, ensure that the actual database tables that any shared formulas refer to have been added to your report before you use the shared formula. Otherwise, you will receive an error message when you check the formula. Second, Crystal Reports versions prior to 9 don't include any sort of automated "change control." It's possible that other users may change shared formulas in the common document. However, your reports won't automatically encompass these changed shared formulas—you'll need to copy the updated formulas back into the report manually.*

Using User Function Libraries

All recent versions of Crystal Reports feature the ability to use User Function Libraries. A *User Function Library* is an external Windows Dynamic Link Library (DLL) that contains custom programming developed in a programming language, such as Visual C++ or Visual Basic. This custom programming can be called from Crystal Reports formulas.

NOTE   *Examples of steps involved to create User Function Library DLLs can be found in Crystal Reports documentation, in various editions of* Crystal Reports: The Complete Reference *(also published by McGraw-Hill/Osborne), or on this book's companion Web site at CrystalBook.com.*

Once a User Function Library has been installed on your computer, specific functions will appear in the Additional Functions category of the Function tree in the Formula Editor. Use these functions the same way you use any other function in the formula language.

NOTE   *If you use a function from a User Function Library in a report, any other Crystal Reports designers who want to run the report will have to have the same User Function Library installed on their computer. Otherwise, any formulas that refer to any User Function Library functions will result in an error.*

1. If necessary, install any custom User Function Libraries on your computer. Depending on how they have been developed, you may simply need to run

a setup program from a network drive or CD. Start Crystal Reports only after you've installed the User Function Library.

2. Create or edit the formula that requires use of a function from the User Function Library.

3. Click the plus sign next to the Additional Functions category of the Formula Editor's function tree. A list of available functions provided by all User Function Library DLLs will appear.

4. Choose the desired function from the list by double-clicking it. Or, just type the function name directly into the formula text box.

5. Supply any required parameters or "arguments" to the function.

6. When finished with your formula, check the formula for errors and save the formula.

Crystal Reports 9 Custom Functions and the Repository

Crystal Reports 9 and later includes new features that make sharing of custom formula logic easier. Custom functions and the repository can be combined to share your particular business logic or custom calculations with other report designers in your organization.

Custom functions are similar to functions exposed by User Function Libraries, discussed earlier in the chapter. However, they don't require an external programming language—you create them in the same Crystal or Basic syntax used in other Crystal Reports formulas. The *repository* is a shared database system that allows custom functions to be shared with others in your organization. The repository includes a change control mechanism, whereby any updated custom functions are automatically used in reports whenever the reports are opened (provided that the Update Repository Objects option is explicitly selected).

Adding a Custom Function to the Repository

1. Add a custom function to your report. You may create the custom function from scratch, or use an existing report formula as a basis for the custom function. For example, you may want to use the formula example from earlier in this chapter for determining a geographic area as the basis for a shared custom function.

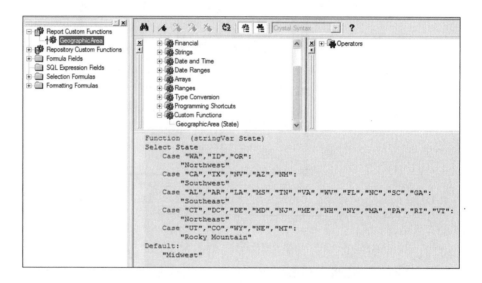

```
Function (stringVar State)
Select State
    Case "WA","ID","OR":
        "Northwest"
    Case "CA","TX","NV","AZ","NM":
        "Southwest"
    Case "AL","AR","LA","MS","TN","VA","WV","FL","NC","SC","GA":
        "Southeast"
    Case "CT","DC","DE","MD","NJ","ME","NH","NY","MA","PA","RI","VT":
        "Northeast"
    Case "UT","CO","WY","NE","MT":
        "Rocky Mountain"
Default:
    "Midwest"
```

NOTE   *Detailed instructions for creating custom functions can be found in Crystal Reports help, or in* Crystal Reports 9: The Complete Reference, *also published by McGraw-Hill/Osborne.*

2. Test the custom function thoroughly to ensure it returns the proper result.

3. Right-click the custom function name in the Formula Workshop tree. Choose Add To Repository from the pop-up menu. Or, you can click the Add To Repository button in the Formula Workshop toolbar.

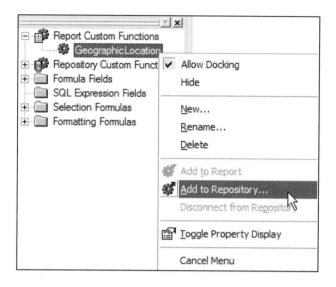

4. Confirm the repository name you wish to add the custom function to from the dialog box and click OK.

5. Alternatively, you may just drag the custom function name from the Report Custom Functions category of the Formula Workshop tree to the Repository Custom Functions category.

6. Note that a small "chain" icon will appear next to the custom function name in the Formula Workshop tree. This indicates that the custom function on your report is now attached to the repository copy.

7. Open the Repository Custom Functions category in the Formula Workshop tree. Note that your custom function is now displaying in the repository.

NOTE   *You may not have permission to add objects to the repository. Check with the person responsible for maintaining the repository to make sure.*

Using a Repository Custom Function in Your Report

1. If you create a new formula, you may use the Formula Expert to base the formula on a repository custom function. You'll choose the repository custom function you want to use from the Custom Function Supplying Logic box in the Formula Expert.

Share Formulas with Others in Your Organization

2. If you want to include more than one function in a new formula, or you wish to edit an existing formula to use a repository custom function, use the Formula Editor. You'll choose the repository custom function you want to use from the Repository Custom Functions category of the Formula Workshop tree.

3. If you are using the Formula Editor, click the plus sign next to the Repository Custom Functions category of the Formula Workshop tree. Navigate through any repository categories until you find the custom function you wish to use.

4. Right-click the desired custom function. Choose Add To Report from the pop-up menu. Or, you can click the Add To Report button in the Formula Workshop toolbar.

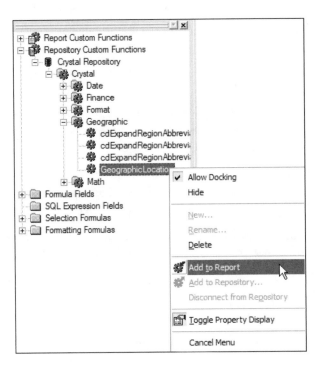

5. Alternatively, you may just drag the custom function name from the Repository Custom Functions category of the Formula Workshop tree to the Report Custom Functions category.

6. The custom function will now appear in the Custom Functions category of the Formula Editor Function tree. Make use of it in your formula as you would any other function, supplying any necessary arguments.

7. For example, if you converted the Select Case logic illustrated earlier in the chapter to a custom function called GeographicArea, you might use it in a formula like this:

```
GeographicArea({Customer.Region})
```

Understand Those Unclear Formula Error Messages

Computer programmers, in general, aren't known for building the most descriptive or logical error messages into their programs. Computer jargon and terminology pervades, despite years and years of supposed "progressive" computer software. Error messages in the Crystal Reports Formula Editor are no exception.

While the error message you receive may not always be exact, your key to troubleshooting the formula problem is where the cursor ends up after the error message. The cursor will usually appear at the point that Crystal Reports stopped understanding the formula.

This is perhaps the least helpful error message of them all. It simply means that Crystal Reports has no idea what the text following the cursor is—it can't resolve it to an existing field, function, operator, or variable name. Simply ensure that what follows the cursor is a properly spelled function name, a field name that includes the curly braces on both sides, or a properly spelled variable declared earlier in the formula.

This error appears when there are mismatched parentheses in the formula. Typically, you've failed to "close out" a function with a right parenthesis somewhere in the formula. From a fundamental perspective, you must always have the same number of right parentheses that you do left parentheses—if you count, you'll probably find that there isn't the same quantity. This error sometimes takes time to resolve, as more complex formulas may "nest" functions within each other, causing parentheses to be mismatched or placed in the wrong position.

This one is right up there with "The remaining text does not appear to be part of the formula" in obscurity. Interestingly enough, the reasons for this error are often the same as the reasons for the other error. Look at where the cursor appears in the formula. Crystal Reports expects there to be some sort of database field, other formula, or variable name to appear where the cursor is. Check spelling and syntax. Ensure that what you've placed in the formula is a field or formula name that includes the curly brace on each side, or a properly spelled variable declared earlier in the formula.

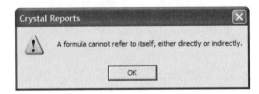

You'll see this message when you attempt to refer to the name of the formula you're currently editing in the formula itself. This often happens when you attempt to include one formula in another and mistakenly choose the formula you're working on from the Field tree. To resolve this, look for the actual formula you really want to include and replace the wrong formula name.

In case you really do want to refer to a formula within itself (perhaps you are creating a type of "recursive" calculation), you won't be able to accomplish the recursion this way—Crystal Reports simply doesn't allow a formula to refer to itself. You may want to try to use a variable in a formula instead (perhaps within some sort of finite loop) to calculate via recursion.

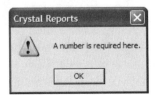

These (and similar messages for other data types) will appear when you inadvertently mix data types where you shouldn't, or supply the wrong type of data to a data type-specific function. For example, you may try to add a string field to a number field with the plus sign operator. Or, you may include fields of different data types in the Then and Else parts of an If-Then-Else formula.

Either replace the incorrect field with the correct field, or use data type conversion functions, such as ToText, ToNumber, or DateValue, if you need to use mixed data types in these situations.

> TIP   *Crystal Reports 8 and later provides the ampersand (&) operator as an alternative to the plus sign for string concatenation. Because the ampersand applies only to string concatenation, it will perform implicit conversion when used with mixed data types in a formula. The ampersand will automatically convert non-string fields to strings when using them in a formula.*

Test for Numbers with Numeric Calculations

In some cases (particularly where older mainframe-based systems may have been converted to new client/server database systems), you'll find numeric data contained in string database fields. This causes difficulty when attempting numeric calculations in formulas because you receive an error message if you try to perform a mathematical calculation on a string field. The first thought you may have is to use the built-in Crystal Reports ToNumber function to convert a string value to a numeric value. By using ToNumber, you can convert the string value to a numeric value for calculations and numeric formatting.

However, Crystal Reports' ToNumber function differs slightly from similar functions in other programming languages or development environments when it encounters nonnumeric characters (such as hyphens or letters) in the string value. While other environments return a zero, or the numeric value they gathered up until they encountered the nonnumeric character, Crystal Reports will generate a runtime formula error (discussed earlier in the chapter).

> DOWNLOAD   *Formula Examples.rpt from CrystalBook.com*

1. Modify the offending formula with use of the NumericText or IsNumber function. You'll most probably want to create an If-Then-Else formula to test for numeric text.

2. Use the NumericText or IsNumber function to test for numeric text before performing the ToNumber function. Supply the string value you want to test for numeric text as the argument to the function.

3. If the function returns numeric text, perform the ToNumber function. If not, return a zero (or other desired value):

```
If NumericText({Orders.PO#}) Then
    ToNumber({Orders.PO#})
Else
    0
```

4. The runtime formula error will no longer occur. Crystal Reports will return a zero if the string contains nonnumeric data.

Convert a String or Numeric Field to a Date

Part of the problem with the "Y2K Computer Crisis" was the way dates were stored in older computer systems. In particular, storing dates with two-digit years instead of four-digit years was cause for concern. Even though most of these problems have been presumably solved, there continue to be reporting requirements for converting string and numeric fields that contain date values into "real" Crystal Reports dates. Date math, flexible date formatting, date sorting and grouping, and use with innovative built-in date functions all become available once these strings or numbers are converted to dates.

 *Formula Examples.rpt from CrystalBook.com*

Converting String Values to Dates

You'll sometimes find dates stored as string fields in a database. Two common types of string fields may contain dates in a YYYYMMDD "unformatted" format, or perhaps the more visually appealing MM/DD/YYYY "formatted" format. In either case, however, you must convert the strings to actual date formats to realize many Crystal Reports benefits.

Unformatted Date Strings

1. Use the DateValue function (the Date function can also be used—it is functionally equivalent).

2. You'll need to supply three arguments: year, month, and day. These arguments need to be numeric values.

3. For each numeric argument, "pick apart" the portion of the unformatted date string you need to supply. For example, you'll need to extract the first

four characters as the year, the fifth and sixth characters as the month, and
the seventh and eighth characters as the day.

4. Use the subscript operator (square brackets) and supply the proper
   beginning and ending characters, separated with the "to" keyword,
   to extract the specific characters from the date string.

5. Convert the extracted string values to numbers with the ToNumber
   function:

```
DateValue(
    ToNumber({@Unformatted Date String}[1 to 4]),
    ToNumber({@Unformatted Date String}[5 to 6]),
    ToNumber({@Unformatted Date String}[7 to 8])
    )
```

Formatted Date Strings

1. Use the DateValue function (the Date function can also be used).

2. Formatted date strings can be supplied as the single argument:

```
DateValue({@Formatted Date String})
```

3. Although the DateValue function understands a fairly wide variety
   of formatted date strings (such as "1/10/99", "Jan 15, 2000", and
   "February 14, 1"), it may not understand peculiar date formats that
   may exist in your data.

4. If the DateValue function encounters a string with a format that it can't
   interpret, a runtime formula error (discussed earlier in the chapter)
   will occur.

5. Use the IsDate function to compensate for the possibility that all date
   strings may not be properly interpreted by the DateValue function:

```
If IsDate ({@Formatted Date String}) Then
    DateValue({@Formatted Date String})
Else
    #1/1/1900#
```

Converting Number Values to Dates

Some databases don't support actual date data types. And, some database
conversions from older systems merely imported the older field types directly
into the new database. In either of these cases, you may encounter dates stored as

numbers. This is often advantageous over dates stored as strings because limited date sorting and matching can still be accomplished with the numeric field.

However, if you simply drag and drop these fields onto the report, you'll rarely be able to achieve the date format you're looking for. For example, the date December 21, 1996, may look like this:

```
19,961,221.00
```

Converting these numeric dates (which typically are in YYYYMMDD format) to actual date data types is a little more challenging than other methods, but still fairly easy to accomplish.

1. Use the DateValue function (the Date function can also be used).

2. You'll need to supply three arguments: year, month, and day. These arguments need to be numeric values.

3. While it may be possible to somehow perform numeric math to "pick out" the year, month, and day portions of the numeric date, you'll probably prefer converting the numeric date to a string and then picking out the pieces.

4. Use the ToText (or CStr) function to convert the number to a string. Supply three arguments to ToText: the numeric value to convert, 0 to indicate no decimal places, and an empty string ("") to indicate no thousands separator.

5. Extract the particular year, month, and day portions of the now-converted string. For example, you'll need to extract the first four characters as the year, the fifth and sixth characters as the month, and the seventh and eighth characters as the day.

6. Use the subscript operator (square brackets) and supply the proper beginning and ending characters, separated with the "to" keyword, to extract the specific characters from the date string.

7. Convert the extracted string values to numbers with the ToNumber function:

```
DateValue(
    ToNumber(ToText({@Numeric Date},0,"")[1 to 4]),
    ToNumber(ToText({@Numeric Date},0,"")[5 to 6]),
    ToNumber(ToText({@Numeric Date},0,"")[7 to 8])
    )
```

NOTE *Although the DateValue function will accept a numeric argument, it expects the number to indicate the number of days since December 30, 1899. If your database contains other Julian-type dates that don't conform to this exact specification, you will need to perform additional conversions or calculations on your numeric field before passing it to the DateValue function.*

Calculate the Interval Between Two Times

Certain real-time database applications can be used to collect time-intensive data, such as times when products enter and exit portions of an assembly line, times that orders are placed and shipped, and so forth. Crystal Reports contains built-in formula features that allow very flexible calculation and manipulation of this time data. For example, you may have two times that you wish to calculate the difference between (how long it took a product lot to proceed from point A to point B in the production line or how long it took to process an order that was ordered and shipped on the same day).

DOWNLOAD *Formula Examples.rpt from CrystalBook.com*

1. Create a new formula to calculate the difference in the two time values.

2. Ensure that just the time portions of the two dates/times are extracted. The Crystal Reports Time function, when supplied with a combined date-time argument, will extract just the time portion.

3. Subtract the earlier time from the later time. Note that math performed on time-only values results in seconds; the subtraction will return a numeric value containing the number of seconds between the two times.

4. To convert the number of seconds into a full time-oriented value (such as 03:10:25 for 3 hours, 10 minutes, 25 seconds), place the original calculation in parentheses, and then add to "midnight," expressed as Time(0,0,0). The resulting formula will look similar to this:

```
Time(0,0,0) +
(Time({@Ship Date With Time}) - Time({@Order Date With Time}))
```

5. This will return a time value that can then be formatted in 24-hour military time format (HH:MM:SS) to show the actual hours, minutes, and seconds between the two times.

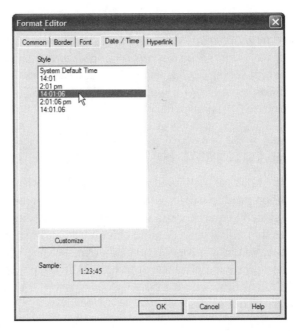

6. If you have a more precise application that requires just the number of seconds to be returned between two times, the formula may be simplified to:

```
Time({@Ship Date With Time}) - Time({@Order Date With Time})
```

7. To determine the number of minutes between two times, divide the results of the subtraction by 60 (turning the number of seconds into minutes). Note that you must perform the subtraction *before* the division for the formula to return the proper results. You may do this by surrounding the subtraction portion of the calculation with parentheses:

```
(Time({@Ship Date With Time}) - Time({@Order Date With Time})) / 60
```

8. To determine the number of hours between two times, divide the results of the subtraction by 3,600 (turning the number of seconds into hours). Note that you must perform the subtraction *before* the division for the formula to return the proper results. You may do this by surrounding the subtraction portion of the calculation with parentheses:

```
(Time({@Ship Date With Time}) - Time({@Order Date With Time})) / 3600
```

> **TIP**   *You may also use the DateDiff function to determine the number of hours, minutes, or seconds between two values. For example:* `DateDiff ("h",{@Order Date With Time},{@Ship Date With Time})` *will calculate the number of hours between the Order Date and Ship Date.*

This returns the number of hours rounded to the nearest whole number.

Calculate the Interval Between Two Dates

Probably more common than time-oriented reporting, is reporting that revolves around date manipulation and evaluation. Determining the number of days, weeks, months, or years between two dates is a fairly common reporting requirement.

While there are many different ways to approach this, probably the most versatile method is by use of Crystal Reports' built-in DateDiff function. DateDiff will return a numeric value indicating the number of "time intervals" between two dates or date/times. The time interval argument is a specific string value, indicating days, weeks, months, or years.

DOWNLOAD *Formula Examples.rpt from CrystalBook.com*

1. Create a new formula to calculate the difference between two dates.

2. Using the DateDiff function, supply three arguments: the time interval to use, the starting date, and the ending date.

3. For example, to determine the number of days between two dates, use a lowercase *d* as the time interval argument, as in:

   ```
   DateDiff("d",{Orders.Order Date}, {Orders.Ship Date})
   ```

4. To determine the number of weeks, months, quarters, or years between the two dates, replace the lowercase *d* with a lowercase *m* (for months), a lowercase *q* (for quarters), or four lowercase *y*'s (for years). For example:

   ```
   DateDiff("yyyy",{Orders.Order Date}, {Orders.Ship Date})
   ```

TIP *While DateDiff is powerful, it doesn't include any built-in functionality to exclude weekends or company holidays from its calculations. To perform these more advanced date calculations, look for the DateDiff function in Crystal Reports online help—an example of how to exclude weekends is included there. Or, use date Custom Functions supplied with the default Crystal Reports 9 repository.*

Check for Null Database Values

Depending on what database you are using, as well as how the database has been designed, you may encounter null values in database fields when you design reports. A *null value* is a value that, in essence, equates to nothing. An important distinction, however, needs to be made between a null and the number zero or an empty string—they are, in fact, different.

Check for Null Database Values

Because of the difference between a null and a zero or an empty string, normal summarizations (such as counts), string concatenations (appending groups of strings together), and tests for empty strings or numeric zero values will often behave unpredictably. There are two approaches to solving null-related problems:

■ Select Convert NULL Field Values To Default options from either the File | Report Options or the File | Options pull-down menu. (In Crystal Reports 9, you can choose to separately convert database null values to default, and non-database, or "other", values to default).

■ Use specific logic to test for nulls and adjust your formula accordingly.

DOWNLOAD *Formula Examples.rpt from CrystalBook.com*

1. Open the formula that appears to be encountering a difficulty with nulls. For example, the following formula may at times return address line 1, followed by a comma and space, and address line 2. At other times, it may return nothing at all:

```
{Customer.Address1} & ", " & {Customer.Address2}
```

2. In this situation, the entire formula will evaluate to null if any of the individual parts (address line 1 or address line 2) are null.

3. If you attempt to check for an empty string with an If-Then-Else statement, as follows, you may not solve the problem, as a null *is not the same as an empty string*:

```
If {Customer.Address2} = "" Then
    {Customer.Address1}
Else
    {Customer.Address1} & ", " & {Customer.Address2}
```

4. Instead, use the IsNull function. IsNull accepts one argument: the field to test for a null value. The following example will work properly:

```
If IsNull({Customer.Address2}) Then
    {Customer.Address1}
Else
    {Customer.Address1} & ", " & {Customer.Address2}
```

Make a Formula Multiline

The freeform design nature of Crystal Reports lends itself to much more innovative reporting than "one record per line" green-bar style reports that used to come off the mainframe. Crystal Reports is perfectly suited for form letters and other more "vertically oriented" reports.

This type of reporting often requires that database values or formulas be stacked vertically on top of each other. If, for example, you want to display a name, address, and city-state-zip combination on three lines, you can place the three fields one below the other. However, you may wish to create a single formula that actually returns a multiline result. You may then simply stretch the formula vertically to accommodate a fixed number of vertical lines, or format the formula with the Can Grow option from the Format Editor to show a variable number of vertical lines.

> **Bike-A-Holics Anonymous**
> **7429 Arbutus Boulevard, Suite 2017**
> **Blacklick, OH 43005**

DOWNLOAD *Formula Examples.rpt from CrystalBook.com*

1. Create a new formula to contain your multiline string values.

2. Use the Chr function to add a specific carriage return character to the formula where you'd like to start a new line. The Chr function accepts one argument: the ASCII character value to return to the formula. The ASCII value for a carriage return is 13.

3. For example, a formula that adds a carriage return between company name, address 1, and city-state-zip might look like this:

```
{Customer.Customer Name} & Chr(13) &
{Customer.Address1} & Chr(13) &
{Customer.City} & ", " &
{Customer.Region} & "   " &
{Customer.Postal Code}
```

NOTE *In Crystal Syntax, you may press the* ENTER *key between operators and other portions of the formula. While the formula will appear on multiple lines in the Formula Editor, carriage returns* will not *be added to the formula. You must explicitly add them with Chr(13).*

4. Manually resize the formula vertically to accommodate the number of lines it will return. Or, format the formula with the Can Grow option from the Format Editor's Common tab to allow the formula to grow vertically automatically.

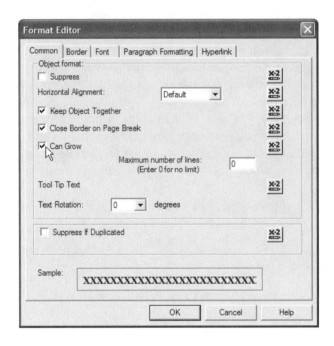

Base a Formula on a Parameter Field

Crystal Reports parameter fields allow the report to be customized every time it is run. A *parameter field* is a value that the report viewer can supply every time the report is refreshed. The value the report viewer supplies can then be used in virtually every part of the report, including record selection, conditional formatting, and formulas.

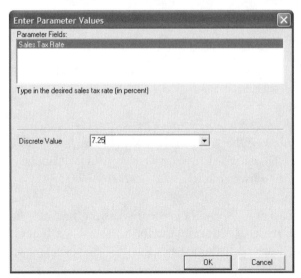

 *Formula Examples.rpt from CrystalBook.com*

1. Create the parameter field to gather the desired value or values from the report viewer when the report is refreshed.

2. Ensure that the parameter field gathers the correct data type for the formula you'll be using it with. For example, define a parameter field as a number if you'll be using it in a numeric formula, a string for string concatenation, or a date for a date-related formula.

3. Create or modify the formula that will make use of the parameter field.

4. In the Field tree of the Formula Editor, scroll down to the bottom of the Report Fields list. You'll notice all parameter fields available for use in the formula (parameter fields will start with a ? character).

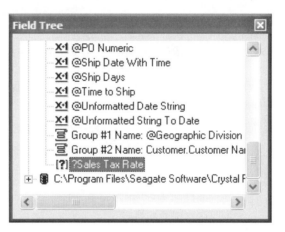

5. Double-click the desired parameter field in the list. It will be added to the formula text box as a database field would be.

6. For example, you may use a parameter field that prompts the report viewer for a sales tax rate in a formula similar to this:

```
{Orders.Order Amount} + {Orders.Order Amount} *
{?Sales Tax Rate} / 100
```

7. Check the formula for errors and save the formula.

Avoid Divide by Zero Errors

As discussed earlier in the chapter, you will sometimes encounter runtime formula errors—where the formula returns an error only after the report starts running, but not when you initially check for the formula with the check button. One of the most common runtime formula errors encountered is when a division formula encounters a zero in the database field or formula being used as the divisor. Solving this problem is as simple as adding a test for a zero divisor with an If-Then-Else statement.

1. Edit the formula that will potentially cause the division by zero error (the Formula Editor may already be displaying the formula if a divide by zero runtime formula error already occurred).

2. Add the test with an If-Then-Else statement. The If portion should test the divisor for a zero value. The Then portion should simply return a zero. The Else portion should perform the division. For example:

```
If {Orders.Quantity} = 0 Then
    0
Else
    {Orders.Total Price} / {Orders.Quantity}
```

NOTE *Eliminating records that contain a zero value in the divisor with record selection may still result in divide by zero errors. This is because formula evaluation may happen before record selection eliminates records. To avoid this situation, place the specific If-Then-Else test in the formula itself, as outlined previously.*

Chapter 4

Charts and Graphs

One of the powerful features of Crystal Reports is its built-in charting capabilities. Displaying data graphically in a pie, bar, line, or other type of chart can provide immediate visual impact when compared to more traditional textual reports.

Crystal Reports charts can be simple or complex—the charting capabilities are quite a bit more sophisticated than they may appear at first glance. Not only can you choose a variety of pleasing chart types, but you can extensively customize the way charts behave and appear.

This chapter covers various fine points of chart creation and modification and will show you how to:

- Change the size and position of various chart elements.

- Interact with certain types of charts, "drilling down" on the chart to view more detailed data.

- Conditionally set the color of chart bars, pie wedges, and so forth (this capability is available only in Crystal Reports 9 or later).

- Replace solid colors of chart elements with pictures or graphics.

- Use a graduated color instead of a solid color for chart elements or the chart background.

Make Cool 3-D Charts

One of the more "cool" chart types is the 3-D chart. This chart type plots multiple data elements in a three-dimensional style. Often, these charts may look like "cityscapes" or pyramids, depending on the type of 3-D chart chosen. Not only can you choose the type of 3-D chart to use, but you can rotate the charts to interesting display angles (even upside down—perhaps not an effective chart display, but cool nevertheless!).

Count of Order ID / Ship Via & Order Date

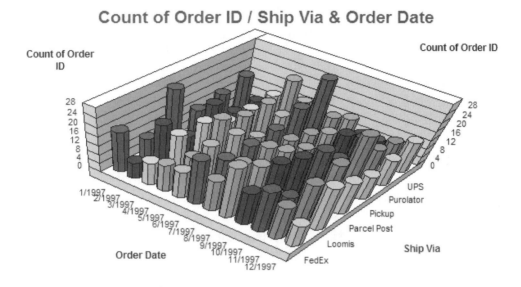

DOWNLOAD *3D Charts.rpt from CrystalBook.com*

1. Create a report that includes at least two major data elements to chart. For example, include two groups on your report, add a cross-tab to the report, or consider two separate data fields that you can choose as "on change of" fields in an Advanced Chart.

2. If you will be creating a group chart, ensure that at least one subtotal or summary field appears in each group footer.

3. Choose Insert | Chart from the pull-down menus or choose the Chart button from the appropriate toolbar. The Chart Expert will appear.

4. Choose either the 3-D Riser or 3-D Surface chart type (depending on whether you want to display elements in a distinct three-dimensional view, or a "topographical" shaded view).

5. If you want more fine control over formatting of the chart, uncheck Automatically Set Chart Options. Click the Data tab to continue.

6. Choose the type of chart you want to create, given the existing layout of your report:

■ To chart how two report groups relate to each other, click the Group button.

■ To chart on a row/column combination from an existing cross-tab or OLAP grid, click the Cross-Tab or OLAP button (these buttons will be dimmed if you don't already have at least one cross-tab or OLAP grid on your report).

■ To create a 3-D chart based on two database fields or formulas that are not already used in report groups, click the Advanced button.

7. If you choose the Group button, choose the two groups you wish to use for the 3-D chart. You *must* choose two groups in the On Change Of drop-down list—choosing a single group won't produce a three-dimensional chart.

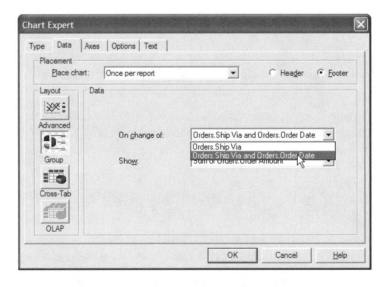

8. If you choose the Advanced button, you must choose On Change Of as the data type and add two fields to the On Change Of list. Or, you can choose any data type (including On Change Of) and add at least two fields to the Show Value(s) list.

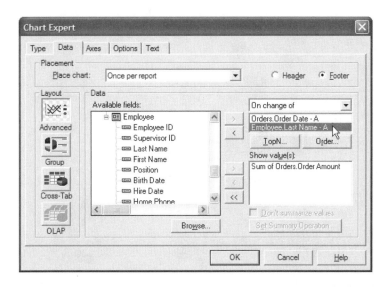

9. If you choose the Cross-Tab or OLAP button, you must choose rows or columns for *both* the On Change Of and Subdivided By drop-down lists.

10. If you unchecked Automatically Set Chart Options on the first Type tab, you will be able to choose more specific chart options on the Axes and Options tabs. Regardless, you'll be able to set options for chart titles, and other textual elements, on the Text tab.

While there are many formatting options that 3-D charts have in common with other chart types, there is one specific formatting option that works with 3-D charts alone. That is the Viewing Angle option.

1. Select the 3-D chart you want to adjust the viewing angle for. Right-click. A pop-up menu will appear.

2. Choose Format Chart | Viewing Angle from the pop-up menu (Chart Options | Viewing Angle in version 9). The Choose Viewing Angle dialog box will appear.

3. Choose one of the predefined viewing angle icons from the dialog. If you'd like more minute control over the viewing angle, click the Advanced Options button. The dialog box will expand to show a tabbed interface for precisely controlling the viewing angle.

Make Cool 3-D Charts

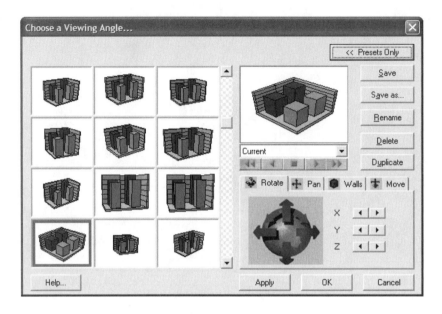

4. Click the Rotate, Pan, Walls, or Move tab to control that particular element of 3-D chart sizing and placement. Make desired changes on each tab.

5. When you're finished with changes, click OK.

6. You'll be asked to supply a Preset name. If you wish to save the viewing angle choices you just made for future use, supply a name for the set of choices and click OK—the choices will be saved in a preset name you can use for future 3-D chart options.

7. If you don't want to save the preset, click Cancel. The viewing angle choices you make will still be applied to the chart, but they won't be saved in a preset name.

Color or Shade the Background

By default, Crystal Reports applies a white background to a chart (or a transparent background, if you make that choice on the Options tab). However, you may desire that the chart display something other than a white background—you may prefer a solid blue, a pattern, or a graduated color combination to appear instead of plain white.

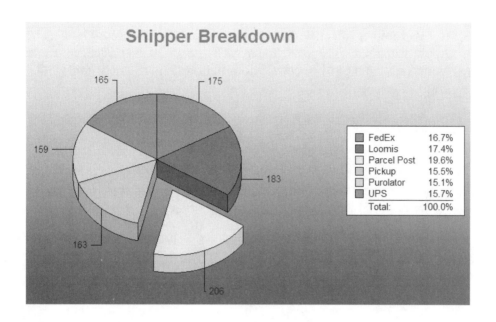

Shipper Breakdown

■	FedEx	16.7%
■	Loomis	17.4%
□	Parcel Post	19.6%
□	Pickup	15.5%
▨	Purolator	15.1%
▨	UPS	15.7%
	Total:	100.0%

DOWNLOAD *General Chart Examples.rpt from CrystalBook.com*

1. Select the chart that you wish to apply the shade, pattern, or graduated background to.

2. If you're using Crystal Reports 8.5, you must display the chart in the Chart Analyzer. Do this by right-clicking on the chart and choosing Chart Analyzer from the pop-up menu, or by selecting the chart and choosing Analyzer | Chart Analyzer from the pull-down menus (there is no more Analyzer in Crystal Reports 9).

3. Click on a blank area of the chart—this will be the chart background. Ensure you don't see a select box on any other chart element, such as a bar, a pie wedge, or the legend.

4. Right-click. Choose Format Chart | Selected Item from the pop-up list (if you're using Crystal Reports 9, choose Chart Options | Selected Item). The Formatting dialog box will appear with the Fill tab already selected.

5. Choose a solid color from the color matrix on the left. If you wish to apply something other than a solid color, click the Pattern, Gradient, Texture, or Picture button.

Color or Shade the Background

6. If, for example, you click the Gradient button, the Choose A Gradient To Apply dialog box will appear. You may choose one of the predefined gradient icons, or click the Advanced Options button to more finely control the gradient you apply.

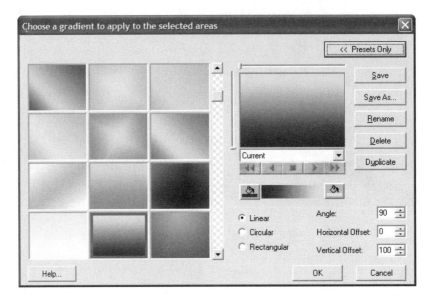

7. You may choose from myriad options: the type of gradient (linear, circular, rectangle), the starting and ending colors for the gradient, the angle of the gradient, and so forth.

8. Once you've made your choices, click OK.

9. You'll be asked to supply a Preset name. If you wish to save the gradient choices you just made for future use, supply a name for the set of choices and click OK—the choices will be saved in a preset name you can use for future gradient options.

10. If you don't want to save the preset, click Cancel. The choices you make will still be applied to the chart, but they won't be saved in a preset name.

TIP

You can use similar techniques to choose something other than a solid color for the legend or for bars or wedges of the chart. Just select the desired legend, bar, or wedge before you choose the Format Chart | Selected Item option (Chart Options | Selected Item in version 9).

Replace Bars or Wedges with Pictures

Typically, individual chart elements (bars, pie wedges, and so forth) are filled with a solid color (Crystal Reports 9 introduces "pleasant" pastel colors by default). This is often appropriate for the quick visual impact that a chart needs to convey. However, for specialized charting requirements (or just to add a certain amount of novelty to a chart), you can replace the solid colors in a chart element with a graphic or picture.

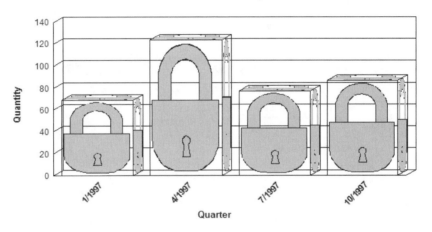

DOWNLOAD *Picture In Chart.rpt from CrystalBook.com*

1. Create a standard chart of the appropriate type. For example, a filled area chart, a bar chart, or a pie chart are appropriate, as their graphical elements take up a relatively large amount of space. A line chart or scatter chart, however, won't be appropriate because of the small amount of space their graphical elements take up.

2. If you're using Crystal Reports 8.5, you must display the chart in the Chart Analyzer. Do this by right-clicking on the chart and choosing Chart Analyzer from the pop-up menu, or by selecting the chart and choosing Analyzer | Chart Analyzer from the pull-down menus. (The Analyzer is no longer included in Crystal Reports 9.)

3. Click on the first desired pie wedge, bar, or other chart element you wish to display with a picture. You'll notice an outline around the item you just selected.

4. Right-click. Choose Format Chart | Selected Item from the pop-up menu (if you're using Crystal Reports 9, choose Chart Options | Selected Item). The Formatting dialog box will appear with the Fill tab selected.

5. Click the Picture button. The Choose A Picture dialog box will appear with one or more "preset" pictures appearing.

6. If you wish to choose from additional pictures that don't appear in the initial preset, click the Advanced Options button. The dialog box will expand with more options.

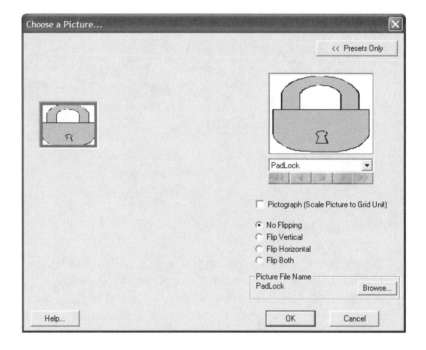

7. Click the Browse button to look for additional pictures. Note that the only type of graphics file that can be used with this feature is a *Windows Metafile* (with a .WMF file extension).

8. When you've chosen an additional .WMF file, a thumbnail image of the file will be added to the dialog box. Click on the actual picture on the left side of the dialog box that you want to appear on the chart element.

9. Choose any desired flipping options with the available radio buttons. If you wish to display the picture in its original orientation, ensure that No Flipping is chosen.

10. If you click the Pictograph check box, the graphic will be repeated over and over within the chart element for each occurrence of a grid line. For example, if you are replacing a bar chart element with a picture and the bar spans four grid lines, the picture will repeat four times—once within each grid line. If you want the picture to appear just once, spanning the entire bar, make sure Pictograph isn't checked.

NOTE   *The Pictograph check box has been eliminated in Crystal Reports 9.*

11. Once you've made your choices, click OK. The Formatting dialog box will reappear with the picture showing in the preview area.

12. Click Apply or OK to change the chart.

13. Repeat steps 3–12 for each additional chart element that you wish to display a picture in.

TIP   *Many versions of Microsoft Office include extensive clip art libraries of .WMF files. Search your hard disk for files with a .WMF extension to see what is already installed on your computer.*

Drill Down on Group Charts

There are many benefits to using Crystal Reports for your organization's reporting needs. One of the main standout features of Crystal Reports is its online reporting options. Once you've designed a report, you can distribute it using a custom Windows application developed with a programming language, or via one of Crystal Reports' many web-reporting options.

One immediate benefit of using an online report distribution method is report interactivity. A report viewer can navigate directly to report groups using the group tree, can search the report for particular text, or can drill down on higher-level group data. *Drilling down* refers to the process of navigating from higher-level summary data to lower-level detail data. Crystal Reports allows drill-down not only on group subtotals and summaries, but on certain types of charts as well.

In particular, a *group chart* (a chart based on existing report group subtotal or summary values) provides drill-down capability. When a viewer points their mouse to a particular chart element, such as a bar or pie wedge, or points to an individual item in the chart legend, the mouse cursor will change to a drill-down cursor, indicating that the viewer may drill down on that group. When the viewer clicks on the desired chart element, the particular group that the user clicked on will appear in its own drill-down tab.

DOWNLOAD   *General Chart Examples.rpt from CrystalBook.com*

1. Open a report containing at least one existing group, or create at least one group on a currently open report.

2. Ensure that you have created at least one subtotal or summary field for each group you wish to chart. A group chart uses a subtotal or summary as the value for chart elements.

3. Add a chart by using the Insert | Chart option from the pull-down menus or the appropriate chart toolbar button. The Chart Expert will appear.

4. Choose the type of chart (bar, pie, and so forth) that you wish to use. If you wish Crystal Reports to automatically set certain choices, check Automatically Set Chart Options.

5. Click the Data tab to choose what data you want your chart based on. Click the Group button to create a group chart (if the Group button is dimmed, it's because you don't have at least one group with at least one subtotal or summary field on your report).

6. Choose the group and subtotal or summary field you want to base the chart on in the On Change Of and Show drop-down lists. Choose where you want the chart to appear with the Place Chart drop-down list and Header and Footer radio buttons.

7. Change any other options you wish for the chart on other tabs in the Chart Expert. When you're finished with the Chart Expert, click OK. The chart will be placed on the report.

8. You may optionally add tool tip text to the chart. Tool tip text will appear when a report viewer "hovers" their mouse over the chart.

9. Select the chart in the Design or Preview tab. Right-click on the chart.

10. If you are using Crystal Reports 8.5, choose Borders And Colors from the pop-up menu. If you are using Crystal Reports 9, choose Format Chart from the pop-up menu. The Format Editor will appear.

11. Click the Common tab. Click the conditional formula button for Tool Tip Text. Enter a string literal or formula to determine what will appear when the report viewer hovers over the chart.

12. Save the formula. Click OK to close the Format Editor.

13. Preview the report. Point your mouse to the chart. Notice that the cursor changes to a magnifying glass drill-down cursor. If you added tool tip text, it will appear.

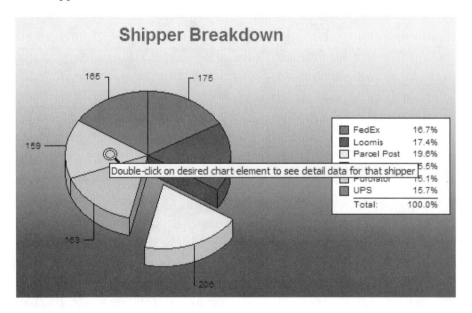

14. Double-click to drill down on the chart (some Web-based report distribution options require only a single click).

Add a Trend Line

Depending on the chart type you choose, and the type of data you chart, a trend line may prove beneficial to the report viewer. A *trend line* shows some sort of statistical trend, such as a mean, standard deviation, or linear regression, across the existing chart. By use of a trend line, a viewer can see not only the actual data elements that make up the chart, but the trend of the data elements over time.

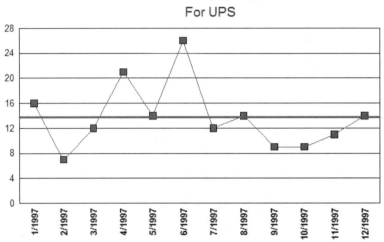

Monthly Shipping Trend
For UPS

 **DOWNLOAD** *General Chart Examples.rpt from CrystalBook.com*

1. Open a report containing an existing chart, or create a new chart.

2. If you're using Crystal Reports 8.5, you must display the chart in the Chart Analyzer. Do this by right-clicking on the chart and choosing Chart Analyzer from the pop-up menu, or by selecting the chart and choosing Analyzer | Chart Analyzer from the pull-down menus. (The Analyzer is no longer included in Crystal Reports 9.)

3. Select one of the data elements that make up the data "series" you want to create the trend line for. For example, select one of the data points that compose a line chart, or select the line itself.

4. Right-click. Choose Trendlines from the pop-up menu. The Trendlines dialog box will appear.

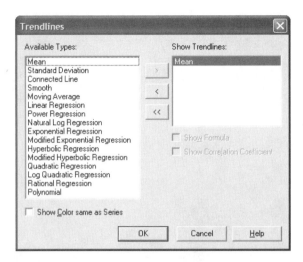

5. Select the desired type of trend line in the Available Types list. Click the right arrow to add the trend line type to the Show Trendlines list. If you wish to add more than one trend line, repeat this step for each type of trend line you'd like to add.

6. Depending on the type of trend line you choose, you may be able to make additional choices—whether to show the formula that creates the line, a "smoothing factor," and so forth. Click the desired trend line in the Show Trendlines list and make these choices.

7. If you check Show Color Same As Series, the trend line will take on the same color as the series data element it's based on. For example, if you base a trend line on a blue line in a line chart, the trend line will also be blue. If you uncheck Show Color Same As Series, you can click the trend line itself inside the chart and change the trend line's color with a Format Chart option.

8. When you're finished choosing trend line options, click OK. The trend line will appear on the chart.

Move the Chart Legend

Certain chart types, such as pie charts, benefit greatly from a chart legend. A *legend* is a box that associates the color of bars, pie wedges, and so forth with the actual data elements that they represent.

By default, Crystal Reports will place the legend in a predetermined location (typically, the right side of the chart). While you can choose from a few specific legend placement choices on the Chart Expert's Options tab, you may find that precise placement of the legend will improve the chart's overall appearance, or prevent the legend from appearing on top of other chart elements.

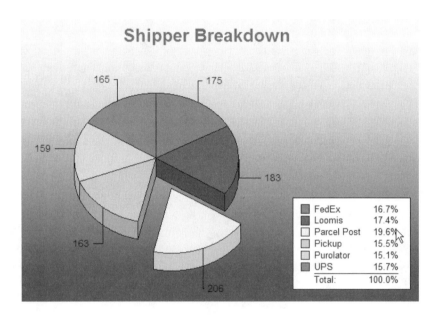

DOWNLOAD *General Chart Examples.rpt from CrystalBook.com*

1. Open a report containing an existing chart, or create a new chart.

2. If you're using Crystal Reports 8.5, you must display the chart in the Chart Analyzer. Do this by right-clicking on the chart and choosing Chart Analyzer from the pop-up menu, or by selecting the chart and choosing Analyzer | Chart Analyzer from the pull-down menus. (The Analyzer is no longer included in Crystal Reports 9.)

3. Click on the border of the chart legend. This will highlight the entire legend.

4. Simply drag the legend to its desired location.

Display a Chart Alongside Data

When creating a chart, you must choose where to place the chart on the report. The Chart Expert gives you limited choices, typically on the top or bottom of data that is being charted. For example, if you create a group chart for Group 1, the only choices in the Chart Expert are "once per report" in the report header or report footer. If you create an Advanced Chart, your choices include once per group, or once per report in a header or footer.

In all cases, the chart must reside at least "one level higher" than the data you are charting. If you create a group chart, the chart must appear at a higher level than the group you are charting. If you create an Advanced chart, you cannot place the chart in the details section—it must reside in a group header or footer, or the report header or footer.

You may think that this limits your chart placement to the top or bottom of a group or report—you can't have the chart appear alongside the data you are charting. In fact, with creative use of the Underlay property within the Section Expert, you can place a chart to appear alongside the data it is charting.

1. Open a report containing an existing chart, or create a new chart.

2. Display the Design tab. Look at the section containing the chart (a group header or footer or the report header or footer).

3. If the chart appears in a group or report header, check to see if other objects are in the same section. If so, you'll need to create a second section to hold just the chart.

4. If the chart appears in a group or report footer, you'll need to move it to a corresponding header section that contains no other objects (you may need to create a second header section).

5. If necessary, create a second group or report header section to contain the chart with no other objects. Do this by right-clicking on the gray section name for the existing header section. Choose Insert Section Below from the pop-up menu.

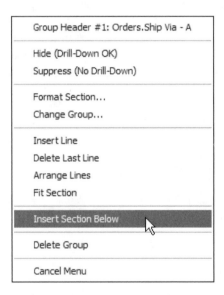

6. You will now see two header sections—the previously existing section labeled a and the new section labeled b (such as Group Header 1a and Group Header 1b).

7. Move the chart into the b header section.

8. Display the Section Expert. Right-click on the b section's gray section name and choose Format Section from the pop-up menu. Or, choose the Format Section option from pull-down menus or the proper toolbar button.

9. Select the b header section you just created. Select the Underlay Following Sections check box.

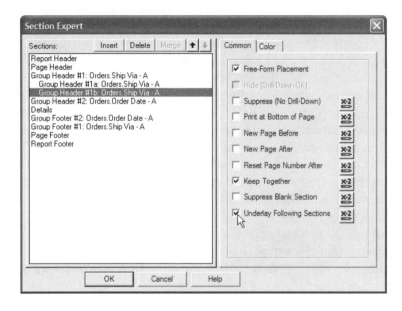

10. Rearrange the chart and objects in sections below the chart so that the chart won't spill directly on top of other objects. For example, move and size the chart so that it takes up the right half of horizontal space in its section. Move and size objects in the sections below so that they take up only the left half of the section.

11. Preview the report. The chart should appear alongside lower report sections that show the data the chart refers to.

12. If necessary, move and resize objects more carefully to avoid the chart appearing directly on top of other objects.

Set Colors Based on Some Data Condition

When Crystal Reports creates a chart, it makes some default choices for chart element colors. In Crystal Reports 8.5, for example, chart colors tend to follow "basic bright" color definitions (yellow, red, blue, magenta, and so forth). Crystal

Reports 9 has replaced basic bright with pastels—however, these are still default color choices you have no initial control over.

Both Crystal Reports 8.5 and 9 provide the ability for you to "manually" change a color for an individual pie wedge, bar, or other chart element. In Crystal Reports 8.5, you may display the chart in the Analyzer, select the desired chart element, right-click, and choose Format Chart | Selected Item from the pop-up menu. In Crystal Reports 9 or later, just click the chart element directly (the Analyzer is no longer included) and choose Chart Options | Selected Item from the pop-up menu.

However, manually changing chart element colors is time consuming and not necessarily consistent. If you want to change colors for many chart elements, you must select each one individually and make the change. And, if the data that populates the chart changes, the settings you made to individual elements may change (for example, additional bars or wedges that appear in the chart will take on default formatting).

Crystal Reports 9 and later provides for conditional chart coloring, whereby the colors of chart elements can be set according to some condition. Perhaps you want each sales rep to always show in the same color. Or, you may want sales amounts that exceed a goal to show in a bright color.

NOTE *The technique discussed here applies only to Crystal Reports 9 or later. Earlier versions of Crystal Reports don't provide for conditional color settings in charts.*

DOWNLOAD *Conditional Chart Color (v9 only).rpt from CrystalBook.com*

1. Open a report containing an existing chart, or create a new chart.

2. Display the Chart Expert for the chart you want to color conditionally. If you've already created a chart, select it, right-click, and choose Chart Expert from the pop-up menu.

3. Ensure that Automatically Set Chart Options is unchecked on the Type tab. Then, click the Options tab.

4. Click the Format button in the Chart Color section. The Chart Color Format Expert dialog box will appear.

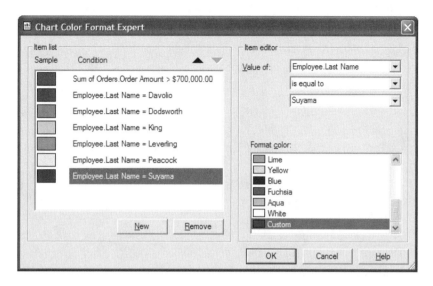

5. Click the New button to add a new condition. A new entry will appear in the Item List.

6. Within the Item Editor section, choose the field or summary you want to base the condition on from the first drop-down list.

7. Choose the comparison condition you want to use from the second drop-down list.

8. In the third drop-down list, either type the value you want to compare to, or choose it from any sample values that appear in the drop-down list.

9. In the Format Color list, choose the desired color for the chosen condition.

10. Click the New button as many times as necessary to add additional conditions for conditional coloring.

11. If two conditions might occur at the same time (perhaps a sales rep condition may be met at the same time a sales threshold condition is met), arrange the conditions on the Item List in the desired priority. Do this by clicking the condition you want to assign a higher priority and click the up arrow to move it above other conditions.

12. Click OK to close the Chart Color Format Expert. Complete any additional necessary options in the Chart Expert. Click OK to close the Chart Expert and display the chart with the conditional colors.

Set Colors Based on Some Data Condition

Chapter 5

Record Selection

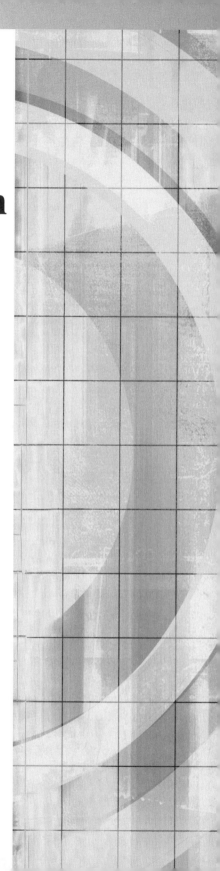

One of the first features of Crystal Reports (or any database reporting or query tool, for that matter) that you should learn about is the filter or record selection tool. *Record selection,* the term used by Crystal Reports, refers to limiting the report to a desired set of records, such as only records for a certain sales rep, date range, or production category.

In particular, if you are writing reports based on a large, industry-standard Structured Query Language database, such as Microsoft SQL Server, Oracle, or Sybase, you'll need to pay very close attention to record selection. As these databases often contain very large data tables (multimillion record tables are typical), careful use of record selection before you preview your report for the first time will prevent thousands, or perhaps millions, of records from coming across the network to your PC.

While you may not consider record selection to be an intricate feature of Crystal Reports, there are actually quite a few fine points to making use of it. Again, if you use a SQL database with large table sizes, a seemingly innocent misstep with record selection can change your report from completing in a few seconds to taking a few hours. And, there are other simple approaches and record selection features that will maximize your use of this important Crystal Reports feature.

Improve Performance with the Select Expert

If you are using an industry-standard SQL database, such as Microsoft SQL Server, Oracle, or Sybase (or any database via an ODBC connection, for that matter), Crystal Reports will ultimately query your database with a Structured Query Language (SQL) statement.

In particular, the record selection criteria you add are used by Crystal Reports to create the SQL WHERE clause, the portion of the SQL statement that tells the database server which subset of records in the database to send back to Crystal Reports. Existence of the WHERE clause can often make the difference between a fast report and a slow one. Inclusion of a WHERE clause will typically result in a much faster report (particularly with large database tables), as a much smaller set of records will come back from the database. If the SQL statement doesn't contain a WHERE clause, the database server will send back *every record* in the tables added to your report—Crystal Reports will have to go through them one at a time to apply your chosen record selection.

To ensure that you always include a WHERE clause in the SQL statement, try to use the Select Expert to create your record selection. Crystal Reports can use most Select Expert options to create a WHERE clause. However, if you manually modify the record selection formula (with the Select Expert's Show Formula button, or the pull-down menu options for the record selection formula), Crystal Reports may not be able to convert the more intricate formula you create to a SQL WHERE clause.

To see if a WHERE clause has been created with the record selection you added to your report, follow these steps:

1. Open or create a report based on a SQL database or ODBC data source.

2. Choose Database | Show SQL Query from the pull-down menus. You may be asked to log on to the database or respond to parameter field prompts. Do so if prompted.

3. The SQL statement will appear in its own dialog box.

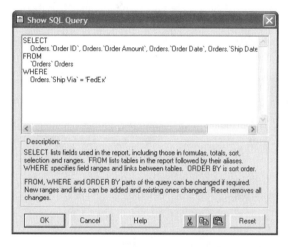

4. Look for the WHERE clause in the displayed SQL statement. In particular, look to see that the fields you specified in the record selection appear in the WHERE clause, along with the values you compared them against.

5. If the WHERE clause doesn't appear, ensure that you use the Select Expert and its built-in operators for record selection. Modifying the record selection formula manually can inadvertently eliminate the WHERE clause.

TIP   *The WHERE clause may also not appear if you've unchecked Use Indexes Or Server For Speed in either the File | Report Options or File | Options dialog box.*

Speed Up Your Report with SQL Expressions

As discussed earlier in the chapter, some seemingly innocent changes made to the record selection formula can eliminate the SQL WHERE clause, which can severely impact report performance. One way to avoid this problem is to limit your report's record selection criteria to only those criteria you add with the Select Expert. However, more sophisticated reports sometimes require more intricate record selection than the Select Expert can provide. In some of these cases, making creative use of SQL Expressions can provide formula-like flexibility in record selection that still maintains a SQL WHERE clause.

A *SQL Expression* is like a regular Crystal Reports formula. The difference, however, is that the SQL Expression makes use of the SQL database language for its calculations, rather than the built-in Crystal Reports formula language. The SQL Expression, therefore, is evaluated by the database server *before* records are sent back from the database, as opposed to being evaluated by Crystal Reports *after* records are sent back from the database. If you place a SQL Expression in a record selection formula, Crystal Reports can often use the SQL Expression in the WHERE clause, eliminating the need for the database to send all records back to Crystal Reports.

DOWNLOAD   *SQL Expression.rpt from CrystalBook.com*

Consider the example of a report that needs to return all orders placed in December, regardless of the year of the order. Because the Select Expert doesn't contain any built-in operator to examine just the month of a date field, you may be tempted to create a formula and include it in Select Expert.

Here's the example:

1. Create a Crystal Reports formula that returns only the month of a date field. The formula might look something like this:

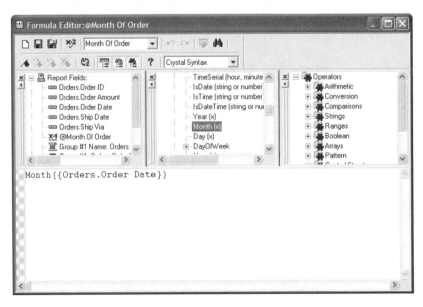

2. Using the Select Expert, compare this formula to the number 12 (the month number for December).

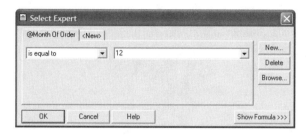

3. Refresh the report. While the correct results will eventually appear on the report, you may notice that the report takes some time to process, with a very large record count appearing in the Crystal Reports status bar.

4. Choose Database | Show SQL Query from the pull-down menus. Notice that the formula you added to the Select Expert *does not* appear in a SQL WHERE clause.

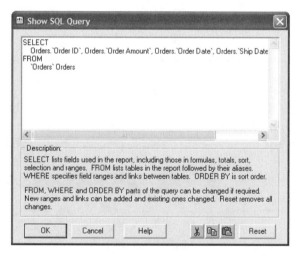

5. Create a SQL Expression to calculate the month of the order. Steps to create a SQL Expression are almost identical to creating a Crystal Reports Formula, except that you choose the SQL Expression category in the Field Explorer (or Formula Workshop in Crystal Reports 9) before you begin.

6. Notice that the choices of operators and functions in the Formula Editor change dramatically when you create a SQL Expression. These functions and operators are those provided by the database server your report is using, not by the Crystal Reports formula language.

Speed Up Your Report with SQL Expressions

7. A similar SQL Expression to calculate the month of an order will look similar to this:

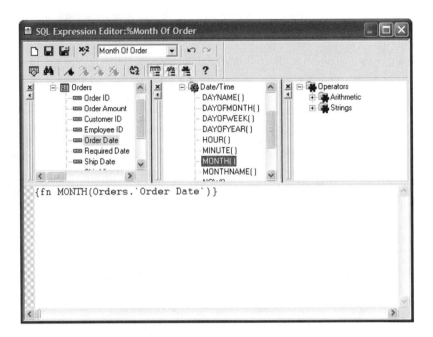

8. Replace the portion of the Select Expert using the Crystal Reports formula with the SQL Expression (if you choose to give the formula and the SQL Expression the same name, notice that the formula is preceded by the @ sign, while the SQL Expression is preceded by the % sign).

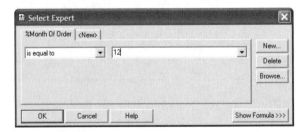

9. Refresh the report. You may notice an improvement in report speed.

10. Choose Database | Show SQL Query from the pull-down menus. Notice that the SQL Expression you added to the Select Expert now appears in a SQL WHERE clause. The database server is now calculating the month and returning only records for December.

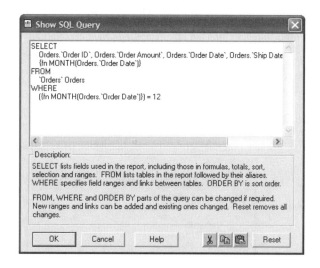

Show Record Selection on the Report

When displaying a report on the screen or a web page, or printing the report on paper, it's a good idea to annotate the report with the record selection that's being used. This informs the report viewer of the limited set of data that appears on the report.

While you can create a text object that merely includes some fixed text, such as "Orders placed in 1997," the contents of the text object won't automatically change along with the record selection you've supplied with the Select Expert. By using a Crystal Reports Special Field, you can actually display the contents of the Crystal Reports record selection formula on the report (perhaps in a page header or footer or a report header or footer). This Record Selection Formula special field will change automatically whenever you make a change to the Select Expert.

```
{Customer.Customer Name} like "*Bike*" and
{Customer.Country} in ["Canada", "Mexico", "USA"] and
{Orders.Order Date} in DateTime (1997, 01, 01, 00, 00, 00) to DateTime
(1997, 12, 31, 00, 00, 00)
```

Order ID	Order Amount	Order Date	Ship Date	Ship Via
7 Bikes For 7 Brothers				
3,054	53.90	5/26/1997	6/4/1997	Parcel Post
Subtotal:	**$53.90**		1 orders	
Against The Wind Bikes				
3,055	479.85	5/26/1997	5/28/1997	Purolator
Subtotal:	**$479.85**		1 orders	
Barry's Bikes				
3,039	52.50	5/21/1997	5/21/1997	Parcel Post
Subtotal:	**$52.50**		1 orders	
Bike Shop from Mars				
1,681	43.80	6/5/1997	6/7/1997	Parcel Post
2,473	71.30	12/10/1997	12/13/1997	Loomis

Record Selection Formula Examples.rpt from CrystalBook.com

1. Open or create the report that you wish to add the Record Selection special field to.

2. Display the Field Explorer.

3. Open the Special Fields category by clicking the plus sign next to it.

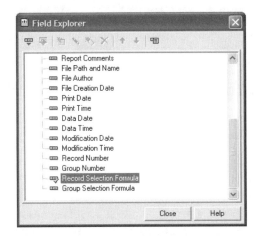

4. Scroll through the Special Fields category until you find the Record Selection Formula special field. Drag and drop it to the desired place on the report.

5. If necessary, resize the field to show its entire contents. If it can potentially become fairly large, use the Can Grow formatting option on the Common tab of the Format Editor to allow it to grow vertically as much as necessary.

NOTE   *The Record Selection Formula special field shows the actual Crystal Reports record selection formula that's used on the report. If you use the tabbed Select Expert, the options you add will be converted to an actual formula before being shown on the report.*

Make Creative Use of Like and Wildcards

One of the main benefits of Crystal Reports is flexible record selection—being able to creatively limit the report to a specifically desired set of database records. One of the Select Expert's operators that helps in this pursuit is the *Like operator.* Like allows the use of *wildcards*: certain special characters that "substitute" for actual characters or groups of characters in a comparison operation.

The two wildcards that work with the Like operator are the question mark and the asterisk:

■   **?**   Substitutes any single character in the position where the ? character is placed. For example, "a?r" will return records where the first character is the letter *a* and the third character is the letter *r,* regardless of what the second character is.

■   *****   Substitutes any number of characters in the position where the * character is placed. For example, *Jones will return records where the last five characters are *Jones,* regardless of what, or how many, characters precede *Jones.* Bill* will return records where the first four characters are *Bill,* regardless of what, or how many characters, follow *Bill.* *Bike* will return records where the characters *Bike* appear *anywhere* in the field, regardless of what, or how many characters, precede or follow *Bike.* This includes situations where Bike is the first four or last four characters in the field, or the only characters in the field.

DOWNLOAD   *Record Selection Example.rpt from CrystalBook.com*

1.   Open an existing report or create a new report that will make use of the Like record selection option.

2.   Display the Select Expert using pull-down menu, pop-up menu, or toolbar button options.

3.   Choose the field you wish to use with the Like operator. Choose "is like" or "is not like" from the operator drop-down list.

4.   Type in the partial string you wish to compare to in the second drop-down list/text box. Use the ? and/or * wildcards where necessary.

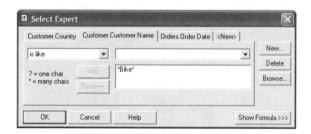

5.   If you wish to add additional comparison strings, type additional strings (including wildcards) and click the Add button.

6. Click OK to close the Select Expert.

The Like operator will appear in the drop-down list of operators only if you've chosen a string field in the Select Expert—Like isn't available with any other data type.

Use Pound Signs for Easy Date Selection

Record selection based on date fields is an important part of many reporting environments. Being able to limit reports to only records from the last month, the current year, or a specific date range dramatically improves the power of Crystal Reports.

While Crystal Reports features the capability to limit records to certain date periods based on your computer's system clock (see "Achieve Automatic Reporting with InThePeriod" later in this chapter), you'll still probably find a need to use Equal To, Less Than, Greater Than, or Is Between Select Expert operators with date fields.

It can sometimes be difficult to provide date or date/time values in a format that the Select Expert accepts. For example, choosing an Is Between Select Expert operator and then typing in beginning and ending values of "1/1/1997" and "12/31/1997" may result in an error from the Select Expert. While you'll eventually rid yourself of the error by typing in dates and times in a very exacting format required by the Select Expert (or by using even more tedious DateTime (yyyy,mm,dd,hh,mm,ss) or Date(yyyy,mm,dd) formula functions), the use of the date literal character makes entering dates far easier. The *# date literal character* can be placed just before and after a date string you supply to the Select Expert. Crystal Reports will interpret what you type between the two # signs as a date or date-time value.

 Record Selection Example.rpt from CrystalBook.com

1. Open or create a report requiring date-based record selection.

2. Display the Select Expert using pull-down menu or pop-up menu options, or the appropriate toolbar button.

3. Add a new criterion based on a date or date-time field.

4. Choose the desired comparison operator in the first drop-down list. Typically, you'll use date literal characters with most available date operators, except InThePeriod.

5. Try typing in a date value in the simple "mm/dd/yyyy" format, including the slashes. Click OK. You may receive an error message.

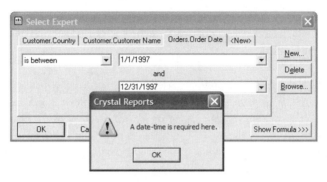

6. Type the value you supplied previously. Even try variations of "free form" date formats. Just make sure that you surround your value with pound signs.

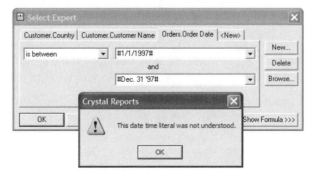

7. While you probably should get in the habit of including four-digit year values, the # date literal character will apply a "sliding scale" to two-digit year values—values between 0 and 29 will assume the 2000 century and values between 30 and 99 will assume the 1900 century.

8. If you type in a value between the pound signs that Crystal Reports doesn't understand, you'll receive an error message indicating such. Try a more conventional format for your date or date/time value.

Use Pound Signs for Easy Date Selection

9. Click OK to save your Select Expert choices. If your date or date/time literals between the pound signs are understood, no error message will appear.

10. Refresh the report to ensure that the proper dates are being supplied to the Select Expert.

While the # date literal character is still fully supported in the Crystal Reports 9 formula language, the Crystal Reports 9 Select Expert is more tolerant of date values typed in without use of the # character. You'll generally need to use the # character only in the Crystal Reports 8.0 or 8.5 Select Expert. The # date literal isn't available in Crystal Reports versions prior to 8.

Use Automatic Weekday Reporting

Depending on your reporting environment, you may encounter a need to report on "yesterday's data" on a regular basis. In many cases, this need is applicable only to data that is gathered on weekdays—Saturday and Sunday processing doesn't occur. This requirement may be particularly important if you run reports automatically on a schedule with such tools as Crystal Enterprise or Seagate Info.

While the Crystal Reports Select Expert's InThePeriod operator supplies many automatic date ranges, "last weekday" isn't one of them. Accordingly, you'll need to go beyond the Select Expert's built-in functions and edit the Crystal Reports record selection formula manually. By making use of the DayOfWeek and CurrentDate built-in formula language functions, you can create a selection formula that will always return records from the previous weekday.

1. Open an existing report or create a new report that requires previous weekday record selection.

2. Choose Report | Edit Selection Formula | Record (Crystal Reports 8.5) or Report | Selection Formulas | Record (Crystal Reports 9). The Record Selection Formula Editor will appear.

3. Type in the following record selection formula (replace the Orders.Order Date field with the actual database field you wish to use in your report):

```
{Orders.Order Date} = (
If DayOfWeek(CurrentDate) = 2 Then
    CurrentDate - 3
Else If DayOfWeek(CurrentDate) = 1 Then
```

```
    CurrentDate - 2
Else
    CurrentDate - 1
)
```

4. Notice that the formula checks the weekday number of the current date (2 indicates Monday and 1 indicates Sunday). The formula subtracts the appropriate number of days from the current date based on the weekday number.

5. Save the record selection formula and refresh the report. You should see only records from the previous weekday on the report.

6. If you wish to use something other than today's date for the CurrentDate function (perhaps you'd like to test the formula for various days of the week, or perform some "point in time" reporting for a previous date), you can change the value of CurrentDate by choosing Report | Set Print Date/Time from the pull-down menus.

NOTE

Although use of this technique breaks the "use only the Select Expert" rule explained earlier in the chapter, this particular record selection formula is still converted to a SQL WHERE clause by Crystal Reports 8.5 and 9. Accordingly, you won't pay a performance penalty for using this technique.

Achieve Automatic Reporting with InThePeriod

Crystal Reports lends itself to creating date-oriented reports, such as those used for accounting, production, forecasting, and sales applications. In many cases, you will want to design reports that automatically include a particular range of dates in record selection. Such examples include reports based on data from the last week, last full month, this month to date, data aged 30 days, data aged 30 to 60 days, and so forth. This type of automatic record selection becomes even handier if you are using an automatic report scheduling tool, such as Crystal Enterprise or Seagate Info.

The Select Expert features the *InThePeriod* operator to provide this kind of automatic date range capability when used with date or date-time fields. By using InThePeriod, your reports will automatically retrieve the correct set of data according to the system clock in your computer (or the computer scheduling the report).

1. Open an existing report or create a new report that requires record selection to be based on an automatic date range.

2. Display the Select Expert using pull-down menu or pop-up menu options, or the appropriate toolbar button.

3. Add a new criterion based on a date or date-time field (the InThePeriod operator won't even appear if you haven't based the criterion on a date or date-time field).

4. Choose Is In The Period or Is Not In The Period from the first pull-down list, depending on whether you want to include or exclude records according to a date range.

5. The second drop-down list will show the available date ranges. Choose the desired date range from the list.

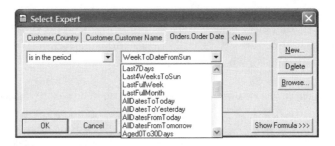

6. Click OK to close the Select Expert. Refresh the report. You should see only records from the chosen date range on the report.

7. If you wish to use something other than today's date in determining the InThePeriod range (perhaps you'd like to perform some "point in time" reporting for a previous date), you can change the date used for determining the InThePeriod value by choosing Report | Set Print Date/Time from the pull-down menus.

Chapter 6

Web Reporting

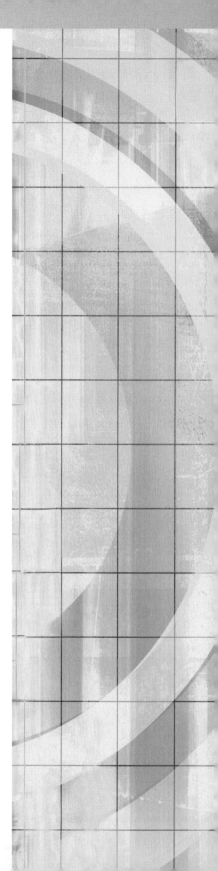

It's hard to argue that the fastest moving, most pervasive method of reporting today is via the World Wide Web. Few, if any, new applications come on the market or are considered in-house without a web interface being an up-front part of the equation.

Crystal Reports has been prepared for the fast movement in this direction for several versions. From the first web access server in version 7 to the web desktop for Seagate Info, to the Report Application Server bundled with Crystal Reports 9, to the complete capabilities of Crystal Enterprise, Crystal Reports has been a part of leading-edge web-based reporting for several years.

Once you've designed your report in Crystal Reports, there are myriad ways to get it to your web-based end users. This chapter covers some of the quickest, easiest, and, sometimes, least widely known ways of getting your reports on the web. You'll also learn how to make the most of your web-based reports, adding interactivity and flexibility along the way.

Create Simple Web Reports with File | Export

Probably the simplest way to get a report on the web is to just export the report as HTML-formatted data. The process for doing this is the same as exporting to other file formats, such as Word documents, Excel spreadsheets, and plain ASCII text files.

You'll have choices of different versions of HTML to export to. HTML 3.2 is an older version of HTML supported by older versions of standard web browsers. The newer HTML 4.0 (also known as Dynamic HTML, or DHTML) is supported by recent versions of Internet Explorer, Netscape, and other web browsers. HTML 4 more faithfully reproduces the original formatting of your report, so you'll probably want to use it whenever possible.

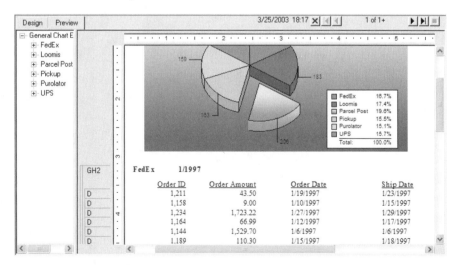

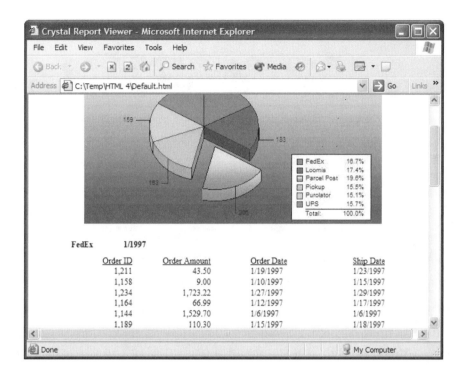

1. Open the existing report or create a new report that you wish to export to HTML.

2. Choose File | Print | Export from the pull-down menus in Crystal Reports 8.5 or File | Export in Crystal Reports 9. You may also click the Export toolbar button. The Export dialog box will appear.

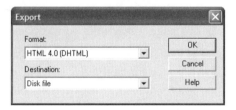

3. Choose the desired HTML format in the Format drop-down list (if your report viewer will be using Internet Explorer or Netscape versions 4 or later, choose HTML4 to maximize accuracy in the HTML page).

4. Choose Disk File in the Destination drop-down list. Click OK.

5. The Export To Directory dialog box will appear.

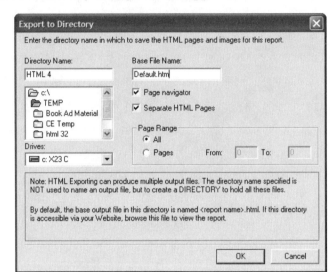

6. In the directory list between the Directory Name and Drives items, navigate to the directory that you want to hold your HTML files. Remember that you will be creating *another* directory that contains your HTML files within the directory you choose.

7. In the Directory Name text box, type in the name of the subdirectory you want to create.

8. In the Base File Name text box, type the name of the HTML file (such as DEFAULT.HTM) that you want to display as the first page of your HTML report.

9. Check Page Navigator if you want Crystal Reports to place First, Last, Next, and Previous page hyperlinks between each report page.

10. Check Separate HTML Pages if you want Crystal Reports to create individual HTML pages for each page of your report. If you don't make this choice, one long single HTML file will result.

NOTE   *If you choose this option, a user won't be able to print the entire report to their printer with their browser's Print function—only the page they are currently viewing will print.*

11. Choose All or type the desired range of report pages you want to export in the Page Range section.

12. Click OK to begin the export.

> NOTE
>
> *While creating web-based reports by exporting to HTML is simple and straightforward, there is a trade-off. Your report won't provide the true interactivity of Crystal Reports (such as use of the group tree or drill down), and will show "static" data—the end user cannot refresh the web report to get a current set of data. Should you wish to provide this kind of interactivity and ad hoc refresh capability, you'll need to use a custom Active Server Page using the Crystal Report Designer Component, Crystal Reports 9 Report Application Server, Crystal Enterprise, or another form of Crystal "native" web reporting.*

Hyperlink to Web Pages or E-Mail Addresses

While Crystal Reports is traditionally considered to be strictly a reporting tool, the term "Crystal Reports" may sometimes be a misnomer. While its history follows traditional report writer directions, more recent versions of Crystal Reports include a good number of web reporting and web interactivity capabilities. One of these features that is very powerful, yet very simple to implement, is hyperlinks. A *hyperlink* is simply a portion of a web page that, when clicked, takes the viewer to another web page or sends an e-mail to a particular e-mail address.

Crystal Reports version 8 and later features a Hyperlink tab right on the Format Editor. This tab, which appears on the Format Editor for every type of object in Crystal Reports (a subreport is the lone exception), allows you to turn the object into a hyperlink to a web page or e-mail address. As you might expect, the hyperlinks will work from web pages that you export to from Crystal Reports (exporting to HTML is discussed earlier in this chapter). Hyperlinks you create in this fashion will also work from "native" Crystal web reporting tools, such as Crystal Reports 9 Report Application Server and Crystal Enterprise.

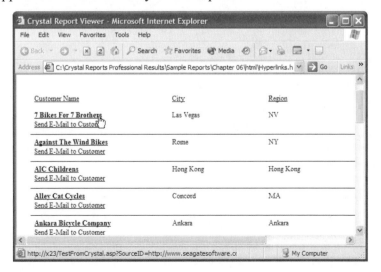

DOWNLOAD   *Hyperlinks.rpt from CrystalBook.com*

1. Open an existing report or create a new report that you wish to hyperlink from.

2. Select the object on the report that you wish to turn into a hyperlink.

3. Right-click the object and choose Format from the pop-up menu. You may also use pull-down menu options or the appropriate toolbar button to display the Format Editor.

4. Click the Hyperlink tab of the Format Editor.

5. To hyperlink to an e-mail address, click the An E-Mail Address radio button. Type the e-mail address you wish to link to in the E-Mail Address text box after the mailto: preface.

6. To hyperlink to a web page, click the A Web Site On The Internet radio button. Type the web URL you wish to link to in the Web Site text box after the http:// preface.

7. Click OK to close the Format Editor.

8. Preview the report. Point to the object you added the hyperlink for. Notice that the mouse cursor changes to a pointing finger.

9. Click on the object. The web page you specified will appear or your e-mail program will launch a Send window with the chosen e-mail address in the To field.

NOTE

After you create a hyperlink for a report object, clicking on the object in the Crystal Reports Preview tab will actually perform the hyperlink, not select the object. To select the object in the Preview tab, right-click on it. Rather than executing the hyperlink, Crystal Reports will just select the object.

Control Hyperlinks with a Formula

While the hyperlink technique discussed previously in the chapter allows fixed web sites and e-mail addresses to be specified, Crystal Reports allows for much more powerful customized hyperlinks using Crystal Reports formulas.

By allowing hyperlinks to be specified with a formula, Crystal Reports unleashes the power of its entire formula language for hyperlink creation. You can base hyperlinks on any database field, use built-in formula functions, or perform calculations and string manipulation to derive a hyperlink.

DOWNLOAD *Hyperlinks.rpt from CrystalBook.com*

1. Open an existing report or create a new report that you wish to hyperlink from.

2. Select the object on the report that you wish to turn into a hyperlink.

3. Right-click on the object and choose Format from the pop-up menu. You may also use pull-down menu options or the appropriate toolbar button to display the Format Editor.

4. Click the Hyperlink tab of the Format Editor.

5. Choose the desired web page or e-mail address hyperlink radio button.

6. Instead of typing a specific web page URL or e-mail address into the corresponding text box, click the formula button next to the text box.

7. Build a formula to create the web URL or e-mail address that you wish to use for the hyperlink. The formula must return a string value—any other data type, such as numbers, will result in an error message when you try save the formula.

Control Hyperlinks with a Formula

8. Use database fields or built-in formula language features as necessary. For example, to replace an old domain name in a database-provided web URL field with a new domain, you might use the following formula:

    ```
    Replace({Customer.Web Site},"seagatesoftware.com","CrystalDecisions.com")
    ```

9. Ensure that a web address formula returns the characters http:// as the first part of the formula (the formula illustrated previously assumes that the {Customer.Web Site} database field contains http:// within the database field itself).

10. Ensure that an e-mail address formula returns the characters mailto: as the first part of the formula. For example:

    ```
    "mailto:" & {Customer.E-mail}
    ```

11. Check the formula with the syntax check button. If you receive no errors, save the formula with the Save button.

12. Notice that the formula button in the Formula Editor hyperlink tab has turned red with the pencil pointing at an angle—this indicates that a formula has been specified to supply the hyperlink.

13. Click OK to close the Format Editor.

14. Preview the report. Point to the object you added the hyperlink for. Notice that the mouse cursor changes to a pointing finger.

15. Click on the object. The web page you specified will appear or your e-mail program will launch a Send window with the chosen e-mail address in the To field.

> **NOTE** *For more detailed information on building Crystal Reports string formulas, consult Crystal Reports documentation. You may also read the* Crystal Reports: The Complete Reference *series, also published by McGraw-Hill/Osborne.*

Pass a Value to Another Page in a Hyperlink

Many web pages make use of URL parameter values passed in the URL along with the web site name and web page filename. You may use Crystal Reports hyperlink features to call these types of web pages, passing specific parameter values to the web page in the URL.

For example, you may wish to link to a web page named OrderPage.asp that accepts a single parameter value, ProductID. The URL might look like this if you wish to order Product # 1104:

```
http://www.OrderXtremeStuff.com/OrderPage.asp?ProductID=1104
```

An example of the power of using a formula for a web page hyperlink is automatically directing a report viewer to the order page, passing the proper product number as a URL parameter.

1. Open an existing report or create a new report that you wish to hyperlink from.

2. Select the object on the report that you wish to turn into a hyperlink.

3. Right-click on the object and choose Format from the pop-up menu. You may also use pull-down menu options or the appropriate toolbar button to display the Format Editor.

4. Click the Hyperlink tab of the Format Editor.

5. Click the A Web Site On The Internet radio button.

6. Instead of typing a specific web page URL into the corresponding text box, click the formula button next to the text box.

7. Build a formula to create the web URL that you wish to use for the hyperlink. The formula must return a string value—any other data type, such as numbers, will result in an error message when you try to save the formula.

8. Use database fields or built-in formula language features as necessary. For example, to build a hyperlink to the OrderPage.asp web page described in the preceding example, you might use the following formula:

```
"http://www.OrderXtremeStuff.com/OrderPage.asp?productid=" &
ToText({Product.Product ID},0,"")
```

NOTE *The ToText function illustrated here converts the numeric Product ID field to a string. When the conversion occurs, no decimal places are used and the thousands separator is set to an empty string.*

9. Check the formula with the syntax check button. If you receive no errors, save the formula with the Save button.

10. Notice that the formula button in the Formula Editor hyperlink tab has turned red with the pencil pointing at an angle—this indicates that a formula has been specified to supply the hyperlink.

11. Click OK to close the Format Editor.

12. Preview the report. Point to the object you added the hyperlink for. Notice that the mouse cursor changes to a pointing finger.

13. Click on the object. The web page you specified will appear with a URL parameter based on data from the report. For example, if you clicked a hyperlink for a product with a product number of 4,104, the following URL would be sent to the browser:

```
http://www.OrderXtremeStuff.com/OrderPage.asp?productid=4104
```

NOTE *Coordinate your Crystal Reports custom hyperlinks with the appropriate web developer to ensure you are building properly formatted URLs.*

Open Crystal Hyperlinks in a New Window

Web pages often contain unique and "tricky" ways of accomplishing things. By using a variety of HTML tags or JavaScript routines, web developers can approximate behavior of more sophisticated Windows development languages in their web pages.

One prevalent feature of web hyperlinks is the ability to open the web page referred to in the hyperlink in a separate web browser window. By use of a simple "target" addition to the standard Anchor HTML tag, you can open a new window to display the web page. However, Crystal Reports hyperlink capabilities described earlier in the chapter don't include a default option to add the target addition—you need to make creative use of a custom hyperlink formula to enable this feature.

Consider the following standard Anchor tag to link to the CrystalBook.com web site:

```
<A HREF="http://www.CrystalBook.com">
Go to CrystalBook.com web site</a>
```

To launch CrystalBook.com in a separate web page window, the Anchor tag will need to be modified with the "target" tag. The value you supply to the target tag is the name of the new window you want to contain the linked page. For example, the following will create a separate browser window (named internally as "NewWindow") to contain the CrystalBook.com web page:

```
<A HREF="http://www.CrystalBook.com" target="NewWindow">
Go to CrystalBook.com web site</a>
```

Enabling this technique with a Crystal Reports hyperlink is not a direct feature within the Crystal Reports Format Editor Hyperlink tab—there is no check box or other feature to open the hyperlink in a new window. However, by creative use of a custom hyperlink formula, you can add the target tag to the Anchor tag.

NOTE *The following technique will work only with Crystal Reports that are displayed in a web browser (via an export to HTML, Crystal Reports 9 RAS, Crystal Enterprise, or other alternative in a web browser). You'll encounter a malformed URL if you attempt to use this technique in a Windows-based environment, such as from the Crystal Reports Preview tab or a custom Windows application containing a Crystal Report.*

1. Open an existing report or create a new report that you wish to hyperlink from.

2. Select the object on the report that you wish to turn into a hyperlink.

3. Right-click on the object and choose Format from the pop-up menu. You may also use pull-down menu options or the appropriate toolbar button to display the Format Editor.

4. Click the Hyperlink tab of the Format Editor.

5. Click the A Web Site On The Internet radio button.

6. Instead of typing a specific web page URL into the corresponding text box, click the formula button next to the text box.

7. Build a formula to create the web URL that you wish to use for the hyperlink. The formula must return a string value—any other data type, such as numbers, will result in an error message when you try to save the formula.

8. Because Crystal Reports adds quotation marks around web URLs in hyperlinks, you need to add additional quotation mark characters, as well as the target tag, to the hyperlink. Add the following text after the portion of the formula that returns the URL to the web site:

```
& chr(34) & " " & "target=" & chr(34) & "NewWindow"
```

9. Use the Chr built-in function to specify an ASCII numeric value for a character. The ASCII value of quotation marks is 34. As Crystal Reports already surrounds the whole Anchor tag with quotation marks by default, the additional two sets of quotation marks will "balance out" the set that Crystal already includes.

10. Check the formula with the syntax check button. If you receive no errors, save the formula with the Save button.

Open Crystal Hyperlinks in a New Window

11. Notice that the formula button in the Formula Editor hyperlink tab has turned red with the pencil pointing at an angle—this indicates that a formula has been specified to supply the hyperlink.

12. Click OK to close the Format Editor.

13. Export the report to HTML (as discussed earlier in the chapter), or add the report to another web-based Crystal Reports system, such as Crystal Reports 9 RAS or Crystal Enterprise.

14. View the report in a web browser.

15. Click on the object that you added the hyperlink for. The web page you specified will appear in a separate web browser window.

> **NOTE**   *This technique can be modified to make use of other HTML features from within a Crystal Reports hyperlink. Consult an HTML reference for detailed information on the Anchor tag, target tag, and other HTML topics.*

Add Tooltips

Tooltips are small bits of text that appear when you "hover" your mouse over a hyperlink in a web page. You may also notice that tooltips are displayed liberally in the Crystal Reports preview window itself when you hover over a particular report object.

Crystal Reports allows you to customize the tooltip that appears when you point to a hyperlink. By using a custom formula in the Format Editor, you may completely customize the appearance of a tooltip. This new tooltip will appear when you view the report in Crystal Reports, or in a web browser.

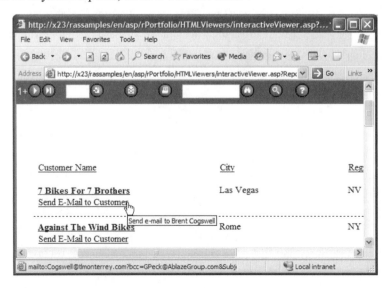

DOWNLOAD *Hyperlinks.rpt from CrystalBook.com*

1. Open an existing report or create a new report that you wish to add a tooltip to.

2. Select the object on the report that you wish to add a tooltip to.

3. Right-click on the object and choose Format from the pop-up menu. You may also use pull-down menu options or the appropriate toolbar button to display the Format Editor.

4. Click the Common tab of the Format Editor.

5. Click the formula button next to the Tool Tip Text property. The Format Formula Editor will appear.

6. Build a formula to create the tooltip that you wish to display. The formula must return a string value—any other data type, such as numbers, will result in an error message when you try save the formula.

7. Use database fields or built-in formula language features as necessary. For example, to display a tooltip indicating "Send e-mail to" followed by the customer first and last names for the current database record, use the following formula:

```
"Send e-mail to " & {Customer.Contact First Name} & " "
& {Customer.Contact Last Name}
```

8. Check the formula with the syntax check button. If you receive no errors, save the formula with the Save button.

9. Notice that the Tool Tip Text formula button has turned red with the pencil pointing at an angle—this indicates that a formula has been specified to supply the tooltip.

10. Click OK to close the Format Editor.

11. Preview the report. Move your mouse over the object you added the tooltip to and wait for a second or two. Notice the customized tooltip that now appears.

Add Tooltips

NOTE

Crystal Reports 8.5 does not include tooltips when exporting to HTML. Tooltips will appear only in Crystal Reports "native" web publishing products, such as ASPs built with the Crystal Report Designer Component or Crystal Enterprise. However, tooltips work properly with all methods of viewing reports in Crystal Reports 9.

Crystal Reports 9 RAS for Simple Web Reports

There are many different ways of displaying reports you design in the Crystal Reports Windows environment in a web browser. One method, described at the beginning of this chapter, is simply exporting reports to HTML format with the File | Export menu option. One of the caveats discussed in that section of the chapter is that this method creates "static" web reports that can't be refreshed in real time by the viewer. And, some of Crystal Reports' more interactive features, such as navigation with the Group Tree and drill-down, aren't accommodated by exporting to HTML.

One of the newer methods to enable fully interactive and real-time web reporting is the Report Application Server (or RAS), supplied with Crystal Reports 9 Professional, Developer, and Advanced Editions. While RAS can be considered a "lite" version of the fuller-featured Crystal Enterprise 9 web-based reporting system, it is simpler to implement and can provide interactive web reporting for a small to medium-sized organization "out of the box."

NOTE

For detailed instructions on fine installation or configuration points on RAS, consult Crystal Reports 9 documentation, or refer to Crystal Reports 9: The Complete Reference, *also published by McGraw-Hill/Osborne.*

Once RAS has been installed, you can quickly connect to it and view sample reports included with the product. Point your web browser to:

```
http://<web server>/rassamples
```

The Report Application Server Launchpad will appear with links to documentation and other RAS-related information. In particular, you'll be interested in *ePortfolio Lite,* the interface that actually provides report viewing in your web browser. Clicking the ePortfolio Lite link will launch it in a separate web browser window.

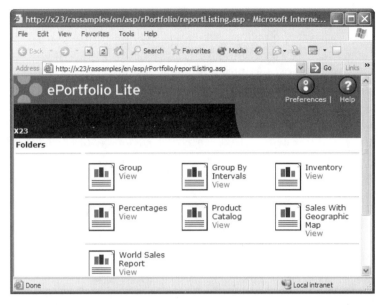

Click a report that you'd like to view. The report will be run against the database with the results displayed in another separate web browser window. If the report was designed with a group tree, it will appear on the left side of the browser window. And, if the report was designed with drill-down capabilities, the mouse will change to the hyperlink "finger" when pointed to a drillable summary or chart.

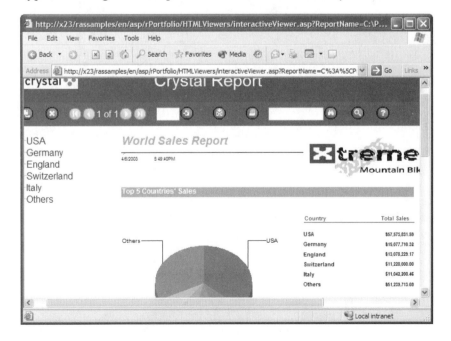

Once you've successfully tested your RAS installation, you may simply point the RAS server to another directory containing the report files that you want to publish to the web. RAS will automatically display the reports in this directory, as well as directories below the initial directory, in the ePortfolio lite.

1. Launch the RAS Configuration Manager. Do this by choosing Crystal Enterprise 9 | Tools | RAS Configuration Manager from the Windows Start button. Or, navigate directly to Program Files\Crystal Decisions\Report Application Server 9 folder and double-click RASCONFIG.EXE. The RAS Configuration Manager dialog box will appear.

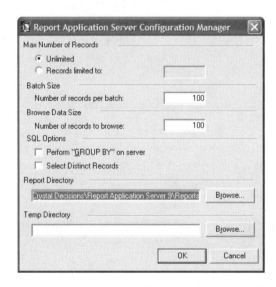

2. Type in the directory where your report files are located in the Report Directory text box. Or, click the Browse button next to the text box and choose the directory from the list.

3. Click OK. You'll receive a message that indicates the need to stop and restart the Report Application Server NT service for the change to take effect.

4. Launch the Windows Control Panel. If necessary, double-click the Administrative Tools icon. Double-click the Services icon. The Services dialog box will appear.

5. Select the Report Application Server in the list of services. Click the Restart button to stop and restart the service.

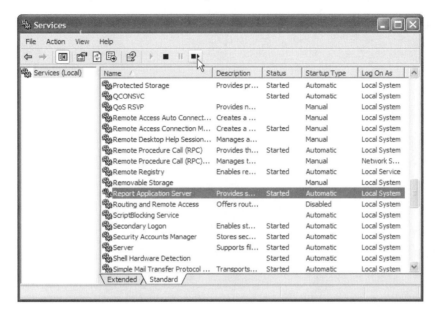

6. Close the Services dialog box and the Control Panel.

7. Start your web browser and type in:

   ```
   http://<web server>/rassamples
   ```

8. The RAS Launchpad will appear. Click the ePortfolio Lite link.

9. The list of reports and subfolders in the folder you supplied to the RAS Configuration Manager will appear.

10. Click a report to run it. If the report requires database logon information or prompts for parameter fields, supply correct values.

11. The report will appear in a separate browser window. You may navigate through the group tree, drill down, and perform other interactive functions using the RAS toolbar at the top of the browser window.

NOTE   *Although RAS supports the newer Crystal Reports 9 file format, it does not require that reports adhere to this format. You can place older Crystal Reports .rpt files in the folder and RAS will display them properly.*

Chapter 7

Parameter Fields

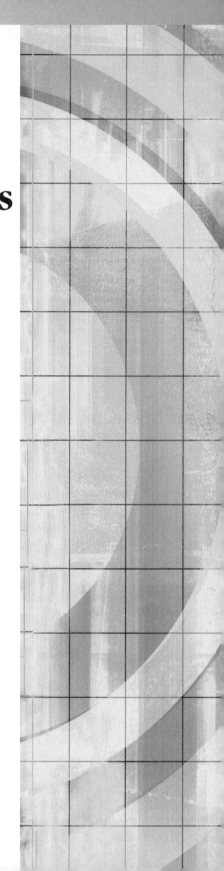

One of the more powerful features of Crystal Reports is the ability to prompt report viewers for values every time they refresh the report. This is accomplished with parameter fields. A *parameter field* is a prompt that asks the viewer to type in a free-form value, or allows the viewer to choose a value from a set of default values. The responses the viewer supplies can then be used in record selection, formulas, conditional formatting, or anywhere a database field or literal value can be used in a report.

This is helpful when using the report in Crystal Reports by itself, as well as when publishing reports with Seagate Info or Crystal Enterprise. Also, it's often helpful to pass values to report parameter fields from within custom code, such as Visual Basic programs or web-based Active Server Pages. There are many techniques you can use with various types of parameter fields that will enhance their features in both stand-alone reports used right from Crystal Reports, as well as when reports are integrated with Crystal Enterprise, Seagate Info, or a custom Windows or web application.

Show All Multivalue Values on the Report

One type of parameter field allows a report viewer to supply more than one value for a single parameter field. For example, by checking the Allow Multiple Values option when you create a parameter field, you allow a report viewer to type or select more than one state to be included on a report.

However, you may be perplexed when you try to display all the values the report viewer has chosen somewhere on the report (you may want to display the values a viewer has supplied in the report header or page header). While just dragging and dropping a single-value parameter field onto the report from the Field Explorer will show the value supplied to the parameter field, a multivalue parameter will show only the *first* value when dragged and dropped on the report.

In order to show all values supplied in a multivalue parameter, you'll need to write a formula and place it on the report. Checking the Allow Multiple Values option when creating a parameter field actually changes the type of value the parameter field returns to the report. The parameter field becomes an *array,* a single object that actually contains more than one value or *element.* By using built-in Crystal Reports formula functions, you can extract the individual elements of the parameter field array and concatenate them together in a single string value.

The technique used in this formula changes substantially depending on the data type of the parameter field. A string parameter field requires simple use of the *Join* function to extract the elements of the parameter field array into a single string value. However, any nonstring multivalue parameter fields (such as numeric or date parameters) require more complex looping logic in the formula to extract the individual elements of the array, convert them to string values, and concatenate them together into a string variable. Contents of the variable can then be returned by the formula.

States Chosen: CA, CO, FL, MD, NY

Order Date	Ship Date	Customer Name
2/1/1998	2/5/1998	Sporting Wheels Inc.
3/12/1998	3/14/1998	Rowdy Rims Company
2/15/1998	2/23/1998	Rowdy Rims Company
1/4/1998	1/5/1998	Sporting Wheels Inc.
2/12/1998	2/15/1998	Rowdy Rims Company

 *Parameters.rpt from CrystalBook.com*

String Multivalue Parameters

If you create a string multivalue parameter field, you can use the Join function to extract and concatenate each individual parameter value.

1. Create a multivalue parameter field to prompt the user for an appropriate string value. Check the Allow Multiple Values option.

2. Choose any other desired parameter options, such as supplying default values, setting edit masks, and so forth.

3. Use the parameter field where necessary on the report, such as in record selection or another formula.

4. To show all the values supplied by the viewer, create a formula that makes use of the Join function. The formula will look similar to the following:

    ```
    "States Chosen: " & Join({?States}, ", ")
    ```

5. The first argument supplied to the Join function should be the multivalue string parameter you want to display.

6. Optionally, supply a second argument in the form of a string literal (the string value should be surrounded by quotation marks or apostrophes) specifying the character or characters you would like to separate each element of the array with.

7. Place the formula on the report. Refresh the report, selecting the option to Prompt For New Parameter Values.

Nonstring Multivalue Parameters

If your multivalue parameter field is any other data type but string, you must undertake more involved looping logic to extract the individual parameter values.

1. Create a multivalue parameter field to prompt the user for an appropriate nonstring value (such as a multiple numbers). Check the Allow Multiple Values option.

2. Choose any other desired parameter options, such as supplying default values, setting edit masks, and so forth.

3. Use the parameter field where necessary on the report, such as in record selection or another formula.

4. To show all the values supplied by the viewer, create a formula that makes use of looping logic. The formula will look similar to the following:

```
NumberVar Counter;
StringVar OrderIDs;
For Counter := 1 to UBound({?Order Numbers})
Do
(
    OrderIDs := OrderIDs &
    ToText({?Order Numbers}[Counter],0,"") & ", "
);
"Order #s: " & Left(OrderIDs, Length(OrderIDs) - 2)
```

5. Declare a numeric variable to hold the counter that will be used to loop through the array elements. Follow the declaration statement with a semicolon.

6. Declare a string variable to hold the contents of the "built-up" concatenated list of parameter values. Follow the declaration statement with a semicolon.

7. Use the For loop statement to increment the numeric counter variable from 1 to the number of elements in the parameter field array (you can determine the number of array elements with the Ubound function).

8. Follow the For statement with the word *Do* and an open parenthesis.

9. "Build up" the contents of the string variable by extracting the individual values of the parameter field and concatenating them to what's already in the string variable.

10. If you wish to format the string values (for example, not display decimal places or a thousands separator) use the ToText or CStr function to convert the individual array element to a string. If default formatting is acceptable, simply use the ampersand (&) concatenate operator to implicitly convert the parameter value to a string.

11. Extract each individual parameter value by supplying the numeric counter variable as the subscript argument (surrounded by square brackets) after the parameter field name.

12. Close off the Do logic by supplying a closing parenthesis. Follow the parenthesis with a semicolon.

13. Return the value of the string variable as the last statement in the formula. If you need to perform any additional manipulation of the string variable (such as stripping off trailing string material), use string functions such as Left and Length in the final formula statement.

14. Place the formula on the report. Refresh the report, selecting the option to Prompt For New Parameter Values.

Show Beginning and Ending Range Values

When you create a parameter field, you'll notice a set of radio buttons at the bottom of the Create Parameter Field dialog box: Discreet Value, Range Value, and Discrete And Range Value (this last option will be available only if you check Allow Multiple Values). The default discrete value choice will allow just a single value to be supplied to a parameter field (or, if you check Allow Multiple Values, one or more single values).

However, certain situations dictate the need for beginning and ending *range values* to be supplied to a parameter. Probably the most notable need for range parameters is with dates. Very often, a report will need to be limited to a date range, rather than just to a single date. Other potential uses for range parameters are a range of customer numbers, a range of product numbers, and so forth. By selecting the Range Value radio button when you create the parameter, you'll be prompted for beginning and ending values when the report is refreshed.

As with a multiple-value parameter field (discussed earlier in this chapter), just dragging and dropping a range parameter field onto the report will not properly show the beginning and ending values supplied to the parameter. In fact, range parameters behave even worse than multivalue parameters in this situation. While a multivalue parameter will at least show the first value in its array on the report, a range parameter won't show anything when dropped onto the report in this fashion.

Show Beginning and Ending
Range Values

In order to extract the beginning and ending values of the range parameter, a formula must be created.

Orders between 1/1/1998 and 4/30/1998

Order Date	Ship Date	Customer Name
2/1/1998	2/5/1998	Sporting Wheels Inc.
3/12/1998	3/14/1998	Rowdy Rims Company
2/15/1998	2/23/1998	Rowdy Rims Company
1/4/1998	1/5/1998	Sporting Wheels Inc.
2/12/1998	2/15/1998	Rowdy Rims Company

DOWNLOAD *Parameters.rpt from CrystalBook.com*

1. Create a parameter field to prompt the user for an appropriate range value (such as a date range). Click the Range Value(s) radio button.

2. Choose any other desired parameter options, such as supplying default values, setting edit masks, and so forth.

3. Use the parameter field where necessary on the report, such as in record selection or another formula.

4. Create a formula that makes use of the Minimum and Maximum functions to extract the beginning and ending values of the range parameter. The formula will look similar to the following:

```
"Orders between " & Minimum({?Date Range})
& " and " & Maximum({?Date Range})
```

5. Use the Minimum function to extract the beginning value of the range parameter.

6. Use the Maximum function to extract the ending value of the range parameter.

7. If you are combining the beginning and ending values with string elements (such as a "Dates chosen" string literal), you may need to convert the minimum and maximum values to strings (if the parameter is defined with a nonstring data type).

8. If you wish to format the beginning and ending string values (for example, spelling out the month names, adding a day-of-week string, and so forth)

use the ToText or CStr function to convert the beginning and ending values to a string. If default formatting is acceptable, simply use the ampersand (&) concatenate operator to implicitly convert the parameter value to a string.

9. Place the formula on the report. Refresh the report, selecting the option to Prompt For New Parameter Values.

Embedding a Parameter in a Text Object

As discussed in previous sections in this chapter, multivalue parameter fields and range parameter fields pose problems when you try to merely drag and drop them on the report. For these types of parameter fields, you need to create formulas to get them to display properly. However, for a single-value parameter field, merely dragging and dropping it on the report will show the value the viewer typed or chose when they ran the report.

However, you may wish to add text around the parameter field to make it easier to understand. For example, instead of just displaying the number "$2,500" on the report, you may wish to display the parameter as "Orders over $2,500 are highlighted." In particular, you'd like the text to flow evenly around the parameter value without any extra white space, regardless of how wide or narrow the value returned by the parameter will be.

There are two ways to accomplish this: create a formula, or embed the parameter in a text object. For some situations, such as the multivalue or range parameter, or if you need to perform some more involved logic, you must use a formula. However, embedding a single-value parameter in a text object can save time and doesn't require that a formula (including possible data type conversions, formatting considerations, and so forth) be created.

Orders over $2,500 are highlighted

Order Amount	Order Date	Ship Date	Customer Name
$559.35	3/22/1998	3/23/1998	Off the Mountaing Biking
$1,439.55	3/12/1998	3/14/1998	Rowdy Rims Company
$296.87	1/4/1998	1/5/1998	Sporting Wheels Inc.
$11,099.25	2/15/1998	2/23/1998	Rowdy Rims Company
$47.00	4/12/1998	4/21/1998	Bike Shop from Mars
$2,699.55	2/12/1998	2/15/1998	Rowdy Rims Company
$29.00	1/18/1998	1/21/1998	Rowdy Rims Company
$1,031.49	3/6/1998	3/6/1998	Changing Gears
$5,219.55	2/7/1998	2/13/1998	Off the Mountaing Biking
$8,819.55	2/26/1998	3/1/1998	Off the Mountaing Biking

1. Create a parameter field to prompt the user for an appropriate value. Ensure that neither the Allow Multiple Values nor Range Value(s) options are selected.

2. Choose any other desired parameter options, such as supplying default values, setting edit masks, and so forth.

3. Use the parameter field where necessary on the report, such as in record selection or another formula.

4. Insert a text object to the report where you'd like the value of the parameter field to be displayed. Begin typing the text you'd like the text object to show to the left of the parameter field, such as "Orders over," followed by a space.

5. If the parameter field was placed on the report previously, you may drag and drop the parameter from the other report location to the text object. If not, display the Field Explorer and drag and drop the parameter into the text object.

6. When you drag the parameter into the text object, you'll notice that the outline of the parameter will disappear and that the cursor will appear inside the text object. Ensure that the cursor inside the text object appears after the space—the parameter will be dropped inside the text object where the cursor appears.

7. Once the cursor appears in the proper place inside the text object, release your mouse button to drop the parameter field inside the text object.

8. The text object will remain in edit mode. Continue typing additional required text, such as " are highlighted" inside the text object. Click outside the text object to end editing.

Formatting the Parameter Within the Text Object

When you drop a parameter field inside a text object, whatever formatting the parameter had before you dropped it inside (either default formatting coming from the Field Explorer or whatever formatting you applied to the parameter on the report before you moved it) will be retained inside the text object. However, you may desire to change the formatting of the parameter field inside the text object. For example, you may prefer that a numeric parameter show no decimal places and have a leading dollar sign.

If you try to perform this type of formatting by just clicking on the whole text object, you won't have any luck—you'll just be formatting text without any decimal place or currency symbol formatting options. To format a parameter inside a text object, you must edit the text object and format the individual parameter field portion within the text object.

1. Edit the text object by double-clicking it.

2. Within the text object, select the parameter field. You'll know you've selected it when the entire parameter field object inside the text object turns black.

3. Right-click. A pop-up menu will appear. Choose Format *parameter field name* from the pop-up menu.

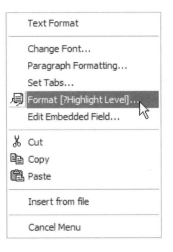

4. The Format Editor will appear. Make any desired formatting changes and click OK.

5. End text object editing by clicking anywhere outside the text object.

NOTE   *Techniques discussed here for embedding and formatting parameters inside text objects will work just as well for embedding other types of objects (such as database fields and formulas) inside text objects.*

Choose from Descriptions Instead of Codes

When you create a parameter field, the value the parameter field needs to return to the report may not always be the most "friendly" from an end-user perspective. For example, the parameter field may need to provide a code or abbreviated value to the Select Expert for database record selection. Or, you may want to supply a series of internal numbers (tax rates, discount rates, and so forth) to a formula. However, the report will be easier to understand if the viewer can pick from a list of more understandable descriptions when the parameter is prompted for.

Crystal Reports features the ability to add descriptions to default values provided to a parameter field. The parameter can then display both the value and the description, or just the description, as a set of choices in a drop-down list when the parameter is prompted for. When the report viewer chooses one of the descriptions, the code or abbreviated value tied to the description is actually supplied to the report for the Select Expert, formula, or other use.

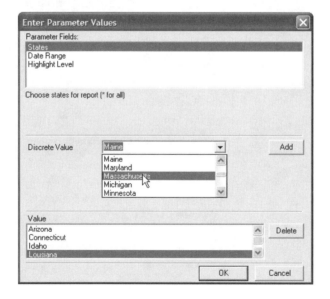

 *Parameters.rpt from CrystalBook.com*

1. Create or edit the parameter field that you'd like to supply a list of descriptions for.

2. Click the Set Default Values button on the Create Parameter Field dialog box. The Set Default Values dialog box will appear.

3. Type in individual default codes you want to be sent to the report in the Select Or Enter Value To Add text box. Click the right arrow after each entry to add the value to the Default Values list.

4. Alternatively, choose a database table and field in the Browse Table and Browse Field drop-down lists. This will fill the list under the Select Or Enter Value To Add text box. Choose individual values and click the right arrow, or click the double right arrow to add all values to the Default Values list.

5. Select a value in the Default Values list that you want to add a description for. Click the Define Description button. The Define Description dialog box will appear.

6. Type in the description you want to appear for the default value. Click OK to save the description and close the Define Description dialog box.

7. Repeat steps 5 and 6 for each value you want to add a description to.

8. In the Display drop-down list, choose how you want default values to display when the parameter field prompts for a value. The options are Value and Description, or just Description.

9. In the Order drop-down list, choose how you want the default values sorted in the drop-down list when the parameter field is displayed. Depending on the data type of the parameter field, choices will include Alphabetical Ascending, Alphabetical Descending, Date Time Ascending, Date Time Descending, or Numeric Ascending.

NOTE *The difference between the Alphabetical and Numeric options is the order in which numeric values will appear. For example, consider the number values 1, 2, and 10. With Alphabetical sorting, the values will appear 1, 10, 2. With Numeric sorting, the values will appear 1, 2, 10.*

Choose from Descriptions Instead of Codes

10. In the Order Based On drop-down list, choose whether you want the default values list sort order to be based on the value or the description.

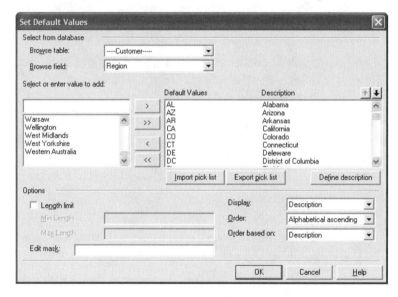

11. Click OK to close the Set Default Values dialog box.

12. Click OK to close the Create Parameter Field dialog box.

13. Refresh the report, selecting the option to Prompt For New Parameter Values. Notice the drop-down list for the parameter field that you just created. Choosing a description from the list will actually pass the value associated with the description to the report.

NOTE   *Building large lists of descriptions can be time consuming. If you have other reports that may contain parameters that will benefit from the same sets of descriptions, you can save the set of values and descriptions to a pick list file with the Export Pick List button. When you create additional parameters that need to use the same list, click the Import Pick List button to populate the descriptions from the pick list file you saved before.*

Control What Can Be Typed in a Parameter

One of the challenges of developing parameter-based reports is providing some level of control over what the report viewer types in to a parameter field prompt. One way of controlling this is by providing default values that the viewer picks from a drop-down list. Another option is to still allow the viewer to type in "free form" values, but to control what the viewer can type in.

Depending on the data type of the parameter field (string, number, date, and so forth), you are given several options for controlling what a viewer can type in. For example, string parameters allow length limits (minimum and maximum number of characters) to be imposed, as well as specification of an *edit mask,* a series of characters that limit the type of characters that can be typed and where. Numeric and date parameters allow range limits to be specified, limiting the lower and upper values that a viewer can type in.

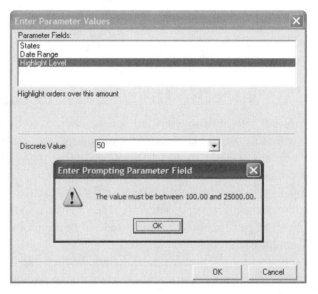

Parameters.rpt from CrystalBook.com

1. Create or edit the parameter field that you'd like to control entry for.

2. Click the Set Default Values button on the Create Parameter Field dialog box. The Set Default Values dialog box will appear.

3. Specify limiting options in the lower-left corner of the Set Default Values dialog box.

   ■ For numeric parameters, you may set minimum and maximum values that can be specified.

   ■ For date parameters, you may set beginning and ending date limits.

   ■ For string parameters, you may set minimum and maximum numbers of characters that must be typed.

   ■ For string parameters, you may specify an edit mask to control specific characters in specific positions. For example, an uppercase *L* will require

Control What Can Be Typed in a Parameter

that a letter be supplied in that position. A greater-than sign will convert subsequent characters in the parameter field to uppercase. For a list of all edit mask characters, consult Crystal Reports online help, or look in *Crystal Reports: The Complete Reference,* also published by McGraw-Hill/Osborne.

4. After specifying limiting options, click OK to close the Create Parameter Field dialog box.

5. Refresh the report, selecting the option to Prompt For New Parameter Values. Ensure that the limits you specified are properly limiting what can be entered into the parameter field.

Create an "All or Specific Item" Parameter

Crystal Reports parameter fields allow several special choices to be made when they are created, such as allowing multiple values, range values, or a combination of both. However, there is no built-in way to allow an "all items" option to be declared with a parameter field that's used in the Select Expert. For example, if the report viewer wants to see all items in the database for a particular parameter field (in essence, the parameter will be eliminated from the Select Expert), or one or more specific values (the parameter will be included in the Select Expert), there is no default way of enabling that behavior.

By creative use of an asterisk parameter value and of the Like operator in the Select Expert, you can add this capability when using string parameters. For other parameter types, such as numbers or dates, modification of the Record Selection formula (instead of using the Select Expert) is required.

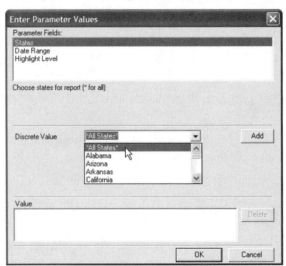

 *Parameters.rpt from CrystalBook.com*

String Parameters

Supplying an asterisk to a string parameter field, in combination with the Like operator in the Select Expert, will return all records for the database field used with the parameter.

1. Edit or create the string parameter field that you want to add an "all" option for.

2. If the viewer will be typing the value in directly (not picking from a list of default values), you may want to provide prompting text indicating that an asterisk will return all records.

3. If you are providing default values for the parameter field, add an asterisk as one of the default values. If you are creating descriptions for the default values, add an "All Records" description for the asterisk.

4. Display the Select Expert. Add a string database field that will be used with the parameter field.

5. Instead of using the Equals operator, use the Like operator. As the Like operator accepts question mark and asterisk wildcards, an asterisk value provided to the Like operator will return all records.

6. Because the Like operator may not properly expose the parameter field in the drop-down list of browsed sample database values, you'll need to type the parameter field name into the Select Expert manually. Include the left and right curly braces around the parameter field name, and make sure to include the question mark character in front of the parameter name.

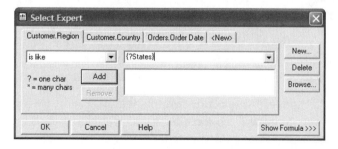

7. Click OK to close the Select Expert. If you are asked to Refresh Or Use Saved Data, you'll probably want to choose the Saved Data option, as

you'll need to manually refresh the report again to be prompted for new parameter values.

8. Refresh the report, selecting the option to Prompt For New Parameter Values. When prompted for the string parameter value, either type an asterisk in directly, or choose the default value that supplies the asterisk. Ensure that all records for that field are returned to the report.

Nonstring Parameters

As there is no equivalent to the Like operator for nonstring fields in the Select Expert, you must modify the Record Selection formula manually to examine some predetermined "all records" value in the parameter, and make changes to the record selection formula accordingly.

1. Edit or create the parameter field that you want to add an "all" option for.

2. If the viewer will be typing the value in directly (not picking from a list of default values), you may want to provide prompting text indicating the predetermined value that will return all records. For example, you may wish to determine that today's date, or the number zero, will be the "all records" value.

3. If you are providing default values for the parameter field, add the predetermined "all records" value as one of the default values. If you are creating descriptions for the default values, add an "All Records" description for this value.

4. You must modify the Record Selection formula manually. Do this either by displaying the Select Expert and clicking the Show Formula button (you can type the formula text in directly, or click the Formula Editor button to display the full Formula Editor), or by bypassing the Select Expert entirely with the Report | Selection Formulas | Record pull-down menu option.

5. Look for any existing reference in the Record Selection formula to the database field/parameter field combination that you will be providing the "all values" capability to. If you find it, remove it.

6. Modify the record selection formula with If-Then-Else logic to accommodate the predetermined "all records" value. For example, if today's date is used as the "all records" value with a date range parameter, you may add the following text to the record selection formula:

```
If Minimum({?Date Range}) = CurrentDate Then
    True
```

```
Else
    {Orders.Order Date} = {?Date Range}
```

7. Make sure that the remainder of the Record Selection formula stays intact, including the "and" or "or" operators that will need to proceed or follow your If-Then-Else logic. A complete Record Selection formula might look like this:

```
{Customer.Country} = "USA" and
{Customer.Region} like {?States} and
If Minimum({?Date Range}) = CurrentDate Then
    True
Else
    {Orders.Order Date} = {?Date Range}
```

8. Save the Record Selection formula. If you are asked to Refresh Or Use Saved Data, you'll probably want to choose the Saved Data option, as you'll need to manually refresh the report again to be prompted for new parameter values.

9. Refresh the report, selecting the option to Prompt For New Parameter Values. When prompted for the just-modified parameter, either type in the predetermined "all records" value directly or choose the default value that supplies it. Ensure that all records for that field are returned to the report.

NOTE   *It's most probable that Crystal Reports will be unable to convert the If-Then-Else portion of the Record Selection formula to SQL. Accordingly, you won't find the database field you've used this technique with appearing in the SQL WHERE clause (you can see the SQL query being sent to the database by choosing Database | Show SQL Query from the pull-down menus). While this technique does add flexibility to parameter fields, it may slow down overall report performance with large databases, as lack of a WHERE clause will require Crystal Reports itself to perform record selection on the parameter-controlled database field.*

Base the N in Top N on a Parameter

Crystal Reports features *Top N reporting*—the ability to sort report groups on the report according to a subtotal or summary value, as opposed to the name of the group. In particular, you can choose to include only the top *N* or bottom *N* groups on the report. This allows you to see only the five best customer groups, or perhaps the ten worst performing regions.

There may be a time when you wish to vary the value of the *N*. For example, a sales manager may wish to run various reports showing top or bottom sales numbers, varying the number of top customers or bottom regions he or she sees each time the report is run. Unfortunately, when you use the standard Top N/Sort Group Expert, the value of N can only be typed in by hand—a parameter field cannot be supplied for this value.

However, by creative use of conditional group suppression and formulas, you may approximate this behavior so that the N can be supplied by a parameter field. While you still make use of the Top N/Sort Group Expert, you will sort all groups by a summary field, not just the top or bottom N. You will then conditionally suppress report sections when comparing the Group Number built-in function to the value of the parameter field.

Top 5 Customer Sales Totals	
Psycho-Cycle totals:	103,535.50
Crank Components totals:	81,477.29
Hooked on Helmets totals:	78,245.79
The Great Bike Shop totals:	76,266.44
Blazing Saddles totals:	76,101.34
Grand Total for Top 5 Customers	**$415,626.36**

DOWNLOAD *Top N With Parameter.rpt from CrystalBook.com*

1. Open or create a report with at least one group that you will use for the Top or Bottom N function.

2. Ensure that at least one subtotal or summary field exists for the group, as the Top N/Sort Group Expert will use a subtotal or summary field to sort the groups.

3. Use the proper toolbar button or menu option to launch the Top N/Sort Group Expert.

NOTE *The Top N/Sort Group Expert is known as the Group Sort Expert in Crystal Reports 9.*

4. Rather than choosing Top N or Bottom N, choose the All option. Choose the desired subtotal or summary field in the Based On drop-down list.

5. If you wish to see the Top *N* groups (the highest group totals first), choose Descending order. To see the Bottom *N* groups (the lowest group totals first), choose Ascending order.

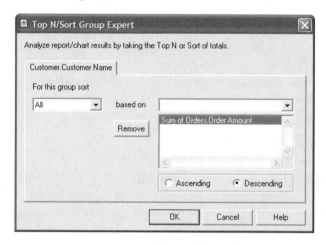

6. Click OK to close the expert. This will sort all groups on the report (not the Top or Bottom *N*) by the subtotal or summary field you chose, in the ascending or descending order you specified.

7. Create a numeric parameter field to prompt for the value of *N*. Add any necessary prompting text to indicate to the report viewer that this will display the Top or Bottom N customers, regions, or so forth.

8. Display the Section Expert to format report sections. This can be done from the Format pull-down menu, with an appropriate toolbar button, or from the appropriate pop-up menu that will appear when you right-click a gray section name.

9. Click the conditional formula button next to the group footer for the group that you want to be suppressed by the parameter value. The Format Formula Editor will appear.

10. Type in a formula that will suppress the section if the Group Number built-in function exceeds the value supplied in the parameter field. The formula may look similar to this:

```
GroupNumber > {?Top N Customers}
```

11. Save the conditional formula. If necessary, suppress other sections (the group header, and so forth) conditionally using this technique.

12. Click OK to close the Section Expert.

Base the N in Top N on a Parameter

13. When prompted, supply the value of *N* to the parameter field. Notice that only the number of groups matching the value appears on the report.

If you are using multiple report groups, comparing the parameter field value to the Group Number built-in function will most probably not work correctly, as the Group Number function will increment for other groups as well. If this occurs, you'll need to create an extra formula that declares and increments a numeric variable in the group header of the Top or Bottom N group. Then, compare the contents of that variable to the parameter field in the conditional suppression formula.

Obtaining Correct Grand Totals

This technique, while providing appropriate report display of the *N* number of groups, will introduce problems if you attempt to show grand totals in the report footer of the report using standard Crystal Reports grand total functions. This occurs because Crystal Reports creates report totals and summaries *before* the Top N/Sort Group Expert sorts report groups. And, the conditional suppression of report sections to limit to the Top or Bottom *N* based on a parameter field occurs after that. As such, grand totals at the end of the report have been calculated long before the parameter field is even used to suppress group footer sections.

When using standard Top *N* reporting, you'll also notice this behavior. However, by using Running Totals instead of Grand Totals, you can avoid this problem. This is because Crystal Reports Running Totals are calculated *after* the Top N/Sort Group Expert limits report groups. Unfortunately, Crystal Reports waits until after Running Totals have been calculated to conditionally suppress report sections. For this reason, even using Running Totals won't provide accurate grand totals when using the Top *N* parameter field method discussed earlier in this section. You must create and maintain your own "running totals" in formulas (using formula variables) in order to display accurate grand totals at the end of the report.

The Top N/Sort Group Expert is known as the Group Sort Expert in Crystal Reports 9.

1. Open an existing report using the method described earlier in this book section. Or, use techniques described earlier in this section to limit display of groups by the Top or Bottom *N* parameter.

2. Create a formula to manually calculate a running total based on the value of the *N* parameter field. It will look similar to this:

```
WhilePrintingRecords;
NumberVar TotalSales;
```

```
If GroupNumber <= {?Top N Customers} Then
    TotalSales := TotalSales +
    Sum ({Orders.Order Amount}, {Customer.Customer Name})
```

3. Force the formula to calculate as the report formats by beginning the formula with the WhilePrintingRecords evaluation time function, followed by a semicolon.

4. Declare a numeric variable to hold the grand total value. If you will be calculating more than one grand total, declare as many variables as necessary to hold each value. End each declaration statement with a semicolon.

5. Add If-Then-Else logic to determine if the grand total should be accumulated. This is determined by the number of groups that have appeared (in the preceding example, the built-in Group Number function is used to make this determination).

6. Save the formula. Place it in the group footer of the group that you want to be totaled. If you don't want the accumulated total to appear in the group footer as the report prints, suppress its display with the Suppress property of the Format Editor.

7. Create another formula to show the contents of the variable that you declared in the preceding formula. It will look similar to this:

```
WhilePrintingRecords;
NumberVar TotalSales
```

8. Force the formula to calculate as the report formats by beginning the formula with the WhilePrintingRecords evaluation time function, followed by a semicolon.

9. Declare the same numeric variable that you used in the preceding formula to hold the grand total value. By simply declaring an existing variable as the last statement in the formula, the formula will return the value of that variable.

10. Save the formula. Add it to the report footer.

11. If you need to show the values of other grand total variables, repeat steps 7–10 for each additional variable you initially declared in the first formula.

12. Refresh the report multiple times, supplying a different value for the Top *N* parameter field. Ensure that the grand total shows the correct grand total value, varying with the number of groups that are shown on the report.

Base the N in Top N on a Parameter

Use a Parameter for Conditional Formatting

When parameter fields are discussed, the first use that often comes to mind is filtering records with the Select Expert. Less often, parameter fields may be discussed for providing values to formulas. However, a parameter field can be used in the report anywhere a database field or formula can be used. So, parameter fields are often overlooked for the flexibility that they provide to a report.

One flexible use for parameter fields is to control conditional formatting on the report. The value returned from a parameter field can be used to change the color of a database field if it falls below a goal, to hide groups if their Group Number is beyond a Top or Bottom *N* value (see "Base the N in Top N on a Parameter" earlier in this chapter for an innovative use of this technique), or to set the background color of a report section according to a condition.

Orders over $2,500 are highlighted

Order Amount	Order Date	Ship Date
$8,819.55	2/26/1998	3/1/1998
$6,005.40	2/19/1998	2/23/1998
$11,099.25	2/15/1998	2/23/1998
$2,699.55	2/12/1998	2/15/1998
$5,219.55	2/7/1998	2/13/1998
$1,031.49	3/6/1998	3/6/1998
$5,300.74	2/1/1998	2/5/1998
$29.00	1/18/1998	1/21/1998
$72.30	1/13/1998	1/17/1998

DOWNLOAD *Parameters.rpt from CrystalBook.com*

1. Open or create a report that will make use of conditional formatting or conditional suppression.

2. Create a parameter field to get a comparison value from the report viewer. Choose the right data type for the parameter field—if you will be comparing it to a string value, choose a string data type, numeric values will require numeric parameters, and so forth.

3. Choose the field or report section that you wish to conditionally format. To format an individual report object, select it and format it with the Format Editor. To format report sections, use the Section Expert.

4. Click the conditional format button for the property that you wish to format. The Format Formula editor will appear.

5. Type in an appropriate formula to set the property conditionally. Make use of the parameter field as necessary in the formula. For example, to set the color of a report section according to a database field compared to a parameter, you will use a formula similar to this:

```
If {Orders.Order Amount} > {?Highlight Level} Then
    crAqua
Else
    crNoColor
```

6. Save the conditional formula. Click OK to close the Section Expert or Format Editor.

7. View the report. You'll be prompted to provide the parameter value.

8. Test with various parameter values to ensure that the conditional formatting is being applied properly in terms of the values you supply to the parameter field.

NOTE   *More information on conditional formatting can be found in Crystal Reports documentation, or in* Crystal Reports: The Complete Reference, *also published by McGraw-Hill/Osborne.*

Use a Parameter for Conditional Formatting

Chapter 8

Sorting and Grouping

One of the most often used features of any reporting or querying tool is sorting and grouping to organize information in an easy-to-follow fashion. In Crystal Reports, sorting simply displays the details records in a particular order based on one or more fields or formulas. Grouping works in a similar fashion but also provides "breaks" whenever the chosen field changes, allowing subtotals, averages, counts, or other summaries to appear when groups change.

Because so much value from Crystal Reports comes from sorting, grouping, and summarizing (grouping and summarizing are particularly important), learning creative ways to use these Crystal Reports features will vastly increase the flexibility you can add to your reports. Being able to manipulate groups in different ways, change or copy summary fields with a few mouse clicks, base sorting and grouping on parameter fields, and take advantage of other unique approaches to sorting and grouping will quickly improve the benefits you get from Crystal Reports.

Sorting/Grouping Based on a Parameter Field

When you initially choose sorting or grouping for a report, you're only given the choice of existing database or formula fields. This may lead you to believe that you must choose to sort or group a report on fixed fields only and can't change sorting or grouping when the report is run, based on a value supplied by the report viewer.

In fact, by creative use of parameter fields and formulas, you can dynamically change sorting and grouping every time the report is refreshed, or when you schedule the report in Seagate Info or Crystal Enterprise. The process simply revolves around changing the value a formula returns based on the parameter field, and then using the formula as the field the sorting or grouping is based on.

Sorting Grouping Based On Parameter.rpt from CrystalBook.com

1. Open or create a report that requires sorting or grouping based on a parameter field.

2. Create the parameter field to prompt the report viewer for the available sorting or grouping options.

3. If you wish, provide the acceptable values (such as "Region" or "Country") as parameter field default values. You may also want to only allow the report viewer to choose from the available default values and not type in their own. Use the appropriate check box on the main Create Parameter Field dialog box to set this limit.

4. Create a formula that uses If-Then-Else, Select Case, or other similar logic to return a different database field or other formula, depending on the value of the parameter field. The formula might look something like this:

```
Select {?Sort By}
  Case "Customer Name":
    {Customer.Customer Name}
  Case "City":
    {Customer.City}
  Case "Last Year's Sales":
    ToText({Customer.Last Year's Sales},"000000.00")
```

NOTE   *In this example, note that a data conversion of the Last Year's Sales field is being performed with ToText. This is necessary to ensure that all values returned by the Select Case formula are of the same data type. Furthermore, the ToText function is formatting the converted numeric field to have a large number of leading zeros. This provides for proper numeric sorting of the now string-based Last Year's Sales field.*

5. Sort or group the report by the formula field you just created.

6. When the report is previewed or printed, the parameter will be prompted for. Choose one of the options and make sure that the report sorts or groups by the value you chose.

Sorting/Grouping Based on a Parameter Field

Limit to Certain Groups with Group Selection

One of the most often used features of Crystal Reports is straightforward grouping and summarizing. By creating a report group based on the desired field, you can then subtotal and summarize various values for each occurrence of that field. By default, Crystal Reports includes every record on the report (based on any record selection added to the report) in one of the report groups.

However, you may wish to further limit the report above and beyond any limitation placed on the report by record selection. Perhaps you want to see only states whose total sales exceed $100,000. This type of selection is known as *group selection,* because it limits data on the report according to a group summary or subtotal field, not to an actual database field.

This is an important distinction. If you limit the report (using record selection) to sales figures that exceed $100,000, only individual detail records that exceed this amount will even appear on the report. However, by limiting the report (with group selection) to groups where the *subtotal* of sales exceeds $100,000, you'll still see smaller individual sales amounts, but only groups that exceed the total.

State Totals

Over $100K States Only

	Customer Name	City	Last Year's Sales
CA			
	Changing Gears	Irvine	26,705.65
	Rowdy Rims Company	Newbury Park	30,131.46
	Off the Mountaing Biking	Irvine	25,000.00
	Sporting Wheels Inc.	San Diego	85,642.56
	Tyred Out	Santa Ana	18,126.33
	Bike Shop from Mars	Newbury Park	25,873.25
		CA State Total:	**211,479.24**
IL			
	Spokes	DeKalb	27,154.90
	Hercules Mountain Bikes	DeKalb	18,000.00
	The Biker's Path	DeKalb	29,036.57
	Crank Components	Champaign	8,030.11
	Deals on Wheels	DeKalb	11,717.24
	Our Wheels Follow Us Everywhere	DeKalb	38,170.65
	Pathfinders	DeKalb	26,369.63
		IL State Total:	**158,479.09**

DOWNLOAD   *Group Selection.rpt from CrystalBook.com*

1. Open or create a report that contains at least one group. The group must also contain at least one subtotal or summary field.

2. Select the summary or subtotal field (such as a subtotal of Last Year's Sales) that you wish to use to limit appearance of report groups.

3. Once the summary has been selected, right-click and choose Select Expert from the pop-up menu. You can also display the Select Expert by using pull-down menu or toolbar options.

4. Supply a condition to limit to groups corresponding to the value of the chosen subtotal or summary field.

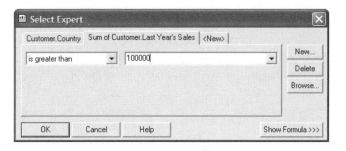

5. Alternatively, you may enter a group selection formula manually, using the Crystal Reports formula language. Either click the Show Formula in the Select Expert, or choose Report | Edit Selection Formula | Group (in Crystal Reports 8.x) or Report | Selection Formulas | Group (in Crystal Reports 9).

6. Type in a valid Boolean formula using a group subtotal or summary field. Check the formula for proper syntax and then save the formula. The formula might look something like this:

```
Sum ({Customer.Last Year's Sales}, {Customer.Region}) > 100000
```

7. When you display the report, only groups that include a summary or subtotal field that meet the criterion will be shown on the report.

Because the group tree (the "hierarchical" group view to the left of the Preview tab) is created before *Group Selection takes place, you'll notice that all groups still appear in the group tree, even though they all won't appear on the report.*
Also, because Group Selection makes use of totals to limit groups, report grand totals will now be inaccurate, as they will have been calculated before Group Selection has taken place. Look for a way around this problem in "Correct Top N/Group Selection Grand Totals" later in the chapter.

Limit to Certain Groups with Group Selection

Show Only the Best or Worst Groups

When you first create a report group and add a summary or subtotal, the groups will still appear on the report in the order of the field the group is based on. In other words, if you create a group based on a State database field and add a subtotal, the groups will still appear with Alabama first and Wyoming last, regardless of the subtotals for the states.

You may wish to show only the ten best states in total sales to send out appreciation rewards. Or, you may wish to show only the 15 worst states in total sales to give to a new salesperson. In either case, you'd prefer that the report groups be sorted by a summary or subtotal field, rather than the group field itself.

The Crystal Reports *Top N/Sort Group Expert* is designed to do just that. By utilizing one or more summary or subtotal fields, report groups can be sorted in order of best to worst or worst to best. And, the Top N/Sort Group Expert also gives you the option to show all groups on the report in this order, or limit the groups to only the top or bottom *N* groups, with you supplying the N (number of groups you want to see).

> **NOTE**   *The Top N/Sort Group Expert is known as the Group Sort Expert in Crystal Reports 9.*

State Totals

Top 10 States Only

Customer Name	City	Last Year's Sales
PA		
Tek Bikes	Philadelphia	301,568.22
Clean Air Transportation Co.	Conshohocken	23,789.25
Backpedal Cycle Shop	Philadelphia	25,162.05
Insane Cycle	Conshohocken	8,000.00
Rocky Roadsters	Conshohocken	28,681.53
	PA State Total:	387,201.05
MA		
Alley Cat Cycles	Concord	298,356.22
Making Tracks	Concord	32,249.55
	MA State Total:	330,605.77
CA		
Changing Gears	Irvine	26,705.65
Rowdy Rims Company	Newbury Park	30,131.46
Off the Mountaing Biking	Irvine	25,000.00
Sporting Wheels Inc.	San Diego	85,642.56
Tyred Out	Santa Ana	18,126.33
Bike Shop from Mars	Newbury Park	25,873.25
	CA State Total:	211,479.24

 *Best 10 Groups.rpt from CrystalBook.com*

1. Open or create a report that contains at least one group. The group must also contain at least one subtotal or summary field.

2. Display the Top N/Sort Group Expert by using pull-down menu options or the correct toolbar button.

3. Alternatively, you may select the summary or subtotal field (such as a subtotal of Last Year's Sales) that you wish to use to sort report groups.

4. Once the summary has been selected, use pull-down menu options or the correct toolbar button to sort records. Because a summary or subtotal field is selected, the Top N/Sort Group Expert will appear.

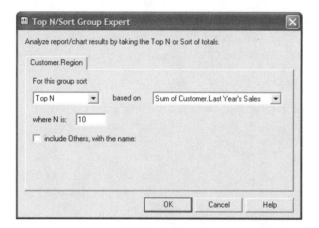

5. If you wish to see all groups from lowest to highest or highest to lowest, leave the For This Group Sort drop-down list set to All.

6. In the Based On drop-down list, choose the summary or subtotal field you wish to base group sorting on.

7. Click the Ascending radio button to see groups from lowest to highest, or the Descending radio button to see groups from highest to lowest.

8. If you wish to sort groups by more than one field, you may repeat steps 6 and 7 for additional summary or subtotal fields.

9. If you wish to limit the report to just the top or bottom *N* groups (perhaps you want to see the top 10 or bottom 15 states), choose Top N or Bottom N in the For This Group Sort drop-down list.

10. In the Based On drop-down list, choose the summary or subtotal field you wish to base the top or bottom N on.

11. In the Where N Is text box, type the number of top or bottom groups that you wish to see.

> NOTE *The N in the Top N/Sort Group Expert can only be typed in directly—you can't supply a formula or parameter field for this value. However, for a creative way to do Top N reporting based on a parameter field, look in Chapter 7 for "Base the N in Top N on a Parameter."*

12. If you want to include additional report records in one "catch all" group beyond the top or bottom N, check the Include Others check box. Then, type in the name of the catch all group in the With The Name text box.

13. Click OK to close the Top N/Sort Group Expert.

14. Preview the report. Notice that the groups are no longer sorted by the name of the group, but by the value of the chosen subtotal or summary field. If you chose Top or Bottom N, only the desired number of groups will appear on the report.

> NOTE *Because the Top N/Sort Group Expert makes use of totals to sort groups, report grand totals will be inaccurate if you don't include all groups. This is because grand totals will have been calculated before the Top N/Sort Group Expert has limited the groups. Look for a way around this problem in "Correct Top N/Group Selection Grand Totals" later in the chapter.*

Sort Groups by an Alternate Field

By default, Crystal Reports sorts report groups by the field the group is based on. For example, if you wish to see sales totals by salesperson, you'll create a group based on salesperson last name in ascending order. In this situation, "Albert" will appear before "Jones," which will appear before "Zimmerman."

However, you may encounter a situation where you want the groups to appear on the report ordered by something other than the field the group is based on. One example of this is best to worst or worst to best (as described earlier in this chapter under "Show Only the Best or Worst Groups"). Another option is sorting the groups by a field other than a total. You may, for example, wish to show salesperson groups in the order of who the salesperson reports to, so that a sales manager can quickly analyze the sales totals of his or her particular sales staff. In this case, you still want the report grouped by salesperson, but you want the groups to appear on the report in a different order.

Similar to the "worst or best" scenario described earlier in the chapter, sorting groups by a field other than the actual field the group is based on is accomplished by using the *Top N/Sort Group Expert.* This feature will sort groups by a summary or subtotal value, as opposed to the actual group field itself. However, rather than using a numeric subtotal or summary as the applicable summarized field, you must create a summary field based on some other field within the group (in the example described previously, the "reports to" name in the salesperson group).

NOTE   *The Top N/Sort Group Expert is known as the Group Sort Expert in Crystal Reports 9.*

Sales Totals

by "Reports To" Last Name

Reports To:	Buchanan	Sales Rep:	Dodsworth	$502,512.02
Reports To:	Buchanan	Sales Rep:	King	$498,528.03
Reports To:	Buchanan	Sales Rep:	Suyama	$530,396.89
Reports To:	Fuller	Sales Rep:	Davolio	$427,432.19
Reports To:	Fuller	Sales Rep:	Leverling	$484,824.53
Reports To:	Fuller	Sales Rep:	Peacock	$440,208.41

DOWNLOAD   *Alternate Group Sorting.rpt from CrystalBook.com*

1. Open or create a report that contains at least one group.

2. Determine the alternate field that you wish to sort the groups by. If it's not already there, add the desired alternate field to the details section.

The alternate field must remain the same within the entire group. For example, if you wish to sort salesperson groups by a "reports to" field, the "reports to" field can't have different values within the same salesperson group—the salesperson must always report to the same sales manager.

3. Select the alternate sort field in the details section. Right-click. Choose Insert | Summary from the pop-up menu.

4. Choose a summary function that will return the actual "sortable" value of the field to the group footer. For example, either a Minimum or a Maximum will return the actual value of the field—a count or distinct count will return a number, which will not be an appropriate value to sort the groups by.

5. Display the Top N/Sort Group Expert by using pull-down menu options or the correct toolbar button.

6. Alternatively, you may select the summary field that you wish to use to sort report groups.

7. Once the summary has been selected, use pull-down menu options or the correct toolbar button to sort records. Because a summary field is selected, the Top N/Sort Group Expert will appear.

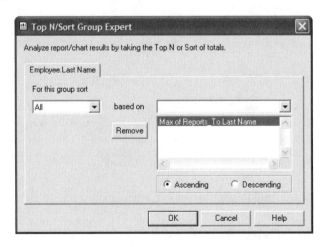

8. In the For This Group Sort drop-down list, choose All.

9. In the Based On drop-down list, choose the summary field based on the alternate sort field. Then choose whether to sort the groups by the alternate field in ascending order or descending order by clicking the desired radio button.

10. If you wish to apply multiple sort levels to the groups, repeat step 9 for any additional summary fields.

11. Click OK to close the Top N/Sort Group Expert.

12. Preview the report and ensure that report groups are now appearing in the desired order.

Correct Top N/Group Selection Grand Totals

Very often, you'll combine both subtotals and summaries at the group level, with grand totals or summaries that are placed in the report footer. This way, you'll be able to analyze not only individual group numbers, but the totals for the entire report. The grand totals are created with the Insert Grand Total option (in Crystal Reports 8.*x*) or the Insert Summary option (in Crystal Reports 9). These choices automatically place the desired total or summary in the report footer.

However, if you use this feature in conjunction with the Top N/Sort Group Expert or Group Selection, you may notice odd behavior with grand totals. In particular, if you use techniques discussed elsewhere in this chapter to limit the number of report groups shown on the report, you may notice that the grand totals don't add up. This may not only be difficult to explain—it could be disastrous if important business decisions are based on the combination of group totals and grand totals being shown on the report.

NOTE   *The Top N/Sort Group Expert is known as the Group Sort Expert in Crystal Reports 9.*

The explanation for this behavior becomes clearer if you consider how the Top N/Sort Group Expert and Group Selection work. Because these features use group subtotals and summaries to determine how many and which groups appear on the report (Group Selection limits display of groups to only those that have subtotals or summaries that meet a criterion, and the Top N/Sort Group Expert limits groups to the Top or Bottom *N* groups based on a subtotal or summary), report totaling must take place *before* the groups are limited.

As grand totaling in the report footer takes place during the same Crystal Reports process that creates totals in group footers, the grand totals are already calculated *before* Group Selection or the Top N/Sort Group Expert limits the groups. As such, the grand totals will always show values for all groups on the report, not just those that are being shown.

One way to solve the problem: don't add grand totals to the report if you are limiting group display with Group Selection or the Top N/Sort Group Expert. However, this may be considered a severe Crystal Reports limitation, if you desire to, for example, show the top ten salespeople in the company, and the associated sales grand total resulting from just the top ten salespeople.

The way to solve this dilemma is by using *running totals.* Running totals are designed to accumulate or "build up" a total as the report progresses. An application for this is when you want to show how sales are "building" as the month or year progresses—you can see a current order amount followed by the total amount accumulated by all orders as of the time the current order was placed. This "building up" capability, however, isn't of value when you're just looking to see correct grand totals at the end of the report. However, a running total will still solve the inaccurate grand total problem for one simple reason: running totals are processed by Crystal Reports *after* Group Selection and the Top N/Sort Group Expert have processed.

DOWNLOAD *Ten Best Groups.rpt from CrystalBook.com*

1. Open or create a report that makes use of the Top N/Sort Group Expert or Group Selection.

2. If you have added a grand total to the report footer with the Insert Grand Total or Insert Summary option, double-check the total. Since you have limited the display to only certain report groups, the grand total will not equal the total of the displayed groups.

3. Create a running total to replace the grand total. Begin by selecting the field in the details section that you wish to base the running total on.

4. Right-click. Choose Insert | Running Total from the pop-up menu. The Create Running Total Field dialog box will appear.

5. Alternatively, you may click on the Running Totals category of the Field Explorer, right-click, and choose New from the pop-up menu. The Create Running Total Field dialog box will appear.

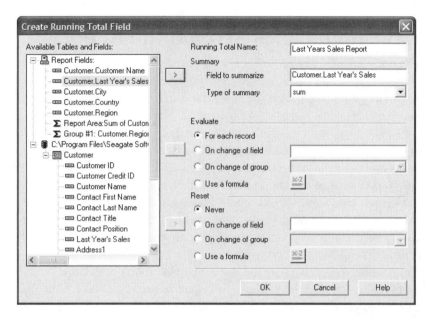

6. Type a meaningful name for the running total in the Running Total Name text box.

7. If you started from the Field Explorer, select the field you want to total in the Available Tables And Fields list. Click the right arrow button next to the Field To Summarize box. If you had already selected a field in the details section, the Field To Summarize box will already contain the field name.

8. Choose the type of summary you want to perform (sum, count, average, and so forth) in the Type Of Summary drop-down list.

9. Leave the Evaluate radio button set to For Each Record.

10. Leave the Reset radio button set to Never.

11. Click OK to save the running total.

12. If you originally selected a field in the details section, the running total will be placed in the details section. Drag it from the details section to the report footer.

13. If you began running total creation from the Field Explorer, drag the running total from the Field Explorer to the report footer.

14. Preview the report and check the value of the running total. It should correctly match the totals of groups that are actually appearing on the report.

Correct Top N/Group Selection
Grand Totals

Copy Totals/Summaries Around the Report

Crystal Reports grouping is of little value if you don't add subtotal or summary fields to the group footer once the group has been created. You'll also often need to create report grand totals with the Insert Grand Total (Crystal Reports 8.*x*) or Insert Summary (Crystal Reports 9) function.

If you desire to show totals for every report group, you may check the Insert Summary For All Groups check box when you first create a subtotal or summary in Crystal Reports 8.*x*. However, as that option has been eliminated from Crystal Reports 9, you'll need to use the Insert Summary option again and again for each new group you create. And, if you create a new group after you've created an initial set of summaries, you may find yourself using the Insert Summary function again for the new group. If you are creating a large number of summaries for each group, this can be quite time consuming.

You may think you need to use the Insert Subtotal, Insert Summary, or Insert Grand Total option to ensure that the proper groups are accommodated for the resulting summary or grand total. But, a closer look at Crystal Reports behavior will reveal that summaries and subtotals don't "belong" to any one group. You can move or copy them around the report and they will automatically adjust to whatever group you placed them in. They'll also automatically adjust if you place them in the report footer.

1. Open or create a report that contains at least one group. If necessary, insert desired subtotal or summary fields into the group footer.

2. Click on one of the subtotal or summary fields that was placed in the group footer. Notice that the Crystal Reports status bar indicates just the summary function and field, such as "Sum of Customer.Last Year's Sales." Notice that the summary *doesn't* indicate any particular group level.

3. Copy the summary object you've selected to the Windows clipboard by choosing Edit | Copy from the pull-down menus or typing CTRL-C.

4. Paste the copied summary by choosing Edit | Paste from the pull-down menus or typing CTRL-V.

5. Once you choose the paste option, notice that an outline appears on the mouse cursor. Move the outline into the desired group footer or report footer section where you want to paste the summary. Click the mouse button when you've reached the desired location to paste the summary there.

6. If you wish to copy multiple summaries and subtotals at the same time, CTRL-click on the multiple summaries, or "elastic box" the summaries and subtotals that you want to copy.

7. Choose Edit | Copy or type CTRL-C to copy all the selected summaries to the clipboard.

8. Choose Edit | Paste or type CTRL-V. Notice the outline that appears on the mouse cursor. Move the mouse to the section where you want all the copied summaries to appear.

9. As the outline indicates the upper-leftmost summary that you've copied, place the mouse cursor where you want the first summary to appear. Click the mouse button to paste all the summaries into the new group or report footer where you placed them.

10. To copy a single summary from one report section to the other, simply click it. Then, hold down the CTRL key and drag the outline to another report section. When you release the mouse button, the single summary will have been copied to its new location.

11. Preview the report. Notice that the copied summaries automatically adjust their values to the new group or report footer where you placed them.

NOTE   *Even though Crystal Reports initially places subtotals, summaries, and grand totals in group footers and the report footer, you don't have to leave them there. If you want totals to appear at the beginning of a group or the beginning of the report, they'll still supply the correct totals. Just move or copy the summaries from group footers or the report footer to group headers or the report header.*

Easily Change the Type of Summary

The true benefits of report grouping are usually realized only when you add summaries or subtotals to the group footer. By using the Insert Subtotal (Crystal Reports 8.x only) or Insert Summary option, you can add helpful sums, averages, counts, and many other types of summary functions to the group footer.

But, what if you initially add a subtotal and want to later change it to an average? Or, is it possible to copy a sum function from the group footer to the report footer, and then quickly change the sum to a count in the report footer? If you have to do this even a few times, it would be helpful to find a more streamlined option than going through the whole "Insert Summary" operation again.

1. Open or create a report that contains at least one group and a summary function that you'd like to change to use a different summary operation.

2. Select the summary that you wish to change. Right-click.

3. Choose Change Summary from the pop-up menu (the pop-up menu will show an Edit Summary choice in Crystal Reports 9).

4. The Change Summary dialog box will appear. It looks very similar to the dialog box you encountered when you first created the summary.

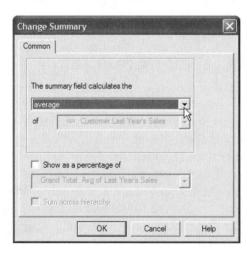

5. Choose the new desired summary operation from the drop-down list called The Summary Field Calculates The. If you wish to make any other changes (such as making the summary a percentage summary field), make the necessary choices.

6. Click OK to close the Change Summary dialog box.

7. Preview the report and notice that the summary function has changed.

Retrieve Only Group Totals from the Database

In many cases, reports are designed to show "the bottom line"—only subtotals or summaries at the end of groups are considered relevant. In these situations, the details sections are often hidden (which allows detail data to be drilled into), or suppressed (which doesn't allow drill down). In either case, the details sections aren't shown when the report is initially previewed.

By default, Crystal Reports still retrieves all the detail data from the database server and performs the subtotaling or summarizing itself on the detail data it received. It then just suppresses the details section and shows the summaries that it calculated. However, if you are using a standard SQL database (Microsoft SQL Server, Oracle, or others) or any database via an ODBC or OLE DB connection, it's possible to have the database server actually do the grouping and summarizing in advance of data ever being sent to Crystal Reports. Only the group summaries are sent to Crystal Reports for formatting.

The advantage of this server-based grouping will be mostly evident with larger reports and larger databases. You may, for example, have a report that returns 25,000 detail lines to the report. The report may be designed to return a relatively small number of groups (perhaps 35 as an example) from this large number of records. Crystal Reports will read all 25,000 records, perform the necessary subtotaling or summarizing, display the summaries in the group footer, and suppress the details section. It may be faster if the database server can perform this summarizing and return only the 35 sets of summaries to Crystal Reports. Network traffic is reduced, and Crystal Reports need only format and display the 35 sets of summaries.

DOWNLOAD *Server Grouping.rpt from CrystalBook.com*

1. Open or create a report that contains at least one group. If necessary, insert desired subtotal or summary fields into the group footer. Summarize on

database fields only—database grouping won't work when groups are based on formulas.

2. Ensure that no other extraneous formulas or database fields are present in the group footer.

3. Hide or suppress the details section by right-clicking on the gray details section name (or the D section name if viewing the report in the Preview tab) and choosing Hide (Enable Drill Down) or Suppress (No Drill Down) from the pop-up menu.

4. If you want to verify that all detail records will still be passed to Crystal Reports, view the SQL Query being sent to the database. Do this by choosing Database | Show SQL Query from the pull-down menus. The SQL Query dialog box will appear.

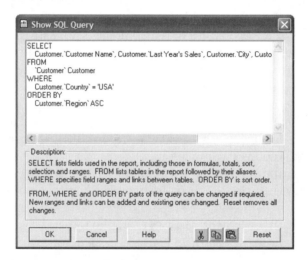

5. Notice that there is no GROUP BY clause in the SQL Query. This indicates that all detail records will be sent to Crystal Reports from the server.

6. Choose Database | Perform Grouping On Server from the pull-down menus. Or, choose File | Report Options and check the Perform Grouping On Server check box in the Options dialog box.

7. If you want to verify that only the group totals will now come down from the server, show the SQL Query again by choosing Database | Show SQL Query.

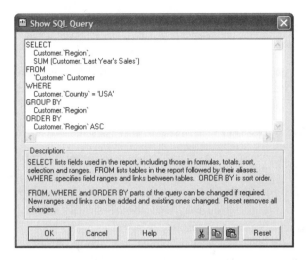

8. Notice that a summary function has been added to the SELECT clause and a GROUP BY clause has been added to the SQL Query. This indicates that the server will perform the grouping and send only summary values to Crystal Reports.

9. Preview the report. Look in the lower right-hand corner of the status bar at the record count. You'll notice that a much smaller number of records has come across the network and has been processed by Crystal Reports.

NOTE *If you want to automatically perform grouping on the server for all new reports in the future, you may choose this setting on the Database tab of File | Options.*

In order for the GROUP BY clause to be added to the SQL Query, your report must meet a certain set of conditions. If you don't see a GROUP BY clause, even after you've chosen the Perform Grouping On Server option, ensure that your report meets these requirements:

- There must be at least one group on the report.
- The details section must be hidden.
- Include only the group fields or summary fields in group headers and footers.
- Don't group on Crystal Reports formulas.
- Running totals must be based on summary fields.

Retrieve Only Group Totals from the Database

- The report cannot contain Average or Distinct Count summaries or Top *N* values.

- Report groups can be sorted only in ascending or descending order. Specified-order grouping won't work.

Customize the Group Name Field

When you create report groups, Crystal Reports automatically places a group name field into the group header. The *group name* field typically just shows the actual value of the database field that the group is based on. For example, if you group on employee last name, the group name field will simply show the last names of the employees that make up each group.

You may not be aware that you can select the group name field in the group header and format it just as you would any other field. Perhaps you've grouped the report on a date or numeric field and want to change the way the date or numbers appear on the report. One problem, however, is that any formatting changes you make to the group name field won't appear in the group tree on the left side of the Preview tab. Also, if you want to customize the way the group name field appears, simple formatting won't provide flexible customization options.

Crystal Reports provides the capability to customize the group name field. With this feature, you can group on a field, such as a date or number, but change the way the group name field appears both on the report and in the group tree. For example, here's a sample group tree from a report that is grouped on Order Date and Employee Number. Notice the spelled-out month name and the employee's full name, despite the actual fields the groups are based on.

```
⊟ Custom Group Name Field.rpt
  ⊟ January 1997
       Nancy Davolio
       Janet Leverling
       Margaret Peacock
       Michael Suyama
       Robert King
       Anne Dodsworth
  ⊞ February 1997
  ⊞ March 1997
  ⊞ April 1997
  ⊞ May 1997
  ⊞ June 1997
  ⊞ July 1997
  ⊞ August 1997
  ⊞ September 1997
  ⊞ October 1997
  ⊞ November 1997
  ⊞ December 1997
```

Custom Group Name Field.rpt from CrystalBook.com

1. Open or create a report that contains a group that you wish to customize.

2. If you are creating a new group, choose Insert | Group from the pull-down menus. If you are changing an existing group, right-click on the group header or group footer gray section name, right-click, and choose Change Group from the pop-up menu. The Insert Group or Change Group Options dialog box will appear.

3. If you are using Crystal Reports 9, click the Options tab in the dialog box.

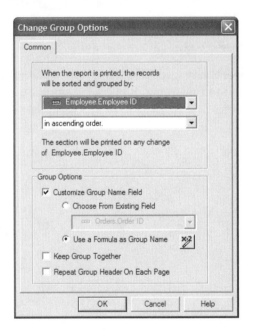

4. Check the Customize Group Name Field check box.

5. Choose how you wish to customize the group name field. You may base the group name field on another database field or a string formula.

6. To base the group name field on another database field, click the Choose From Existing Field radio button. Then, choose the other database field you want to appear in the group name field from the drop-down list.

7. To base the group name field on a formula, click the Use A Formula As Group Name radio button. Then, click the custom formula button to the right of the radio button. The Group Name Formula Editor will appear.

Customize the Group Name Field

8. Type in a string formula to display in the group name field. For example, to spell out the name of the month, followed by a space, followed by the four-digit year, you might type a formula like this:

    ```
    ToText({Orders.Order Date}, "MMMM yyyy")
    ```

    Or, to show the full first and last name (separated by a space) of a salesperson, even though the group is based on an employee number, you might type a formula like this:

    ```
    {Employee.First Name} & " " & {Employee.Last Name}
    ```

9. Once you've typed in the formula, check and save the formula. The Group Options dialog box will reappear with the custom formula button colored in red.

10. Click OK to close the Group Options dialog box.

11. Preview the report and notice that the group name fields on the report, as well as the group tree, reflect the custom formatting.

Chapter 9

Subreports

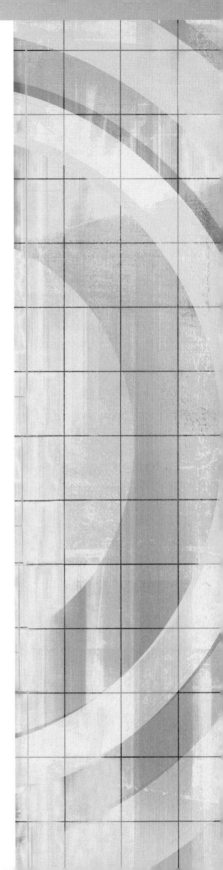

One Crystal Reports feature that tends to win both the "most beneficial" and "most confusing" award is the subreport. A *subreport,* in essence, is one report placed inside another report. Both the main report (the report you create first) and the subreport (that you put inside the main report) have their own separate database connections, their own separate design tabs, and their own separate sets of fields and records. However, the subreport eventually just prints at a certain place inside the main report.

Subreports are invaluable when you encounter situations where database organization precludes your creating the report you need with a single database connection. "Unlinkable" data, many-to-many table relationships, and other similar situations often require that you use a subreport to get the end result you need. And, when you do use a subreport, there are a few techniques you may find useful to add even more flexibility to your reports.

Hide the Border Around a Subreport

Whenever you add a subreport to your main report, Crystal Reports places a border around the subreport. You can't change this default Crystal Reports behavior—there's no default formatting option for subreports on the File | Options dialog box.

Eliminating the border on the subreport is simply a matter of formatting the subreport object in the main report with the Format Editor.

USA

City Cyclists
Mr. Chris Christianson, Sales Manager
7464 South Kingsway
Suite 2006
Sterling Heights, MI 48358

1998 Orders Subreport

Order ID	Order Amount	Order Date
2,640	2,939.85	01/26/1998
2,659	659.70	01/30/1998
2,682	931.05	02/02/1998
2,687	27.00	02/04/1998
2,772	2,294.55	02/28/1998
2,900	5,549.40	04/09/1998
2,982	63.90	04/29/1998

 *Subreport Borders.rpt from CrystalBook.com*

1. Open an existing report containing a bordered subreport or add a new subreport to an existing report. Notice the border around the subreport.

2. Ensure that the main report Design or Preview tab is selected (don't select the subreport Design or Preview tab).

3. Click the subreport. You'll notice that the lower left of the Crystal Reports status bar shows that a subreport has been selected.

4. Right-click. From the pop-up menu, choose Border And Colors. The Format Editor will appear with the Border tab chosen. (In version 9, choose Format Subreport from the pop-up menu, then click the Border tab.)

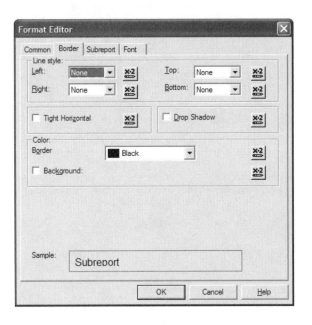

5. Choose None as the line style for the left, right, top, and bottom borders.

6. Click OK to close the Format Editor. Notice that the subreport no longer displays a border.

Showing the Border Only When There Is Subreport Data

The technique shown previously will eliminate the border on every subreport instance—whether the subreport contains any data or not. However, you may wish to "conditionally" add a border to a subreport only when the subreport contains data. If the subreport doesn't contain data, you'd prefer that no border appear.

You may be tempted to try to conditionally set the left, right, top, and bottom line style properties on the Border tab of the Format Editor. But, if you click the Conditional Formula button to the right of the line style drop-down lists, you'll find nothing in the Format Formula Editor that you can use to test for the existence or nonexistence of subreport data. Therefore, you need to be a little more "creative" to include borders only around subreports that actually contain data.

BBS Pty
Miss Victoria Ashworth, Sales Representative
45 Fauntleroy Circus
London, England

1998 Orders Subreport

Order ID	Order Amount	Order Date
2599	19.96	01/14/1998
2824	659.70	03/17/1998
2935	1,139.55	04/18/1998
2936	107.80	04/18/1998
2946	6,209.55	04/19/1998

Cycle City Rome
Mr. Paolo Accorti, Sales Representative
Via Monte Bianco 34
Torino, Italy

1998 Orders Subreport

----

1. Perform the steps outlined earlier in this topic to eliminate the border on the subreport object in the main report.

2. Select the subreport Design tab. If you don't see the subreport Design tab, return to the main report Design tab and double-click the desired subreport object. The subreport Design tab will appear.

3. Choose File | Report options. This will display the Report Options dialog box.

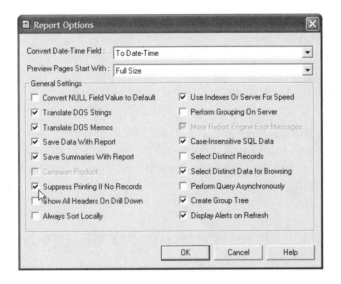

4. Check the Suppress Printing If No Records option. Click OK to close the dialog box. This will suppress any subreport printing if there are no records in the subreport.

5. Choose Insert | Box from the pull-down menus (or click the box drawing toolbar button). The mouse cursor will turn into a pencil.

6. Begin drawing the box in the upper left-hand corner of the first "unsuppressed" report header section.

7. End the box drawing in the lower right-hand corner of the last "unsuppressed" report footer section.

8. Ensure that the box encompasses all the visible report objects in the subreport.

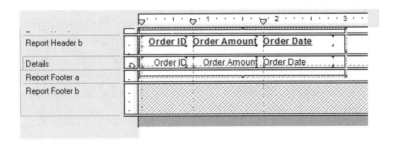

TIP *By default, Crystal Reports adds multiple report header and footer sections to subreports. If you have eliminated extra report header and footer sections, just draw the box from the single report header section through the single report footer section. If you've suppressed those sections, show them for the box to appear properly.*

9. Redisplay the main report Preview tab. Notice that subreports that contain data will appear with a box drawn around them, while subreports that don't contain data don't appear at all, and no borders appear.

"No Records" Message with an Empty Subreport

By default, Crystal Reports simply processes each subreport it encounters. If the subreport contains data, the various subreport sections are formatted and the subreport appears within the main report. If the subreport doesn't contain data (linked subreports, for example, may not return any records for a particular occurrence of a linked field), then empty subreport sections, such as a subreport report header containing field titles, will still appear on the main report.

You may prefer to display a message indicating "No Records" (or something similar) in place of subreports that contain no data. In your endeavors toward this end, you might, for example, try placing a "no records" text object alongside the subreport object in the main report. You would then try to conditionally suppress the subreport object and the text object in accordance with the number of records being returned from the subreport. However, when you click the Conditional Formula button next to the Suppress check box, you won't find any formula functions that indicate whether a subreport is empty or not, or how many records a subreport may return. No matter how hard you try, you won't be able to determine whether a subreport contains data or not from within the main report.

In order to display a "No Records" message, you must actually create logic in the subreport itself to determine if there are no records. Having determined this, you can display this message in a subreport, hiding any other subreport sections that would usually show objects. The subreport will always appear in the main report, but it will either show data or the no records message, depending on logic in the subreport.

```
Warsaw Sports, Inc.
Mr. Pavel Ropoleski, Owner
ul. Nowogrodzka 94/96
Warsaw, Poland
```

1998 Orders Subreport

Order ID	Order Amount	Order Date
2668	8,902.95	02/01/1998
2683	43.50	02/02/1998
2771	107.80	02/28/1998
2787	3,222.90	03/04/1998
2842	2,339.70	03/21/1998
2882	29.00	04/02/1998
2998	1,082.50	05/02/1998

```
Greenlane Bicycles
Mr. Hank Binford, Sales Representative
41 King Street
Dublin, Ireland
```

1998 Orders Subreport

No 1998 Orders for this customer

No Records Message.rpt from CrystalBook.com

1. Open an existing report containing a subreport or add a new subreport to an existing report.

2. Select the subreport Design tab. If you don't see the subreport Design tab, return to the main report Design tab and double-click the desired subreport object. The subreport Design tab will appear.

3. In an empty report header or report footer, add a text object that contains a "No Records" message. There should be no other objects in this report section. Insert an extra report header or footer section, if necessary, for this text object.

4. Conditionally suppress the section containing the "No Records" message—it should not appear if there *are* records on the report. A way to test for the existence of records is to test for a non-null value for an always-expected report field. You may, for example, conditionally suppress the report section with a formula that looks like this:

```
Not IsNull({Orders.Order ID})
```

NOTE
You may experiment with other ways of determining record counts. However, be aware that checking the value in the RecordNumber built-in formula function, using a Count function, or other similar methods may actually result in a null value rather than a numeric result, if there are no records on the report.

5. Conditionally suppress all remaining report sections with an "opposite" formula that suppresses the sections if there *are not* records on the report. You might use a formula that looks like this:

```
IsNull({Orders.Order ID})
```

NOTE
If you wish to conditionally suppress multiple report sections (such as Report Header a and Report Header b), you may simply suppress the overall report header area. You do not have to conditionally suppress each report header section.

6. Redisplay the main report Preview tab. Notice that subreports that contain data will show sections that actually show data, while subreports that don't contain data will show only the report section containing the "No Records" text object.

NOTE
Ensure that the "Suppress Printing If No Records" option from File | Report options is not selected. If you choose this option, the "No Records" message won't appear with an empty subreport.

Pass Data from Subreport to Main Report

In many situations, you will need to pass one or more values from a subreport back to the main report. This is necessary if you need to accumulate totals from subreports to show on the main report, or use a value from the subreport in a formula on the main report.

Passing a value from the subreport back to the main report requires the use of formulas and shared variables. A *shared variable* is a variable (a variable, in essence, is a small piece of computer memory set aside to hold data) that retains its value throughout the entire main report/subreport processing cycle. If you place a value in a shared variable in a subreport and use a main report formula that declares the same shared variable, the variable will contain the value that was placed in it by the subreport. Other Crystal Reports variable "scopes," such as local and global, won't retain values when they are passed between a subreport and the main report.

Passing one or more values from a subreport to the main report requires three basic steps:

■ Create a formula in the subreport that declares a shared variable and places a value in it.

■ Create a formula in the main report that declared the same shared variable to retrieve the value from it.

■ If necessary, create another formula in the main report that resets the value of the shared variable to empty or zero, in case certain occurrences of subreports don't process. In this case, the shared variable won't retain its value from previous subreport occurrences.

Mountain View Sport
Mr. Fran Durant, Sales Manager
1443 Main Street
Suite 990
Auckland, New Zealand

1998 Orders Subreport

Order ID	Order Amount	Order Date
Total		

1998 Running Total   957,189.52

Total 1998 Order Amount **$ 957,189.52**

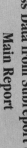

DOWNLOAD *Passing Data To Main Report.rpt from CrystalBook.com*

1. Open an existing report containing a subreport or add a new subreport to an existing report.

2. Select the subreport Design tab. If you don't see the subreport Design tab, return to the main report Design tab and double-click the desired subreport object. The subreport Design tab will appear.

3. Create a formula in the subreport that declares a shared variable and places a value in it. It might look similar to this (using Crystal Syntax):

```
WhilePrintingRecords;
Shared NumberVar OrderTotal;
OrderTotal := Sum ({Orders.Order Amount})
```

4. Begin the formula with the WhilePrintingRecords evaluation time statement. Ensure that this statement ends with a semicolon.

NOTE *If you are using a shared variable, WhilePrintingRecords is actually not required, as a shared variable processes in the WhilePrintingRecords report pass by default. However, it's a good idea to make a habit of forcing most formulas that use variables to this pass to ensure that all related formulas will evaluate in the same report pass.*

5. Begin the next formula line with the Shared keyword, followed by a variable declaration function for the desired type of variable (number, string, and so forth).

6. Follow this function with the name of the variable you wish to use. Variable names must not begin with a number or contain spaces. Also, they cannot appear in a blue color when you type them—they cannot share a name with a built-in Crystal Reports function.

7. If you simply declare the variable name and assign it a value later, end the declaration statement with a semicolon. Optionally, you may declare a variable and assign it a value on the same line, such as:

13. Begin the formula with the WhilePrintingRecords evaluation time statement. Ensure that this statement ends with a semicolon (as mentioned earlier, WhilePrintingRecords is optional with a shared variable, but still recommended).

14. Begin the next formula line with the Shared keyword, followed by the same variable declaration function and variable name as used in the subreport.

15. Perform any additional necessary formula logic with the shared variable, such as using another variable to accumulate the values coming from all subreports.

16. Check and save the formula.

17. In order for the formula to process properly (because it will be processing in the WhilePrintingRecords report pass), it must be physically placed on the main report in the proper report section. You may suppress display of the formula if you don't want it to actually appear when the subreport prints.

NOTE
Any main report formulas that retrieve values from the subreport must *appear in a separate report section that* follows *the subreport—you won't be able to retrieve the correct value from a formula placed in the same section as the subreport itself. For example, if the subreport appears in Group Footer #1a, the formula that retrieves the value from the shared variable must appear in Group Footer #1b or later.*
This is because Crystal Reports processes subreports after *it processes report formulas. Therefore, the formula in the same main report section as the subreport will retrieve a value from the shared variable* before *the subreport places a value in that variable.*

18. Create any additional formulas as necessary to calculate or show values being passed from the subreport.

19. View the report and ensure that the proper values are being returned from the subreport to the main report.

Resetting the Shared Variable

If the possibility exists that some instances of the subreport that's "stuffing" the shared variable won't process, you may need to reset the value of the shared variable in the main report. If you don't, the shared variable will retain its value from previous subreport instances that did process. Main report logic (accumulations, for example) may be incorrectly affected by a shared variable that retains a value even though a subreport isn't placing anything in it.

Pass Data from Subreport to
Main Report

To reset the contents of the shared variable:

1. Create a main report formula to reset the shared variable. It may look something like this (in Crystal Syntax):

```
WhilePrintingRecords;
Shared NumberVar OrderTotal := 0
```

2. Begin the formula with the WhilePrintingRecords evaluation time statement. Ensure that this statement ends with a semicolon (as mentioned earlier, WhilePrintingRecords is optional with a shared variable, but still recommended).

3. Begin the next formula line with the Shared keyword, followed by the same variable declaration function and variable name as used in the subreport.

4. Follow the variable name with an equals assignment operator (:=), followed by a zero for a numeric variable, an empty string ("") for a string variable, and so forth.

5. Check and save the formula.

6. In order for the formula to process properly (because it will be processing in the WhilePrintingRecords report pass), it must be physically placed on the main report in the proper report section. Because formulas process before subreports, you may place the reset formula in the same section as the subreport.

7. You may suppress display of the formula if you don't want it to actually appear when the subreport prints.

NOTE   *Techniques discussed in this section involve more complex formula and variable creation. You may find a more involved discussion of formulas and variables to be helpful. Consult Crystal Reports online documentation, or consider the* Crystal Reports: The Complete Reference *series, also available from McGraw-Hill/Osborne.*

Pass Data from Main Report to Subreport

The previous section of this chapter discusses how to pass data from a subreport back to the main report for accumulations, formulas, and so forth. You may also have a need to pass data from the main report to the subreport. There can be many reasons for this. You may need to perform some sort of subreport calculation based on a value passed from the main report. Or, you may wish to display some sort of message in the subreport (such as a "No Records for *<customer>*" message) that uses a value passed from the main report.

While the "shared variable" method discussed in the previous book section can also be used to pass a value from the main report to a subreport, it involves a fair amount of formula creation and manipulation. A simpler way is to use subreport links. A *subreport link* is a field chosen in the main report to link to a field in a subreport. Typically, these links are used to pass a value from the main report to use in subreport record selection. With the simple unchecking of a box, a subreport link can be used to pass a value to a subreport that doesn't impact subreport record selection. The resulting parameter field in the subreport can be used in a formula, embedded in a text object, or otherwise used just like any other parameter field.

Pass Data from Main Report to Subreport

Tom's Place for Bikes
Mr. Jimmy Hatch, Sales Representative
545 Peachtree Road
Johannesburg, South Africa

1998 Orders Subreport

No 1998 Orders for Tom's Place for Bikes

Coastal Line Bikes
Ms. Caron Ryans, Owner
22th Flr Safren House
Johannesburg, South Africa

1998 Orders Subreport

No 1998 Orders for Coastal Line Bikes

 *Passing Data To SubReport.rpt from CrystalBook.com*

1. Open an existing report containing a subreport or add a new subreport to an existing report.

2.   Right-click the subreport object in the main report Design tab. Choose
     Change Subreport Links from the pop-up menu.

3.   The Subreport Links dialog box will appear. If you've already linked the
     subreport to the main report on one or more fields, you'll see the links
     already appear in the dialog box.

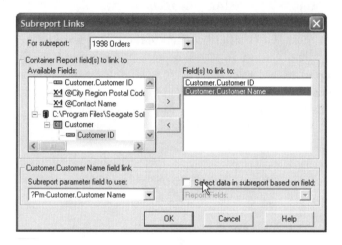

4.   In the Available Fields list, choose the main report field or formula that
     you want to pass to the subreport. Click the right arrow to add it to the
     Field(s) To Link To list.

5.   Notice that a parameter field name will be generated and will appear in
     the Subreport Parameter Field To Use drop-down list. Also notice that
     Select Data In Subreport Based On Field check box will be automatically
     checked.

6.   Uncheck the Select Data In Subreport Based On Field check box. This
     will create a parameter field in the subreport but will not use the parameter
     field in the subreport's record selection formula.

7.   Select the subreport Design tab. If you don't see the subreport Design tab,
     return to the main report Design tab and double-click the desired subreport
     object. The subreport Design tab will appear.

8.   Display the Field Explorer. Expand the Parameter Fields category.

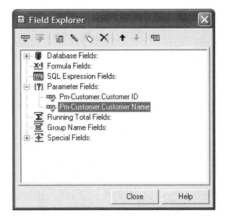

9. Notice that the parameter field that appeared in the Subreport Links dialog box in the main report has been created in the subreport.

10. Make use of this parameter as necessary to get the passed value from the main report. Embed it in a text object, create a formula that makes use of it, or just drag and drop it onto the subreport.

11. Return to the main report and preview the report. Ensure that values are being properly passed to the subreport from the main report.

Avoid Subreports with a Not Equal Join

A subreport is a helpful feature that is often required to deal with certain situations where data organization makes regular report design techniques inadequate for your reporting requirements. Many-to-many data relationships, "unlinkable" fields, and other similar situations may require the use of subreports to solve your ultimate reporting requirements. However, subreports have an immediate downside as well. They increase processing time—sometimes dramatically so.

Even when subreport performance is not an issue (perhaps you just have a need for a single unlinked subreport in the main report's report header), creating a subreport requires a bit of extra work, in that a whole separate report design process must be undertaken. For these types of situations, you may be able to avoid use of a subreport by using a database linking technique known as a not equal join. By using a *not equal join*, you can link two database tables together on a noncommon field that won't ever be the same in the two database tables. In this case, records will be returned from both database tables when the linked fields *are not equal to each other.*

A common use for this technique is when you wish to include information on a report from two database tables that don't relate to each other at all. For example, you may have standard "transactional" database tables that contain order, customer, client, or salesperson information that you wish to base a report on. The same database may contain a table that exposes a set of company information for the company that will actually be running the report, such as company name, address, and so forth. By joining one of the transactional tables to the company info table on a noncommon field with a not equal join, the same record from the company info table will join up to every record in the transactional tables. You need then only add fields from the company info table to the report header or page header to get the intended result—no subreport is required.

NOTE   *Crystal Reports 8.5 limits the choice of SQL Join Type to reports based on SQL, ODBC, or OLE DB databases. Because of this, the technique described here won't work if you are using another type of database. In this case, you must still use a subreport. This limitation has been eliminated from Crystal Reports 9.*

Xtreme Mountain Bikes, Inc.
2001 Meridian Way
Vancouver, BC V6G 3G6
6046813435

Customer Listing

Customer Name	City	Country	Last Year's Sales
7 Bikes For 7 Brothers	Las Vegas	USA	8,819.55
Against The Wind Bikes	Rome	USA	2,409.46
AIC Childrens	Hong Kong	China	5,879.70
AlleyCat Cycles	Concord	USA	298,356.22
Ankara Bicycle Company	Ankara	Turkey	43,000.50
Arsenault et Maurier	Clermont-Ferrand	France	12,535.70
Aruba Sport	Oranjestad	Aruba	3,239.85
Athens Bicycle Co.	Athens	Greece	11,100.90
Auvergne Bicross	Vichy	France	5,179.98
Backpedal Cycle Shop	Philadelphia	USA	25,162.05
Bangkok Sports	Bangkok	Thailand	70,000.50
Barbados Sports, Ltd.	Bridgetown	Barbados	4,443.80
Barry's Bikes	Dover	USA	33.90
BBS Pty	London	England	500,000.00
Beach Cycle and Sport	Nassau	Bahamas	14,463.35
Beach Trails and Wheels	Hamilton	New Zealand	2,944.00
Belgium Bike Co.	Brussels	Belgium	200,000.00
Bendai Mountain Bikers	Tokyo	Japan	14,076.80
Benny - The Spokes Person	Huntsville	USA	6,091.96
Berg auf Trails GmBH.	Düsseldorf	Germany	2,939.29
Berlin Biking GmBH.	München	Germany	2,989.35
Bicicletas de Montaña Cancun	Cancun	Mexico	1,551.18
Bicicletas Buenos Aires	Buenos Aires	Argentina	55,664.35
Bicicletas de Montaña La Paz	La Paz	Bolivia	6,269.25

 *Not Equal Join.rpt from CrystalBook.com*

1. Open or create a report that requires data from an unrelated table.

2. Choose Database | Add Database To Report from the Crystal Reports 8.x pull-down menus. If you are using Crystal Reports 9, choose Database | Database Expert.

3. Add the desired table to the report.

4. If you are using Crystal Reports 8.x, the Visual Linking Expert will appear automatically once you've closed the Data Explorer. Or, if you are using Crystal Reports 9, click the Links tab in the Database Expert once you've added the table.

5. Drag and drop from an unrelated field in one of the transaction tables to an unrelated field in the new table. Note that both fields must still be the same data type.

6. Once the link line appears, ensure that the link line is selected (it will appear in a highlighted color). Click the Link Options button. The Link Options dialog box will appear.

7. In Crystal Reports 8.x, click the Not Equal (!=) radio button in the SQL Join Type section.

In Crystal Reports 9, click the Inner Join radio button in the Join Type section, and the != (not equal) radio button in the Link Type section.

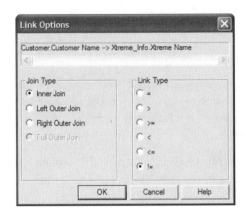

8. Click OK to close the Link Options dialog box. Then, click OK to close the Visual Linking Expert or Database Expert.

9. Add fields from the new table to the appropriate report section (for the company info example mentioned previously, you would add company info fields to the report header or page header).

10. Preview the report. Notice that the new fields will appear where they were placed and that transactional data continues to appear.

11. Pay careful attention to record counts and totals—if there is more than one "nonmatching" record in the new table, you'll encounter a many-to-many table relationship that will skew transactional totals. If this happens, limit the new table to a single record with record selection.

Place a Subreport Alongside Main Report Data

When you add a subreport to a report section, it will follow any report objects that appear above it in the same report section, as well as following objects in any report sections above its own section. And, any report sections that follow the section containing the subreport will print below the subreport.

While this "vertical orientation" is standard Crystal Reports behavior, you may wish to alter report formatting so that a subreport will print alongside data above it, as opposed to printing below this data. This is handy, for example, when you want to print some data in the main report that relates to a subreport and have the subreport print alongside the main report data. By placing the subreport in its own report section and using the Section Expert's "Underlay" formatting option, you can achieve this result.

City Cyclists
Mr. Chris Christianson, Sales Manager
7464 South Kingsway
Suite 2006
Sterling Heights, MI 48358

1998 Orders Subreport

Order ID	Order Amount	Order Date
2640	2,939.85	01/26/1998
2659	659.70	01/30/1998
2682	931.05	02/02/1998
2687	27.00	02/04/1998
2772	2,294.55	02/28/1998
2900	5,549.40	04/09/1998
2982	63.90	04/29/1998

Pathfinders
Miss Christine Manley, Sales Representative
410 Eighth Avenue
DeKalb, IL 60148

1998 Orders Subreport

Order ID	Order Amount	Order Date
2577	43.80	01/07/1998
2606	1,083.04	01/15/1998
2652	2,429.10	01/29/1998
2653	2,451.85	01/29/1998
2719	953.35	02/13/1998
2739	48.51	02/19/1998
2777	1,529.70	03/01/1998
2837	659.70	03/20/1998
2857	503.35	03/23/1998
2969	3,185.42	04/26/1998

DOWNLOAD *Subreport Beside Data.rpt from CrystalBook.com*

1. Open an existing report containing a subreport or add a new subreport to an existing report.

2. Determine the report objects that you want to appear side by side with the subreport. Resize and move them far enough left or right on the report to accommodate the width of the subreport on the opposite side.

3. Resize the subreport object so that it will fit in the allotted horizontal space.

4. Insert a new report section separate from main report objects to contain the subreport. For example, if the main report data is located in the details section, insert another details section below the section containing the main report objects.

5. Swap the details sections so that the new details section is *above* the section containing the main report objects.

6. Move the subreport object to the new details section above the main report objects. Position the subreport so that there won't be any horizontal "conflict" with main report objects.

7. Right-click the gray section name for the details section containing the subreport. Choose Format Section (Crystal Reports 8.x) or Section Expert (Crystal Reports 9) from the pop-up menu. You may alternatively use the Format | Section menu option (Crystal Reports 8.x) or Report | Section Expert menu option (Crystal Reports 9), or the corresponding toolbar button. The Section Expert will appear.

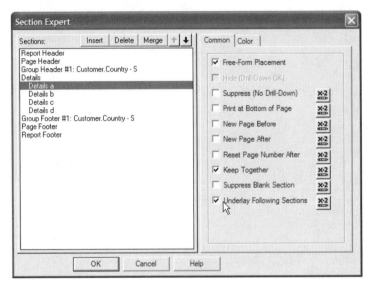

8. Select the section containing the subreport in the Sections list. Click the Underlay Following Sections check box.

9. Click OK to close the Section Expert.

10. Preview the report. Notice that the subreport will appear alongside the main report data.

11. Make any necessary horizontal sizing or placement adjustments with main report objects and the subreport object for a more pleasant appearance.

Better Performance with On-Demand Subreports

While subreports are an undeniable benefit to using Crystal Reports (more complex reports that encounter database-related linking issues can't be designed without them), they often introduce one serious consequence to reporting: performance degradation. This issue becomes even more critical with online, real-time reports (in web pages, custom Windows applications, and so forth), as a viewer must wait for subreports to process.

This performance problem is endemic to the subreport processing model. Consider a single report without any subreports—only one query must run against the database to populate the report with data (and, that one query still may take an extended period of time to complete). However, if you then add a subreport (say, for example, a linked subreport in each group footer), the number of queries increases significantly. In the "one subreport per group footer" scenario just discussed, the number of database queries increases from 1 to 51 if there are 50 groups on the report. If the subreport query also takes an extended time to process, the resulting degradation in performance can be excruciating.

One way that online reporting can enjoy vastly improved performance, as well as an increasing degree of interactivity, is with the on-demand subreport. An *on-demand subreport* actually processes only when a user clicks it—when the main report is first displayed online, only a hyperlink-like "placeholder" exists. When the viewer clicks a particular placeholder hyperlink, then (and only then) will that one particular subreport process. Considering the 50-group scenario described earlier, use of an on-demand subreport will return the initial report to requiring only a single database query to initially display. Then, when the viewer chooses one of the 50-group subreport hyperlinks, that one subreport for the chosen group will run in real time. The subreport will appear in its own separate tab next to the main report Preview tab.

City Cyclists
Mr. Chris Christianson, Sales Manager
7464 South Kingsway
Suite 2006
Sterling Heights, MI 48358

Click to see 1998 orders for City Cyclists

Pathfinders
Miss Christine Manley, Sales Representative
410 Eighth Avenue
DeKalb, IL 60148

Click to see 1998 orders for Pathfinders

Bike-A-Holics Anonymous
Mr. Gary Jannis, Sales Associate
7429 Arbutus Boulevard
Suite 2017
Blacklick, OH 43005

Click to see 1998 orders for Bike-A-Holics Anonymous

 *On-Demand Subreport.rpt from CrystalBook.com*

Better Performance with On-Demand Subreports

1. Open an existing report containing a subreport or add a new subreport to an existing report.

2. Select the subreport object in the main report design or Preview tab. Right-click.

3. From the pop-up menu, choose Format Subreport. You may also use the Format menu option or toolbar button to format the subreport.

4. The Format Editor will appear. Click the Subreport tab.

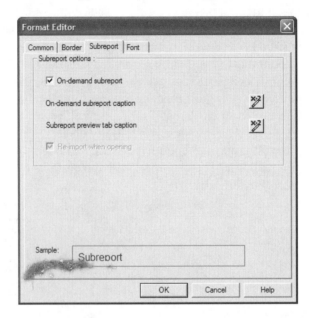

5. Click the On-Demand Subreport check box.

6. If you wish to customize the text that appears in the subreport hyperlink, click the On-Demand Subreport Caption formula button. The Formula Editor will appear.

7. Create a string formula that will control display of the hyperlink. You may use a formula similar to this:

    ```
    "Click to see 1998 orders for " & {Customer.Customer Name}
    ```

8. Check the formula for proper syntax and save it. The Format Editor will return.

9. If you wish to customize the caption that appears on the tab that will appear about the subreport preview window, click the Subreport Preview Tab Caption formula button. The Formula Editor will appear.

10. Create a string formula that will control display of the Preview tab for the subreport. You may use a formula similar to this:

```
{Customer.Customer Name} & " 1998 Orders"
```

11. Check the formula for proper syntax and save it. The Format Editor will return.

12. Click OK to close the Format Editor.

13. Preview the report. Notice that the actual contents of the subreport no longer appear within the main report—only the hyperlink appears.

14. Click a desired hyperlink. Only the single subreport you chose will process, appearing in its own Preview tab.

15. Click the red X next to the page navigation controls to close the on-demand subreport Preview tab.

Better Performance with On-Demand Subreports

Chapter 10

Cross-Tabs

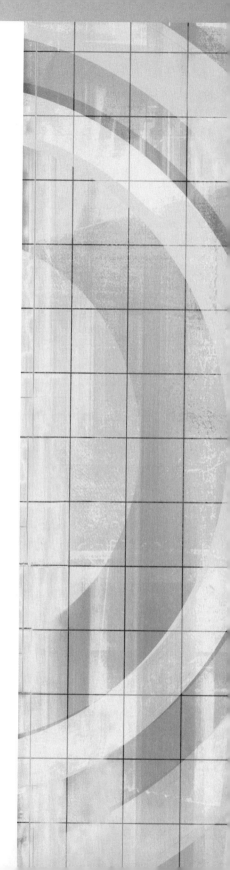

Crystal Reports designers often find themselves creating database reports that progress "vertically" down the page, or down multiple pages. These standard "vertically oriented" reports print as data from the database is read and sorted or grouped. If the report is grouped by two fields—perhaps calendar quarter within sales rep—the report viewer may have difficulty in comparing one group to the next, or analyzing all subgroups and all "parent" groups (such as all quarters for all sales reps) within a concise, easy-to-understand format.

This down-the-page format may cause report viewers to lament, "Can we export this report into Microsoft Excel and reformat it into a spreadsheet format?" While exporting to Excel is an option, Crystal Reports cross-tabs can often provide the same level of row-and-column organization as a simple Excel spreadsheet. By summarizing data in a row/column/cell format, down-the-page totals can be displayed in a row and column format for easier side-by-side analysis.

While Crystal Reports doesn't even pretend to be a spreadsheet program—it's not designed to provide the level of flexibility that comes with a true spreadsheet program—cross-tabs can often satisfy an analytical need without requiring an Excel export. The items discussed in this chapter will help you gain even more value from Crystal Reports cross-tabs.

Add a Legend to a Cross-Tab

Crystal Reports cross-tabs aren't limited to a single summarized field value. You may add as many summarized fields as you like (counts, averages, sums, and so forth), based on as many data elements as you like, to the summarized fields box in the Cross-Tab Expert.

One of the difficulties you'll encounter when you use more than one summarized field, however, is determining exactly what the multiple sets of numbers in each cell represent. For example, if you add a summarized field based on the count of a field, and another summarized field based on the sum of a field, it may not be apparent to the report viewer exactly what the two numbers represent.

One way to resolve this problem is to format each summarized field in a particular way that differentiates it from another summarized field (different colors, fonts, or so forth). You may then create your own cross-tab "legend" using a combination of text objects (or other similarly formatted visual elements) placed in the upper left-hand corner of the cross-tab.

1997 Quarterly Analysis

by Sales Rep

| ■ Order Count | | | | | |
Gross Revenue	1/1997	4/1997	7/1997	10/1997	Total
Davolio, Nancy	52 87,741.84	78 162,951.53	60 102,177.32	61 97,995.14	251 $450,865.83
Dodsworth, Anne	59 132,435.81	81 143,288.42	65 144,839.47	50 92,981.82	255 $513,545.52
King, Robert	56 116,156.38	99 153,103.81	69 123,314.42	73 119,831.99	297 $512,406.60
Leverling, Janet	43 101,513.66	90 157,316.45	55 86,818.77	66 101,586.31	254 $447,235.19
Peacock, Margaret	44 77,645.46	68 144,866.30	64 101,166.52	70 122,472.28	246 $446,150.56
Suyama, Michael	50 117,106.69	89 104,506.80	60 156,497.11	61 118,770.88	260 $496,881.48
Total	304 $632,599.84	505 $866,033.31	373 $714,813.61	381 $653,638.42	1,563 $2,867,085.18

DOWNLOAD *Cross-Tab Legend.rpt from CrystalBook.com*

1. Open a report containing a cross-tab or add a cross-tab to an existing report. The cross-tab should have more than one summarized field specified in the Cross-Tab Expert.

2. Within the cross-tab object, select and format each summarized field with a separate, distinct formatting choice. For example, use different colors for each summarized field or format each with other different formatting options (bold, italics, and so forth).

3. In the Design tab, create a text object for each summarized field. The text should indicate what the summarized field represents (such as Order Count or Gross Revenue).

4. Format each corresponding text object with the same attributes (color, font, bold, italics, and so forth) as the summarized field it represents.

Add a Legend to a Cross-Tab

5. Place the text objects close together vertically and arrange them in the upper left-hand corner of the cross-tab object (even though the cross-tab may overlay the text objects slightly, they'll still show through).

6. If color is the differentiating characteristic of the summarized field, you may optionally add box objects for each summarized field. Choose Insert | Box from the pull-down menus and draw a small box.

7. Format each box with a fill color identical to the summarized field the box refers to.

8. Place the colored boxes next to the text objects that represent what the summarized fields contain.

9. Preview the report. Notice that the "legend" appears in the upper left-hand corner of the cross-tab.

NOTE *Crystal Reports 9 features the new Show Labels check box on the Cross-Tab Expert's Customize Style tab. While this feature may negate the need for the technique illustrated here, you may still prefer the look of a color-coded legend in the upper left-hand corner of a cross-tab, instead of the Crystal Reports 9 labels.*

Conditionally Format Cells

If you develop even a small number of Crystal reports, you're probably aware of the standard conditional formatting capabilities provided by the Highlighting Expert and the conditional formula buttons in the Format Editor. These choices allow you to change colors, fonts, font attributes, and other visual properties, depending on the contents of the field you're formatting, or other fields and conditions on the report.

What you may not be aware of is that cells in cross-tabs can be conditionally formatted as well. If you wish to have certain cell values stand out from others (perhaps you want to highlight sales amounts that qualify a sales rep for a bonus), you have complete conditional control over the appearance of a cross-tab cell.

1997 Monthly Analysis
by Sales Rep

Bonus Amount in red	1/1997	2/1997	3/1997	4/1997	5/1997	6/1997
Davolio, Nancy	31,063.32	19,693.11	36,985.41	48,779.07	30,023.46	84,149.00
Dodsworth, Anne	41,023.04	57,639.73	33,773.04	43,971.49	19,236.58	75,080.25
King, Robert	29,123.17	39,920.40	47,112.81	26,806.45	46,386.58	79,430.78
Leverling, Janet	36,842.10	45,470.19	18,201.37	30,245.85	50,603.15	76,467.65
Peacock, Margaret	29,538.45	35,968.66	12,140.35	13,532.91	49,586.62	81,746.77
Suyama, Michael	43,675.02	41,678.76	31,754.91	33,850.62	21,332.44	49,323.74
Total	$211,265.10	$240,366.85	$180,967.89	$202,186.19	$217,648.93	$446,198.19

 *Conditional Cross-Tab Formatting.rpt from CrystalBook.com*

Simple Conditional Formatting with the Highlighting Expert

If you just want to change the font color, background color, or simple border style of a cross-tab cell, and if you don't need to determine which actual row or column the cell is in, you may use the Highlighting Expert to conditionally format cross-tab cells. The Highlighting Expert is designed to provide limited conditional formatting capabilities to a report designer who isn't familiar with the Crystal Reports formula language.

1. Open a report containing a cross-tab, or add a new cross-tab to your report.

2. In either the Design or Preview tab, click the cell that you wish to conditionally format. It can be a row/column "intersection" cell, or a row or column total cell.

3. Right-click the cell and choose Highlighting Expert from the pop-up menu. You can also use Format | Highlighting Expert from the pull-down

menus, or the appropriate toolbar button. The Highlighting Expert will appear.

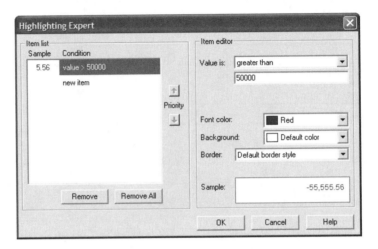

4. Choose a desired comparison in the Value Is drop-down list.

5. Type in the value you want to compare the cell to in the text box below the Value Is drop-down list.

6. Choose the font color, background color, and border style you'd like to display if the cell's contents meet the criterion you selected.

7. If you wish to test for an additional criterion (say another bonus level) and display different formatting, click "new item" at the bottom of the Item List. Repeat steps 4 through 6.

8. Click OK to close the Highlighting Expert.

9. Preview the report to ensure that the cross-tab cells that meet your criteria are appropriately formatted.

More Sophisticated Conditional Formatting with the Format Editor

While the Highlighting Expert allows simple conditional formatting in a cross-tab, you may find slightly more complex requirements that it won't provide for. For example, you may want to test the actual row or column that the cell belongs to in addition to, or instead of, the cell's value. Or, you may want to include parameter field values or Crystal Reports formula functions in your test. For these more sophisticated requirements, you'll need to use the conditional formula buttons in the Format Editor to conditionally format the cell.

1. Open a report containing a cross-tab, or add a new cross-tab to your report.

2. In either the Design or Preview tab, click the cell that you wish to conditionally format. It can be a row/column "intersection" cell, or a row or column total cell.

3. Right-click the cell and choose one of the desired formatting options from the pop-up menu. You can also use options from the Format pull-down menu, or the appropriate toolbar button. The Format Editor will appear.

4. If necessary, click the Format Editor tab that contains the property you wish to set conditionally.

5. Rather than choosing one of the "absolute" property values, click the conditional formula button next to the property you wish to set conditionally. The Format Formula Editor will appear.

6. Build the conditional formula that you wish to use to format the cell. The formula might look like this:

```
If GridRowColumnValue ("Orders.Order Date") = #12/1/1997# And
    CurrentFieldValue > 30000 Then crRed
Else If CurrentFieldValue > 50000 Then crRed
Else crBlack
```

7. Notice the specific cross-tab functions that exist in the Function tree. GridRowColumnValue allows you to test the row or column that a cell appears in. Row or column names that you supply to GridRowColumnValue appear in the Function tree. And, CurrentFieldValue will return the actual numeric value of the cell.

8. Check the formula for proper syntax. Save the formula.

9. Click OK to close the Formula Editor.

10. Preview the report to ensure that the cross-tab cells that meet your criteria are appropriately formatted.

Automatic Object Placement

When you add a cross-tab to the Crystal Reports design tab, it takes up a relatively small amount of space—only enough space to represent one row, column, and

Automatic Object Placement

summarized field added to the cross-tab, along with row and column totals. However, when you preview the report, the cross-tab will grow both horizontally and vertically to show all the actual data that it contains—many additional rows and columns will typically appear. Should you change record selection or should records be added or removed from the database, the vertical and horizontal size of the cross-tab can change again, depending on the number of records it represents.

This variable width and height behavior makes it difficult to place additional objects, such as text, graphics, or database fields, around the cross-tab so that they always appear close to the bottom or right side of the cross-tab. If you place objects to the bottom or right of the cross-tab in the same report section, the cross-tab will often spill right over the top of the objects when the report actually prints. Attempts to vertically expand the section the cross-tab is in, or to place objects at some predetermined horizontal position in the same section, will work only if the cross-tab expands to the exact same width and height every time it prints.

Placing objects so that they appear just below the cross-tab (regardless of how far the cross-tab grows vertically) is a fairly straightforward process in all versions of Crystal Reports. Placing objects to adjust to appear just to the right of a variable-width cross-tab is a little more challenging. In fact, in Crystal Reports 8.x, it's not possible. Crystal Reports 9 has introduced new capabilities to solve this problem, however.

Automatic Vertical Adjustment

If the vertical size of a cross-tab changes depending on the data it's showing, you'll find that attempting to place an object or objects just below the cross-tab in the same section will often be a futile effort—either the cross-tab will print over the top of the objects, or an excessive amount of vertical white space will appear between the bottom of the cross-tab and the objects.

However, by inserting an additional report section below the section containing the cross-tab, you'll always be able to achieve perfect spacing between the bottom of the cross-tab and the objects that follow it.

 *Conditional Cross-Tab Formatting.rpt from CrystalBook.com*

1. Open an existing report containing a cross-tab, or add a new cross-tab to your report.

2. Point to the gray line at the bottom of the report section (report header, group header, and so forth) containing the cross-tab. The mouse cursor will change into the "double-line/double-arrow" section sizing cursor.

3. Push the line up until it stops at the bottom of the cross-tab. Alternatively, you can right-click in the gray section name and choose Fit Section from the pop-up menu.

4. Insert another occurrence of the same report section (such as Report Header b or Group Header #1 b) by right-clicking in the gray section name of the section containing the cross-tab. Choose Insert Section Below from the pop-up menu.

5. An additional report section will appear below the cross-tab. Add the objects that you want to print below the cross-tab to this section.

6. Make any necessary size and placement adjustments to the objects in the new section.

7. Preview the report. Ensure that the objects you added to the section below the cross-tab have automatically appeared right below the cross-tab.

Automatic Horizontal Adjustment (Version 9 Only)

There may be situations where you want to place another report object (text, graphic, database field, and so forth) so that it will appear *to the right* of a cross-tab. If the cross-tab's width can vary depending on the data it shows, exact object placement to the right of it is virtually impossible in Crystal Reports versions prior to 9.

Crystal Reports 9 introduces the Relative Positions option in the Section Expert. When you turn this option on, other objects in the same section as the cross-tab will automatically move right depending on the horizontal size of the cross-tab.

DOWNLOAD *Automatic Horizontal Adjustment (v9 Only).rpt from CrystalBook.com*

1. Open an existing report containing a cross-tab, or add a new cross-tab to your report.

2. While still displaying the Design tab, add or move any other report objects you wish to appear to the right of the cross-tab to the right side of the cross-tab object in the same report section as the cross-tab.

3. Right-click in the gray section name of the section the cross-tab is in. Choose Format Section from the pop-up menu. The Section Expert will appear

Automatic Object Placement

(you may also choose pull-down menu options or the appropriate toolbar to display the Section Expert).

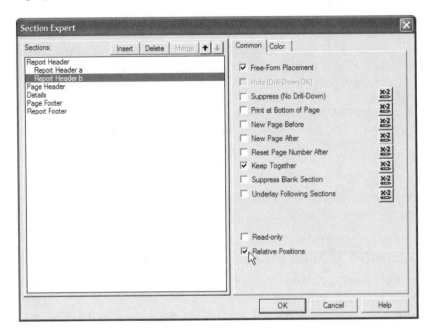

4. Check the Relative Positions check box.

5. Click OK to close the Section Expert.

6. Preview the report. Ensure that the objects you added to the section to the right of the cross-tab appear to the right of the cross-tab in the Preview tab, regardless of how wide the cross-tab grows.

NOTE *If there are other objects that you wish to display with the cross-tab that you* don't *wish to adjust horizontally, you'll need to place them in another report section above or below the cross-tab. Use the Insert Section Below approach discussed previously in the chapter under "Automatic Vertical Adjustment" to create additional report sections.*

Change the Type of Cross-Tab Summary

When you initially create a cross-tab, you add fields to the Summarized Fields box that you wish to summarize in the "cell" that appears at every row/column intersection.

When you add these summarized fields, you may change the type of summary used (sum, average, count, and so forth) by selecting the summarized field in the Summarized Fields list and clicking the Change Summary button.

However, if you've already added a cross-tab to your report and want to quickly change the type of summary for a cell, you may think you need to re-display the Format Cross Tab dialog box to do it. In fact, a much smaller set of steps that doesn't even require display of the Format Cross Tab dialog box will allow you to change the type of summary for a cell value.

1. Open an existing report containing a cross-tab, or add a new cross-tab to your report.

2. Preview the report. Notice the cross-tab displaying the summary values you added to the Summarized Fields list.

3. Click one of the summarized values right in the cross-tab in the Preview tab. Notice that other cells will also show an outline, indicating that you've, in essence, selected them too.

4. Right-click. Choose Change Summary from the pop-up menu (in version 9, choose Edit Summary from the pop-up menu).

Bonus Amount in red	1/1997	2/1997	3/1997	4
Davolio, Nancy	31,063.?			48,?
Dodsworth, Anne	41,023.			48,?
King, Robert	29,123.			26,8
Leverling, Janet	36,842.			30,4
Peacock, Margaret	29,538.			13,?
Suyama, Michael	43,675.			33,8
Total	$211,265.			02,1

Field: Sum of Orders.Order Amount
Format Field...
Border and Colors...
Font...
Highlighting Expert...
Change Summary ...
Object Size and Position...
Paste
Cancel Menu

Bonus sales: Greater than $50,000, wit   s gr

5. The Change Summary dialog box will appear. Choose the new desired summary from the drop-down list.

6. Click OK to close the Change Summary dialog box. Notice that the cross-tab immediately displays the new summary values in cells.

Avoid Truncation

When you create a cross-tab, Crystal Reports makes some default choices of how wide to make cross-tab columns and how tall to make cross-tab rows. In some cases, the width and height that Crystal Reports chooses are insufficient to show the entire contents of row or column labels, or summarized fields in cells.

Sometimes it's obvious that labels are being truncated—words stop appearing in the middle of a letter, names aren't complete, and so forth. And, some of the same obvious truncation may appear with the summarized values in cross-tab cells. Some of these truncation issues are merely annoying. However, a more dangerous problem can result if truncation of the numeric values in cross-tab cells isn't readily apparent. In this case, a cell actually containing 435,750.21 may be truncated to appear as 750.21. Needless to say, making important business decisions with truncated cross-tab cells can be disastrous.

Fairly simple techniques exist to deal with both of these problems. While the "Can Grow" feature on the Common tab of the Format Editor doesn't work with a cross-tab, you can do some manual formatting and object resizing to reduce label truncation. And, if you turn off the Allow Field Clipping option in the Format Editor, numeric cell values that are truncated will appear as pound signs, indicating that there isn't enough horizontal space to show the cell's actual value.

Avoiding Label Truncation

It may not be readily apparent how to change the width or height of cross-tab columns or rows. Unlike in a spreadsheet program, there are no obvious column or row "headings" that can easily be stretched. And, if you display the Format Cross Tab dialog box, you won't find any column width or row height settings that you can change.

Because Crystal Reports cross-tabs are actually collections of individual report objects, you must select the individual objects that make up the cross-tab and resize them horizontally or vertically if you desire to make a row, column, or summarized cell wider or taller.

1. Open an existing report containing a cross-tab, or add a new cross-tab to your report.

2. Preview the report. Look carefully to see if any row or column labels are being truncated.

3. If they are, select the label that's not displaying in its entirety. Notice the small blue "sizing handle blocks" on four sides of the label.

4. To widen the label, point to the right sizing handle block until your mouse changes into a two-way arrow cursor. Hold down the mouse button and stretch the object horizontally.

5. To make a label taller, point to the bottom sizing handle block until your mouse changes into a two-way arrow cursor. Hold down the mouse button and stretch the object vertically.

6. Once you've stretched a label horizontally or vertically, notice that the entire cross-tab has adjusted to accommodate the new width or height you chose. If you stretched horizontally to a sufficient degree, the label will no longer be truncated. If you stretched vertically, truncated labels will word-wrap where a space occurs, appearing on multiple vertical lines.

7. If you need to make further width or height adjustments (perhaps you over-stretched the label), select the desired label and use the sizing handle blocks to reduce or increase horizontal or vertical size.

Replacing Truncated Cell Values with Pound Signs

Microsoft Excel, by default, replaces cell values that are truncated with pound signs. Crystal Reports, however, will actually truncate numbers in cross-tab cells if there is insufficient horizontal space to show the entire value. You can change this default value by turning off the Allow Field Clipping option in the Custom Style dialog box from the Format Editor.

1997 Quarterly Analysis
by Sales Rep

■ Order Count
▨ Gross Revenue

	1/1997	4/1997	7/1997	10/1997	Total
Davolio, Nancy	52	78	60	61	251
	87,741.84	162,951.53	102,177.32	97,995.14	$450,866
Dodsworth, Anne	59	81	65	50	255
	132,435.81	143,288.42	144,839.47	92,981.82	$513,546
King, Robert	56	99	69	73	297
	116,156.38	153,103.81	123,314.42	119,831.99	$512,407
Leverling, Janet	43	90	55	66	254
	101,513.66	157,316.45	86,818.77	101,586.31	$447,235
Peacock, Margaret	44	68	64	70	246
	77,645.46	144,866.30	101,166.52	122,472.28	$446,151
Suyama, Michael	50	89	60	61	260
	117,106.69	104,506.80	156,497.11	118,770.88	$496,881
Total	304	505	373	381	1,563
	##########	##########	##########	##########	$2,867,085

Avoid Truncation

1. Open an existing report containing a cross-tab, or add a new cross-tab to your report.

2. In either the Design or Preview tab, click a cell that you wish to format to show pound signs.

3. Right-click. Choose Format Field from the pop-up menu. The Format Editor will appear.

4. Since no field clipping choices are available on the main Number tab, you must customize the formatting style to make this choice.

5. Click the Customize button. The Custom Style dialog box will appear.

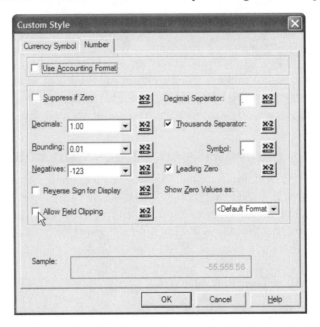

6. Uncheck the Allow Field Clipping option on the Number tab. Click OK to close the Custom Style dialog box.

7. Click OK to close the Format Editor.

8. Notice if any cross-tab cells contain pound signs.

9. If so, select the individual cell. Notice the four "sizing handle blocks" that appear on the selected cell.

10. Move your mouse over the right sizing handle block until the mouse cursor changes to a two-way arrow cursor. Hold the mouse button down and stretch the cell to the right. The entire cross-tab will adjust according to the new width.

11. Ensure that the cell now displays the entire numeric value and not pound signs. Make any additional adjustments to other cross-tab columns, if necessary.

Changing the Default Allow Field Clipping Setting

When you first install Crystal Reports, the Allow Field Clipping option is turned on by default. This may cause number values in cross-tabs, as well as those displayed by other numeric fields and formulas, to be truncated if the cross-tab cell or numeric object isn't wide enough. You may change this default behavior so that Allow Field Clipping is turned off by default.

1. Choose File | Options from the pull-down menus.

2. Click the Fields tab on the options dialog box.

3. Click the Number and/or Currency buttons to display the default formatting for each type of field.

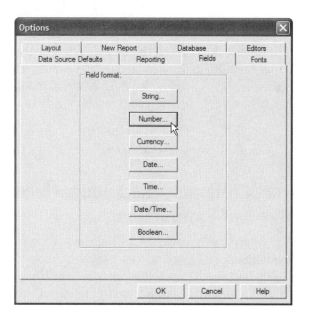

4. Click the Number tab on the default Format Editor.

5. Since no field clipping choices are available on the main Number tab, you must customize the formatting style to make this choice.

6. Click the Customize button. The Custom Style dialog box will appear.

7. Uncheck the Allow Field Clipping option on the Number tab. Click OK to close the Custom Style dialog box.

8. Click OK to close the Format Editor.

9. Click OK to close the Options dialog box.

Changes to default formatting made with File | Options will affect only new fields added to reports from the time you make the change forward. Any existing objects in existing reports will retain their original formatting.

Cross-Tabs with Formulas and Parameters

When you initially create a Crystal Reports cross-tab, you may be tempted to include only database fields in the Rows, Columns, and Summarized Fields boxes of the Format Cross-Tab dialog box. This, however, can place a serious limit on the flexibility you can gain with cross-tabs.

By using formulas with cross-tabs, you gain a substantial amount of flexibility in customizing cross-tab rows, columns, and summarized fields. And, if you use Crystal Reports parameter fields to control the formulas, you go one step further. Creative use of parameter fields can give you the ability to prompt the report viewer for choices for row, column, and summarized field values, allowing the cross-tab to be customized on the fly. You can also base cross-tab conditional formatting on the parameter field values, adding yet more flexibility to cross-tab creation.

DOWNLOAD *Cross-Tab with Parameters and Formulas.rpt from CrystalBook.com*

Basing Rows, Columns, and Summarized Fields on Formulas and Parameters

By basing row, column, or summarized field values on formulas instead of database fields, you gain an immediate increase in cross-tab flexibility. However, basing these formulas on parameter fields lends even more flexibility to the mix. You can prompt report viewers for pertinent information to customize the rows, columns, and summarized fields that appear in the cross-tab.

1. Open an existing report or create a new report that you wish to contain a customized cross-tab.

2. Add parameter fields to the report to prompt the report viewer for pertinent information. For example, you may wish to create "desired

row," "desired column," and "summary field" parameters to allow the viewer several choices.

3. Create formulas related to each parameter field that return certain database fields or calculations based on the values supplied in the parameter fields. For example, the row formula may look like this:

```
If {?Row Field} = "Product Name" Then
    {Product.Product Name}
Else
    {Product.Product Class}
```

The column field may look like this:

```
If {?Column Field} = "Month" Then
    ToText({Orders.Order Date}, "yyyy-MM")
Else
    {Employee.Last Name} & ", " & {Employee.First Name}
```

And, the summary field formula may look like this:

```
If {?Summary Field} = "Quantity Sold" Then
    {Orders_Detail.Quantity}
Else
    {Orders_Detail.Unit Price} * {Orders_Detail.Quantity}
```

4. Create the cross-tab, adding the appropriate formulas to the Rows, Columns, and Summarized Fields boxes of the Format Cross-Tab dialog box.

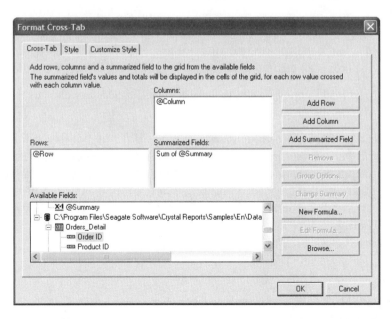

Cross-Tabs with Formulas and Parameters

5. Run the report, supplying various values for the parameter field prompts. Ensure that the formulas the cross-tab is based on behave as expected with various parameter values.

Conditionally Format Cross-Tabs Based on Parameter Fields

Although a cross-tab may look like a single object when you look at the report in the Design or Preview tab, it actually consists of several "subobjects," such as the row and column labels, row and column totals, and summarized field in the "cell." All these individual objects can be formatted—either absolutely or conditionally. Absolute formatting can be done with the Formatting toolbar or the Format Editor. Conditional formatting is accomplished with the Highlighting Expert or conditional formula buttons in the Format Editor (Crystal Reports 8.x can format numeric totals or cell values only with the Highlighting Expert—labels must use conditional formatting from the Format Editor).

Using the same parameter fields that already control the row, column, and summary behavior of the cross-tab, you can also conditionally format cross-tab elements. This provides great flexibility for changing not only the fields and values the cross-tab shows, but how it shows them.

1. Select the individual row or column label, row or column total, or summary value "cell" that you wish to conditionally format.

2. To perform simpler conditional formatting using the Highlighting Expert, choose Format | Highlighting Expert from the pull-down menus. You can also click the appropriate Highlighting Expert toolbar button or right-click the cross-tab element and choose Highlighting Expert from the pop-up menu.

3. The Highlighting Expert will appear. Make necessary choices to conditionally format the object and click OK.

4. To perform more complex conditional formatting, or to conditionally format properties that the Highlighting Expert doesn't support (such as number of decimal places), choose Format | Format Field from the pull-down menus. You can also click the appropriate Format toolbar button or right-click the cross-tab element and choose Format Field from the pop-up menu. The Format Editor will appear.

5. Click the appropriate tab containing the property that you wish to format conditionally. If necessary, click the Customize button on a tab to more closely customize a property (such as number of decimal places from the Number tab).

6. Click the conditional formula button next to the property that you want to customize. The Format Formula Editor will appear.

7. Create an appropriate formula to conditionally format the cross-tab object. For example, to change the number of displayed decimal places based on a parameter field, you might use a formula similar to this:

```
If {?Summary Field} = "Quantity Sold" Then 0 Else 2
```

8. Check and save the formula. Notice that the conditional formatting button turns red.

9. Click OK to close dialog boxes, including the Format Editor.

10. Refresh the report with various responses to parameter prompts. Ensure that the conditional formatting behaves as expected.

Customize the Cross-Tab Group Name Field

When you create standard Crystal Reports groups, a *group name field* is placed in the group header automatically. Typically, this group name field just prints the value the group is based on, such as Country, Sales Rep Name, or Month. However, if you wish to customize the way the group name field appears (perhaps you have grouped on Sales Rep Number but want to show Sales Rep Name), you can use the Customize Group Name Field option from the Group Options dialog box.

What you may not be aware of is that cross-tabs, in essence, create their own "groups" to create the rows and columns that make up the cross-tab. The row or column labels behave similarly to group name fields in regular report groups. And, as with regular report groups, the row and column labels in the cross-tab can be customized just like group name fields in regular report groups.

You gain even more flexibility by customizing cross-tab group name fields according to parameter values supplied by the report viewer. This allows the cross-tab not only to display different values in rows and columns according to parameter fields, but to customize the way the row and column labels appear according to the same parameter fields.

1. Select the entire cross-tab object that you wish to customize the row or column labels for (click a border line between cells, or the small white space between the upper row and column).

2. Right-click and choose Format Cross-Tab from the pop-up menu (the pop-up menu will display Cross-Tab Expert in Crystal Reports 9). The Format Cross-Tab dialog box will appear.

3. Select the row or column field in the Rows or Columns box that you wish to customize the label for. Click the Group Options button. The Cross-Tab Group Options dialog box will appear.

4. Click the Customize Group Name Field check box (if you are using Crystal Reports 9, you'll need to select the Options tab first).

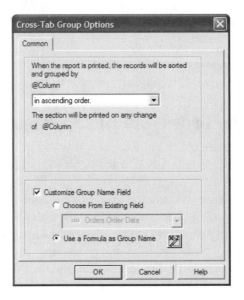

5. To base the column or row label on another report formula, click the Choose From Existing Field radio button and choose the field in the drop-down list.

6. To base the column or row label on a formula, click the Use A Formula As Group Name radio button. Then, click the conditional formula button. The Formula Editor will appear.

7. Create a string formula to determine how the row or column label will appear. For example, to base the formula on a parameter field, you might use a formula similar to this:

```
If {?Column Field} = "Month" Then
    {@Column}[6 to 7] & "/" & {@Column}[1 to 4]
Else
    {@Column}
```

NOTE

Even though parameter fields don't appear in the Field tree of the Formula Editor when customizing the group name field, you can still use them in the formula. Just type the parameter field names in manually, including the curly braces and question mark.

8. Check and save the formula. Notice that the conditional formula button in the Cross-Tab Group Options dialog box turns red.

9. Click OK to close the Cross-Tab Group Options dialog box. Click OK on the Format Cross-Tab dialog box to close it.

10. View the report with appropriate responses to parameter fields to ensure that the row or column labels are customized appropriately given the parameter values.

Cross-Tabs with Formulas and Parameters

Appendix

Formula Reference

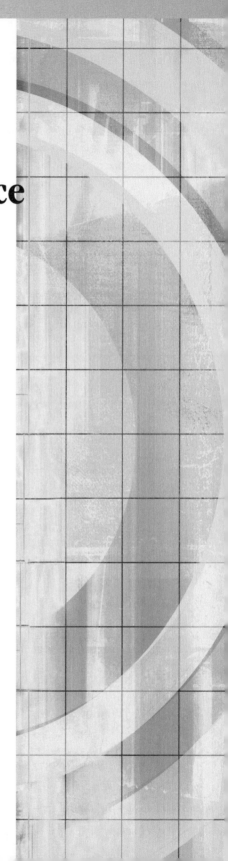

This appendix provides detailed information for each Crystal Reports formula language function and operator. Functions and operators are categorized by usage (string, numeric, financial, and so forth). The purpose of each function or operator is discussed, along with explanations of various function arguments. An example of each function and operator is provided.

Consider the following points when making use of this reference:

- Crystal Syntax is used in this reference. Basic Syntax is not covered, as Visual Basic and Visual Basic for Applications (which Basic Syntax is based on) are commonly documented languages. In many cases, the Basic Syntax version of the function or operator is identical or very similar to the Crystal Syntax version documented here.

- Some more esoteric functions, such as statistical and financial functions, may not be explained in great detail. It is assumed that report designers who need to use these specialized functions will already possess a basic understanding of their usage.

- Some functions or operators are available only in Crystal Reports 9. These are so noted. Any differences in syntax between Crystal Reports 8.x and 9 will be so noted.

- Although most of the examples in this appendix use "literal" arguments, you may easily substitute database fields, other formulas, and so forth, for function arguments.

- Formatting in examples that follow each function or operator assume standard U.S. settings in the Windows control panel. If you've changed these settings, your default output formatting may be different.

Functions: Additional Functions

This category of the Function tree exposes functions that are provided to Crystal Reports by a set of external dynamic link libraries (DLLs). These DLLs, known as User Function Libraries (UFLs) within Crystal Reports, can be developed in a Windows programming language to provide extensible functions to the Crystal Reports formula language.

In Crystal Reports 9, UFL functions are categorized by the UFL filename. In Crystal Reports 8.x, they are all merely lumped together within the Additional Functions category.

If you have upgraded from previous versions of Crystal Reports, or you have downloaded additional User Function Libraries from Crystal Decisions (or other sources), you'll find additional entries in the Additional Functions category of the Function tree.

ByteToText

Converts a number to a descriptive string indicating disk or memory storage used.

ByteToText is useful when reporting on the Local File System (or other data source that requires amounts of computer storage to be included on the report). Values less than 1,204 are returned in bytes, values between 1,204 and 1,048,576 are abbreviated to "KB", and values above 1,048,576 are abbreviated to "MB".

ByteToText (n)

n – numeric value.

```
ByteToText(1000)
```

returns "1000 bytes".

```
ByteToText(10000000)
```

returns "9 MB".

DateTimeTo2000

Converts a date-time value that may not be year 2000–compliant to a year 2000–compliant date-time with a four-digit year.

DateTimeTo2000 is "left over" from previous versions of Crystal Reports that may not have dealt with date-time values properly. It is largely not required with current versions, unless you may be dealing with older databases that don't return full four-digit years in date-time fields.

DateTimeTo2000 (dt, n)

dt – date-time value with a two- or four-digit year.
n – numeric value to act as a "sliding scale" year window.

```
DateTimeTo2000(DateTimeValue("1/1/90 1:03 pm"), 95)
```

returns 1/1/2090 1:03:00 PM

DateTimeToDate

Returns only the date portion of a date-time value.
This function is "left over" from previous versions of Crystal Reports and has been replaced by the CDate and DateValue functions. See **DateValue** for details.

DateTimeToSeconds

Extracts the number of seconds that have passed since midnight.
DateTimeToSeconds evaluates the time portion of the supplied date-time value and returns the number of seconds that have passed since midnight.

DateTimeToSeconds (dt)

dt – date-time value.

```
DateTimeToSeconds(CurrentDateTime)
```

returns 49,980 for a current date-time value that includes the time 1:53:00 P.M.

DateTimeToTime

Returns only the time portion of a date-time value.
This function is "left over" from previous versions of Crystal Reports and has been replaced by the CTime and TimeValue functions. See **TimeValue** for details.

DateTo2000

Converts a date value that may not be year 2000–compliant to a year 2000–compliant date with a four-digit year.
DateTo2000 is "left over" from previous versions of Crystal Reports that may not have dealt with date values properly. It is largely not required with current versions, unless you may be dealing with older databases that don't return full four-digit years in date fields.

DateTo2000 (d, n)

d – date value with a two- or four-digit year.
n – numeric value to act as a "sliding scale" year window.

```
DateTo2000(#1/1/90#, 95)
```

returns 1/1/2090.

DTSTo2000

Returns a string value from a date string or date-time string with a two- or four-digit year.

DTSTo2000 will convert a string formatted in a specific year-month-day-hour-minute-second format to another string with a four-digit year. This function includes a sliding-scale year argument to ready two-digit dates for year-2000 compliance.

DTSTo2000 (s, n)

s – string containing a date in the format "yyyy/mm/dd" or "yy/mm/dd" or date-time in the format "yyyy/mm/dd hh:mm:ss.00" or "yy/mm/dd hh:mm:ss.00".
n – numeric value to act as a "sliding scale" year window.

```
DTSTo2000("90/10/01",95)
```

returns the string "2090/10/01".

DTSToDate

Converts a string formatted in a specific date-time format to a true date value.

DTSToDate is functionally equivalent to CDate and DateValue. See **DateValue** for more information.

DTSToDateTime

Converts a string formatted in a specific date-time format to a true date-time value.

DTSToDateTime is functionally equivalent to CDateTime and DateTimeValue. See **DateTimeValue** for more information.

DTSToSeconds

Extracts the number of seconds that have passed since midnight.

DTSToSeconds evaluates the time portion of the supplied date-time string and returns the number of seconds that have passed since midnight.

DTSToSeconds (s)

s – string containing a date-time in the format "yyyy/mm/dd hh:mm:ss.00" or "yy/mm/dd hh:mm:ss.00".

```
DTSToSeconds("2003/05/28 13:53:00.00")
```

returns 49,980 (the number of seconds between midnight and 1:53 P.M.).

Functions: Additional Functions

DTSToTimeField

Converts a string formatted in a specific date-time format to a true time value.
DTSToTimeField is functionally equivalent to CTime and TimeValue. See
TimeValue for more information.

DTSToTimeString

Returns a string containing just the time portion of a date-time string.
DTSToTimeString simply extracts the text after the eleventh character of a
string (which does not actually have to be formatted as a date-time string).

DTSToTimeString (s)

s – string containing a date-time in the format "yyyy/mm/dd hh:mm:ss.00".

```
DTSToTimeString("1998/05/28 13:53:00.00")
```

returns the string "13:53:00.00".

NOTE   *The preceding series of date-time string (DTS) functions are "left over"
from previous versions of Crystal Reports that may not have dealt with
date-time values properly. For example, Crystal Reports 6 did not
properly recognize a true date or date-time value from a database
but returned these values as string fields in a certain format. While
you can still make the choice to convert date or date-time values to
strings, these DTS functions are largely not required with current
Crystal Reports versions.*

EventNumber

Returns a text description of a Microsoft Exchange event number.
EventNumber is helpful when reporting from Microsoft Exchange data sources.
Certain supplied event numbers are significant (for example, 1,000 indicates local
delivery). Those that aren't recognized will return "unknown event" results.

EventNumber (n)

n – numeric value representing a Microsoft Exchange event number.

```
EventNumber(1000)
```

returns "Local Delivery".

ExchGetId

Extracts the e-mail address from an X400- or X500-formatted string.

ExchGetID is helpful when reporting from Microsoft Exchange data sources. These data sources return certain e-mail address strings that can be passed to ExchGetID to return just the e-mail address.

ExchGetId (s)

s – string containing an X400- or X500-formatted address.

```
ExchGetID("c=US; a= ;p=Ablaze Group;
o=AblazeServer;dda:smtp=Info@AblazeGroup.com")
```

returns "Author@CrystalBook.com".

ExchGetOrganization

Extracts the organization string from an X400- or X500-formatted string.

ExchGetOrganization is helpful when reporting from Microsoft Exchange data sources. These data sources return certain organization strings that can be passed to ExchGetOrganization to return just the organization.

ExchGetOrganization (s)

s – string containing an X400- or X500-formatted address.

```
ExchGetOrganization("c=US; a= ;p=Ablaze Group;
o=AblazeServer;dda:smtp=Info@AblazeGroup.com")
```

returns "Ablaze Group".

ExchGetPath

Extracts the destination path string from an X400- or X500-formatted string.

ExchGetPath is helpful when reporting from Microsoft Exchange data sources. These data sources return certain destination strings that can be passed to ExchGetPath to return just the destination path.

ExchGetPath (s)

s – string containing an X400- or X500-formatted address.

```
ExchGetPath("c=US;a= ;p=Ablaze Group;ou1=Info;
ou2=Ablaze Group;o=AblazeServer;dda:smtp=Info@AblazeGroup.com")
```

will return "OU1=INFO; OU2=ABLAZE GROUP;".

ExchGetSite

Extracts the site string from an X400- or X500-formatted string.

ExchGetSite is helpful when reporting from Microsoft Exchange data sources. These data sources return certain site strings that can be passed to ExchGetSite to return just the site.

ExchGetSite (s)

s – string containing an X400- or X500-formatted address.

```
ExchGetSite("c=US;a= ;p=Ablaze Group;ou1=Info;ou2=Ablaze Group;
o=AblazeServer;dda:smtp=Info@AblazeGroup.com")
```

will return "AblazeServer".

ExtractString

Extracts the portion of a string that appears between two other strings.

ExtractString will search a string, returning the portion that falls between two other search strings. If the first search string is not found, ExtractString returns an empty string. If the second search string is not found, ExtractString will return the entire portion of the source string after the first search string.

ExtractString (s1, s2, s3)

s1 – source string to be searched.
s2 – first string to search for.
s3 – second string to search for.

```
ExtractString("The rain in Spain falls on the plain",
"rain", "plain")
```

returns "in Spain falls on the".

FRAccRecTurnover

Returns the average turnover of accounts receivable in numeric days.

FRAccRecTurnover calculates the average "turnover" of accounts receivable by dividing accounts receivable by sales, and multiplying the result by the number of days in the year.

FRAccRecTurnover (n1, n2, n3)

n1 – numeric value of total accounts receivable.

n2 – numeric value of total sales.
n3 – numeric value indicating the number of days in a year (default is 360).

```
FRAccRecTurnover(10000,100000,360)
```

returns 36 days.

FRCashFlowVsTotalDebt

Returns the ratio between cash flow and total debt.

FRCashFlowVsTotalDebt determines the ratio of cash flow to debt by dividing cash flow by total debt.

FRCashFlowVsTotalDebt (n1, n2)

n1 – numeric value indicating total cash flow.
n2 – numeric value indicating total debt.

```
FRCashFlowVsTotalDebt(100000,10000)
```

returns a cash flow–to–debt ratio of 10.

FRCurrentRatio

Returns the ratio between current assets and current liabilities.

FRCurrentRatio determines the ratio of current assets to current liabilities by dividing assets by liabilities.

FRCurrentRatio (n1, n2)

n1 – numeric value indicating total current assets.
n2 – numeric value indicating total current liabilities.

```
FRCurrentRatio(100000,10000)
```

returns an asset-to-liability ratio of 10.

FRDebtEquityRatio

Returns the ratio between total liabilities and total equity.

FRDebtEquityRatio determines the ratio of total liabilities to total equity by dividing liabilities by equity.

FRDebtEquityRatio (n1, n2)

n1 – numeric value indicating total liabilities.
n2 – numeric value indicating total equity.

```
FRDebtEquityRatio(10000,100000)
```

returns a liability-to-equity ratio of .1.

FRDividendYield

Returns the ratio between dividend and market price.

FRDividendYield determines the ratio of dividend to market price by dividing dividend by market price.

FRDividendYield (n1, n2)

n1 – numeric value indicating dividend amount.
n2 – numeric value indicating share market price.

```
FRDividendYield(10,50)
```

returns a dividend–to–market price ratio of .2.

FREarningsPerCommonShare

Returns the ratio of net profit distributable to shareholders to the number of shares.

FREarningsPerCommonShare determines the ratio of net profit to number of shares by subtracting the preferred dividend amount from net profit, and dividing the result by the number of common shares.

FREarningsPerCommonShare (n1, n2, n3)

n1 – numeric value indicating net profit.
n2 – numeric value indicating dividend paid to preferred shareholders.
n3 – numeric value indicating number of issued common shares.

```
FREarningsPerCommonShare (100000, 10, 10000)
```

returns a profit-to-share ratio of 10.

FREquityVsTotalAssets

Returns the ratio between total equity and total assets.

FREquityVsTotalAssets determines the ratio of total equity to total assets by dividing equity by assets.

FREquityVsTotalAssets (n1, n2)

n1 – numeric value indicating total equity.
n2 – numeric value indicating total assets.

```
FREquityVsTotalAssets(100000,500000)
```

returns a equity-to-assets ratio of .2.

FRGrossProfitMargin

Returns the ratio between gross profit and sales.

FRGrossProfitMargin determines the ratio of gross profit to sales by dividing gross profit by sales.

FRGrossProfitMargin (n1, n2)

n1 – numeric value indicating gross profit.
n2 – numeric value indicating sales.

```
FRGrossProfitMargin(10000,100000)
```

returns a profit-to-sales ratio of .1.

FRInterestCoverage

Returns the ratio between cash flow and interest expense.

FRInterestCoverage determines the ratio of cash flow to interest expense by dividing cash flow by interest expense.

FRInterestCoverage (n1, n2)

n1 – numeric value indicating cash flow.
n2 – numeric value indicating interest expense.

```
FRInterestCoverage(100000,2500)
```

returns a cash flow–to–interest expense ratio of 25.

FRInventoryTurnover

Returns the average turnover of inventory in numeric days.

FRInventoryTurnover calculates the average "turnover" of inventory by dividing inventory by sales, and multiplying the result by the number of days in the year.

FRInventoryTurnover (n1, n2, n3)

n1 – numeric value of total inventory.
n2 – numeric value of total sales.
n3 – numeric value indicating the number of days in a year (default is 360).

```
FRInventoryTurnover(10000,100000,360)
```

returns 36 days.

FRNetProfitMargin

Returns the ratio between net profit and sales.

FRNetProfitMargin determines the ratio of net profit to sales by dividing net profit by sales.

FRNetProfitMargin (n1, n2)

n1 – numeric value indicating net profit.
n2 – numeric value indicating sales.

```
FRNetProfitMargin(10000,100000)
```

returns a profit-to-sales ratio of .1.

FROperatingProfitMargin

Returns the ratio between operating profit and sales.

FROperatingProfitMargin determines the ratio of operating profit to sales by dividing operating profit by sales.

FROperatingProfitMargin (n1, n2)

n1 – numeric value indicating operating profit.
n2 – numeric value indicating sales.

```
FROperatingProfitMargin(10000,100000)
```

returns a profit-to-sales ratio of .1.

FRPriceEarningsRatio

Returns the ratio between share market price and earnings per share.

FRPriceEarningsRatio determines the ratio of share market price to earnings by dividing share market price by earnings per share.

FRPriceEarningsRatio (n1, n2)

n1 – numeric value indicating share market price.
n2 – numeric value indicating earnings per share.

```
FRPriceEarningsRatio (10,100)
```

returns a price-to-earnings ratio of .1.

FRQuickRatio

Returns the ratio between current assets (less inventory) and current liabilities.

FRQuickRatio determines the ratio of current assets (less inventory) to current liabilities by subtracting inventory from assets and dividing the results by liabilities.

FRQuickRatio (n1, n2, n3)

n1 – numeric value indicating current assets.
n2 – numeric value indicating inventory.
n3 – numeric value indicating current liabilities.

```
FRQuickRatio (100000, 10000, 5000)
```

returns a quick ratio of 18.

FRReturnOnCommonEquity

Returns the ratio between net profit and common equity.

FRReturnOnCommonEquity determines the ratio of net profit to common equity by subtracting the dividend amount from net profit, and dividing the result by common equity.

FRReturnOnCommonEquity (n1, n2, n3)

n1 – numeric value indicating net profit.
n2 – numeric value indicating the total preferred dividend amount.

Functions: Additional Functions

n3 – numeric value indicating common equity.

```
FRReturnOnCommonEquity (10000, 15, 100000)
```

returns a return on common equity ratio of .1.

FRReturnOnEquity

Returns the ratio between net profit and total equity.
FRReturnOnEquity determines the ratio of net profit to total equity by dividing net profit by equity.

FRReturnOnEquity (n1, n2)

n1 – numeric value indicating net profit.
n2 – numeric value indicating total equity.

```
FRReturnOnEquity (10000,100000)
```

returns a profit-to-equity ratio of .1.

FRReturnOnInvestedCapital

Returns the ratio between net profit and invested capital.
FRReturnOnInvestedCapital determines the ratio between net profit and invested capital by dividing net profit by the sum of bank debt and equity.

FRReturnOnInvestedCapital (n1, n2, n3)

n1 – a numeric value indicating net profit.
n2 – a numeric value indicating total bank debt.
n3 – a numeric value indicating total equity.

```
FRReturnOnInvestedCapital (10000,5000,100000)
```

returns a return on invested capital ratio of .1.

FRReturnOnNetFixedAssets

Returns the ratio between net profit and net fixed assets.
FRReturnOnNetFixedAssets determines the ratio of net profit to fixed assets by dividing net profit by fixed assets.

FRReturnOnNetFixedAssets (n1, n2)

n1 – numeric value indicating net profit.
n2 – numeric value indicating net fixed assets.

```
FRReturnOnNetFixedAssets (10000,100000)
```

returns a profit-to-assets ratio of .1.

FRReturnOnTotalAssets

Returns the ratio between net profit and total assets.

FRReturnOnTotalAssets determines the ratio of net profit to total assets by dividing net profit by total assets.

FRReturnOnTotalAssets (n1, n2)

n1 – numeric value indicating net profit.
n2 – numeric value indicating total assets.

```
FRReturnOnTotalAssets (10000,75000)
```

returns a profit-to-assets ratio of .13.

LooksLike

Returns a Boolean (true or false) value based on whether the "mask" is found in the source string.

LooksLike uses DOS-style "wildcards" (the asterisk and question mark) to determine if the source string contains the characters specified in the wildcard-based mask. This is helpful for checking for partial text matches.

LooksLike (s1, s2)

s1 – the source string to be searched.
s2 – the mask string to search against. The mask can include a question mark wildcard to indicate a single-character substitution and/or an asterisk to indicate a multiple-character substitution.

```
LooksLike("George Peck", "G?orge*")
```

returns True.

Functions: Additional Functions

Now

Returns the current time from the system clock as a text string.

    This function is "left over" from previous versions of Crystal Reports and is similar to the CurrentTime function. The only difference between Now and CurrentTime is the data type returned. CurrentTime returns a time data type, while Now returns a string data type.

Picture

Formats a string based on the supplied formatting "mask" string.

    Picture reformats a string value, inserting literal characters supplied within the "mask" formatting string. Picture is helpful for adding characters to an existing string, such a parentheses and hyphens to string database phone numbers without such punctuation.

Picture (s1, s2)

s1 – source string to format.

s2 – string "mask" to base formatting on. Any occurrence of an "x" character in the mask will substitute a single character from the source string. Any character other than "x" will simply be added to the output string.

```
Picture("8007733472", "Phone: (xxx) xxx-xxxx")
```

returns "Phone: (800) 773-3472".

Soundex

Returns a four-character string indicating how the source string "sounds".

    Soundex uses a character-based algorithm to assign a "sound" to the source string. Similar-sounding strings, such as "George" and "gorge", will return the same four-character Soundex result. You may use Soundex in If-Then-Else statements, or similar constructs, where you want to compare the sound of two or more strings.

Soundex (s)

s – a string value to perform the Soundex algorithm on.

```
Soundex("George")
```

returns the string "G620".

```
If Soundex("George") = Soundex("gorge") Then
   "Sound the same"
Else
   "Different sound"
```

returns "Sound the same".

> **NOTE** *An involved description of the Soundex algorithm can be found in Crystal Reports online help.*

Functions: Alerts

This set of functions exposes Crystal Reports Alerts to formulas. Alerts are created with either Report | Create Alerts (Crystal Reports 8.5) or Report | Alerts (Crystal Reports 9).

> **NOTE** *Alerts are not included in Crystal Reports 8.0 or earlier.*

AlertMessage

Returns a string containing the message portion of an alert.

AlertMessage returns the message portion of an alert when a particular report record has triggered the alert. If the record has not triggered the alert, AlertMessage returns an empty string.

AlertMessage (s)

s – a string value indicating the name of the alert.

```
AlertMessage("Order Over 5K")
```

returns "Orders over $5,000 exist" (the message for the Order Over 5K alert) if the report record has triggered the Order Over 5K alert.

AlertNames

Shows the name of each alert included in the report.

The AlertNames category of the Function tree (within the Alerts category) will show the names of each alert that has been created on the report. These alert names can be supplied as arguments to other Alert functions (described later in this section). If no alerts have been created, this function category won't appear in the Function tree.

IsAlertEnabled

Returns a Boolean (true or false) value indicating whether or not the "Enabled" check box is checked for the specified alert.

IsAlertEnabled tests to see if an alert will "fire" if records meet its criteria. An alert can be enabled or disabled when the alert is edited.

IsAlertEnabled (s)

s – a string value indicating the name of the alert.

```
If IsAlertEnabled("Order Over 5K") Then
    "Over 5K orders will be tested for"
```

returns "Over 5K orders will be tested for" if the enabled check box is checked in the Order Over 5K alert dialog box.

IsAlertTriggered

Returns a Boolean (true or false) value indicating whether or not an alert is triggered.

IsAlertTriggered is used within a formula to see if a particular alert has "fired" for the current record. The formula can base the remainder of its logic on whether or not the record has triggered the alert.

IsAlertTriggered (s)

s – a string value indicating the name of the alert.

```
If IsAlertTriggered ("Order Over 5K") Then
    "Congratulations--Great Order!"
```

returns "Congratulations—Great Order!" if the Order Over 5K alert is triggered when the formula evaluates.

Functions: Arrays

This category of functions applies to arrays. An *array* is a collection of data items stored in a single "bucket," such as a single variable. If an array contains 15 items, it is said to have 15 *elements*. Arrays can contain any supported Crystal Reports data type, such as number, string, date-time, and so forth.

Average

Returns a number containing the average of the numeric elements in the array.

Average (a)

a – an array. The array must be numeric.

```
Average([1,5,10,20,10])
```

returns 9.2.

Count

Returns a number containing the number of elements in the array.

Count is helpful when performing looping logic through an array. By using Count, you can determine how many array elements to loop through.

Count (a)

a – an array. The array can be of any data type.

```
Count([1,5,10,20,10])
```

returns 5.

NOTE   *Count is functionally equivalent to UBound when dealing with arrays.*

DistinctCount

Returns a number containing the number of unique entries in the array.

DistinctCount is different from Count in that a duplicated entry in the array (for example, a second occurrence of the same element) will not increment the count when using DistinctCount, whereas it will with Count.

DistinctCount (a)

a – an array. The array can be of any data type.

```
DistinctCount(["George","Paul","George","John","Ringo","John"])
```

returns 4.

MakeArray

Creates an array.

MakeArray will create an array of values. It can be used to assign an array to a variable or pass a "literal" array to another array-based function. Supplying array elements within square brackets is the equivalent of MakeArray.

MakeArray (v1, v2...)

[v1, v2…]

v1 and v2 – literal values, separated by commas, that become array elements. The literal values can be any Crystal Reports data type, as long as they are all of the same data type. An array can contain, at maximum, 1,000 elements.

```
StringVar Array Beatles :=
    MakeArray("George","Paul","John","Ringo");
Beatles[3]
```

returns "John".

```
StringVar Array Beatles :=
    ["George","Paul","John","Ringo"];
Beatles[3]
```

returns "John".

> **NOTE** *Basic syntax contains the Array function in addition to MakeArray. Array and MakeArray are functionally equivalent in Basic syntax.*

Maximum

Returns the last entry in an array.

Maximum will return the "last" entry in an array. What constitutes the "last" entry is based on the type of data in the array. Maximum will return the highest number in a numeric array, the last string value alphabetically in a string array, and so forth.

Maximum (a)

a – an array. The array can be of any data type.

```
Maximum([#1/1/1990#,#12/15/85#,#5/13/03#,#7/4/2000#])
```

will return 5/13/2003 12:00:00 A.M. as a date-time value.

Minimum

Returns the first entry in an array.

   Minimum will return the "first" entry in an array. What constitutes the "first" entry is based on the type of data in the array. Minimum will return the lowest number in a numeric array, the first string value alphabetically in a string array, and so forth.

Minimum (a)

a – an array. The array can be of any data type.

```
Minimum(["Paul","George","John","Ringo"])
```

will return "George".

PopulationStdDev

Returns a number containing the population standard deviation of an array.

PopulationStdDev (a)

a – an array. The array must be numeric.

```
PopulationStdDev([1,10,15,20,25])
```

returns 8.28 (rounded to two decimal places).

PopulationVariance

Returns a number containing the population variance of an array.

PopulationVariance (a)

a – an array. The array must be numeric.

```
PopulationVariance([1,10,15,20,25])
```

returns 68.56 (rounded to two decimal places).

StdDev

Returns a number containing the standard deviation of an array.

StdDev (a)

a – an array. The array must be numeric.

```
StdDev([1,10,15,20,25])
```

returns 9.26 (rounded to two decimal places).

Sum

Returns a number containing the sum of array elements.

Sum (a)

a – an array. The array must be numeric.

```
Sum([1,10,15,20,25])
```

returns 71.

UBound

Returns the number of elements in the array.

UBound is helpful when performing looping logic through an array. By using UBound, you can determine how many array elements to loop through.

UBound (a)

a – an array. The array can be of any data type.

```
UBound([1,5,10,20,10])
```

returns 5.

NOTE   *UBound is functionally equivalent to Count when dealing with arrays.*

Variance

Returns a number containing the variance of an array.

Variance (a)

a – an array. The array must be numeric.

```
Variance([1,10,15,20,25])
```

returns 85.70 (rounded to two decimal places).

Functions: Conditional Formatting

This category of functions appears in the Function tree only when you display the Format Formula Editor by clicking a Conditional Formatting Formula button from another Crystal Reports dialog box. Some of these functions will appear only in the proper "context"—for example, the Color or RGB functions will be available only when you are setting a color property conditionally.

Color

Returns a specific red-green-blue color combination.

Color allows you to specify intricate color values for font color, background color, and so forth. Rather than choosing from the limited set of default colors (such as crRed, crAqua, and so forth), you may specify any combination of red-green-blue colors with this function.

Color (n1, n2, n3)

n1 – a numeric value specifying the amount of red. The value must be between 0 and 255.

n2 – a numeric value specifying the amount of green. The value must be between 0 and 255.

n3 – a numeric value specifying the amount of blue. The value must be between 0 and 255.

```
If {Orders.Order Amount} > 5000 Then crRed Else Color(10,100,244)
```

will set the font color to a light blue shade (consisting of a red value of 10, green value of 100, and blue value of 244) if the order amount is not over 5,000.

NOTE
The RGB function is functionally equivalent to Color. RGB also accepts three arguments and may be used interchangeably with Color.

CurrentFieldValue

Returns the contents of the field being formatted.

CurrentFieldValue will return the value contained in the field being formatted. The data type can vary, depending on the field being formatted. CurrentFieldValue is particular valuable when conditionally formatting Cross-Tab or OLAP grid cells, as the cells themselves cannot be directly referred to in a formatting formula.

CurrentFieldValue

```
If CurrentFieldValue > 5000 Then crRed Else crBlack
```

will set the color property to red if the value of the object being formatted is greater than 5,000.

DefaultAttribute

Returns the setting of the formatting property from the originating dialog box.

DefaultAttribute returns the value set in the calling dialog box. For example, if you set the "absolute" font color to aqua but then click the Conditional Formatting Formula button, you will be able to recall the aqua value in the formatting formula by using DefaultAttribute.

DefaultAttribute

```
If {Orders.Order Amount} > 5000 Then crRed Else DefaultAttribute
```

will set the font color to that selected in the absolute font color property of the Format Editor if the order amount is not greater than 5,000.

GridRowColumnValue

Returns the value of the row or column name in a cross-tab or OLAP grid object.

GridRowColumnValue will return the contents of a "title" cell of a row or column in a cross-tab or OLAP grid object. By using this function, you may determine which row or column is currently formatting and change formatting logic accordingly.

GridRowColumnValue (s)

s – string value indicating row or column name to query.

```
If GridRowColumnValue ("Orders.Employee ID") = 3 Then
    crRed
Else
    crBlack
```

will determine if the Employee ID row in a cross-tab contain employee number 3. If so, the cell will be formatted in a red color.

Row Or Column Names

Names of the rows or columns in a cross-tab or OLAP grid object.

This category of the Function tree will appear only when you are conditionally formatting a cross-tab or OLAP grid object. The category will contain the names given to rows or columns in the cross-tab or OLAP grid. You may use these values with the GridRowColumnValue function to determine which row or column is currently formatting.

Functions: Date and Time

This set of functions deal with date and time manipulation, including extracting the current date and time from your computer's internal clock, performing date-time math, converting date-time functions to other data types, and so forth.

CurrentDate

Returns a date value with the current date from your computer's internal clock.

CurrentDate

```
CurrentDate
```

returns 5/30/2003 if the current date is May 30, 2003.

CurrentDateTime

Returns a date-time value with the current date and time from your computer's internal clock.

CurrentDateTime

```
CurrentDateTime
```

returns 5/30/2003 2:48:32PM if the current date is May 30, 2003 and the current time is 2:48 P.M.

CurrentTime

Returns a time value with the current time from your computer's internal clock.

CurrentTime

```
CurrentTime
```

returns 2:48:32PM if the current time is 2:48 in the afternoon.

Date

Returns a date value when supplied with various other data types.

Date is functionally equivalent to DateValue. See **DateValue** for details.

DateAdd

Returns a date-time value in the past or future, depending on supplied arguments.

DateAdd is handy for calculating dates in the past or future, based on a certain number of days, weeks, years, and so forth. DateAdd automatically handles leap years, months with less than 31 days, and so forth.

DateAdd (s, n, dt)

s – string value indicating interval type (days, weeks, and so forth). See **Interval Types** later in this section for recognized values.

n – a numeric value indicating number of intervals to add to the source date-time. This can be a negative or positive number.

dt – a date or date-time value indicating the source date-time to add intervals to.

```
DateAdd("d",5,CurrentDate)
```

returns 6/4/2003 12:00:00AM if the current date is May 30, 2003.

```
DateAdd("m",-2,#1/1/2003 10:00AM#)
```

returns 11/1/2002 10:00:00AM.

DateDiff

Returns a number indicating the number of "intervals" between two dates.

DateDiff is helpful in determining a specified amount of time that has elapsed between two date or date-time values. DateDiff can return the number of years, months, days, minutes, and so forth.

DateDiff (s, dt1, dt2)

s – string value indicating interval type (days, weeks, and so forth). See **Interval Types** later in this section for recognized values.
dt1 – a date, date-time, or time value indicating the start date-time to compare.
dt2 – a date, date-time, or time value indicating the end date-time to compare.

```
DateDiff ("h",#5/2/2003 10:00 AM#,#5/3/2003 2:00 PM#)
```

returns 28.

DateDiff (s, dt1, dt2, n)

s – string value indicating interval type (days, weeks, and so forth). See **Interval Types** later in this section for recognized values.
dt1 – a date, date-time, or time value indicating the start date-time to compare.
dt2 – a date, date-time, or time value indicating the end date-time to compare.
n – a numeric value or constant indicating the first day of the week. If not supplied, Sunday is assumed to be the first day of the week. See **First Day of Week Constants** later in this section for recognized constants or numbers for this argument.

```
DateDiff ("ww",#5/1/2003#,#6/1/2003#,crMonday)
```

returns 4.

DatePart

Returns a number indicating the individual "part" (month, hour, year, and so forth) of a date, date-time, or time value.

DatePart will return just the year, month, day, hour, minute, or second of a supplied date-time value. Other functions that work similarly to DatePart are Year, Month, Day, Hour, Minute, and Second.

DatePart (s, dt)

s – string value indicating interval type (day, week, hour, and so forth). See **Interval Types** later in this section for recognized values.
dt – a date, date-time, or time value to extract the interval from.

```
DatePart ("m",CurrentDate)
```

returns 5, if the current date is May 30, 2003.

DatePart (s, dt, n)

s – string value indicating interval type (day, week, hour, and so forth). See
Interval Types later in this section for recognized values.

dt – a date, date-time, or time value to extract the interval from.

n – a numeric value or constant indicating the first day of the week. If not supplied,
Sunday is assumed to be the first day of the week. See **First Day of Week Constants**
later in this section for recognized constants or numbers for this argument.

```
DatePart ("w",#May 30, 2003#,crMonday)
```

returns 5, considering that May 30, 2003, is a Friday.

DatePart (s, dt, n1, n2)

s – string value indicating interval type (day, week, hour, and so forth). See
Interval Types later in this section for recognized values.

dt – a date, date-time, or time value to extract the interval from.

n1 – a numeric value or constant indicating the first day of the week. If not
supplied, Sunday is assumed to be the first day of the week. See **First Day of
Week Constants** later in this section for recognized constants or numbers for
this argument.

n2 – a numeric value or constant indicating the first week of year. If not supplied,
the week containing January 1 is assumed to be the first week of the year. See
First Week of Year Constants later in this section for recognized constants or
numbers for this argument.

```
DatePart ("ww",#6/1/2003#,crSunday,crFirstJan1)
```

returns 23.

DateSerial

Returns a date value based on year, month, and day arguments.

DateSerial provides similar functionality to a specific usage of CDate, Date,
and DateValue. DateSerial differs from these other functions in one significant
way: the arguments supplied do not have to fall into a strict "month between 1 and
12, day between 1 and 31" requirement. By supplying other values, such as negative
numbers, calculations, and so forth, arguments will be evaluated "relatively."

DateSerial (n1, n2, n3)

n1 – a numeric value indicating the year.

n2 – a numeric value indicating the month.
n3 – a numeric value indicating the day.

```
DateSerial(2003, 6, 1)
```

returns 6/1/2003.

```
DateSerial(2003, 6-10, 1-30)
```

returns 7/2/2002 (10 months before June—which equates to August 1, 2002, and 30 days before the first day of the month, which equates to July 2, 2002).

DateTime

Returns a date-time value based on one of several sets and types of arguments.

DateTime is functionally equivalent to CDateTime and DateTimeValue. See **DateTimeValue** for more information.

DateTimeValue

Returns a date-time value based on one of several sets and types of arguments.

DateTimeValue can accept a wide variety of arguments that will be converted to a date-time. DateTimeValue comes in handy when you need to convert other data types to date-time, such as database fields from older systems that stored dates as strings. DateTimeValue is functionally equivalent to DateTime and CDateTime.

DateTimeValue (d)

d – a date value that will be converted to a date-time value with midnight as the time.

```
DateTimeValue(CurrentDate)
```

returns 5/30/2003 12:00:00AM if today's date is May 30, 2003 (in essence, converting the CurrentDate date-only value to a date-time value).

DateTimeValue (d, t)

d – a date value that will become the date portion of the resulting date-time value.
t – a time value that will become the time portion of the resulting date-time value.

```
DateTimeValue(CurrentDate, Time(#10:30 am#))
```

returns 5/30/2003 10:30:00AM if today's date is May 30, 2003.

DateTimeValue (n)

n – a numeric value indicating the number of days since December 30, 1899.

```
DateTimeValue(35000)
```

returns 10/28/1995 12:00:00AM (35,000 days from December 30, 1899).

DateTimeValue (s)

s – a string value that will be evaluated for particular date and time equivalents.

```
DateTimeValue("January 1, 2003 15:50")
```

returns 1/1/2003 3:50:00PM.

DateTimeValue (n1, n2, n3)

n1 – a numeric value indicating the year.
n2 – a numeric value between 1 and 12 indicating the month.
n3 – a numeric value between 1 and 31 indicating the day of month.

```
DateTimeValue(2002,10,15)
```

returns 10/15/2002 12:00:00AM.

DateTimeValue (n1, n2, n3, n4, n5, n6)

n1 – a numeric value indicating the year.
n2 – a numeric value between 1 and 12 indicating the month.
n3 – a numeric value between 1 and 31 indicating the day of month.
n4 – a numeric value between 0 and 23 indicating the hour of day.
n5 – a numeric value between 0 and 59 indicating the minute.
n6 – a numeric value between 0 and 59 indicating the second.

```
DateTimeValue(2002,10,15,14,35,50)
```

returns 10/15/2002 2:35:50PM.

DateValue

Returns a date value based on one of several sets and types of arguments.

DateValue can accept a wide variety of arguments that will be converted to a date. DateValue comes in handy when you need to convert other data types to date, such as database fields from older systems that stored dates as strings. DateValue is functionally equivalent to Date and CDate.

DateValue (dt)

dt – a date-time value that you wish to strip the time portion away from.

```
DateValue(CurrentDateTime)
```

returns 5/30/2002 if the current date is May 30, 2003, regardless of what time of day.

DateValue (n)

n – a numeric value indicating the number of days since December 30, 1899.

```
DateValue(35000)
```

returns 10/28/1995 (35,000 days from December 30, 1899).

DateValue (s)

s – a string value that will be evaluated for particular date equivalents.

```
DateValue("January 1, 2003")
```

returns 1/1/2003.

DateValue (n1, n2, n3)

n1 – a numeric value indicating the year.
n2 – a numeric value between 1 and 12 indicating the month.
n3 – a numeric value between 1 and 31 indicating the day of month.

```
DateValue(2002,10,15)
```

returns 10/15/2002.

Day
Returns a numeric value indicating the day of the month.

Functions: Date and Time

Day (dt)

dt – a date or date-time value.

```
Day(CurrentDate)
```

returns 30 if the current date is May 30, 2003.

DayOfWeek

Returns a numeric value indicating the day of the week.

DayOfWeek returns the day of the week. By default, DayOfWeek assumes Sunday is equal to 1. However, you may provide an extra argument to DayOfWeek indicating a different starting day. DayOfWeek is functionally equivalent to WeekDay.

DayOfWeek (dt)

dt – a date or date-time value.

```
DayOfWeek(CurrentDate)
```

returns 6 if the current date falls on a Friday.

DayOfWeek (dt, n)

dt – a date or date-time value.
n – a numeric value or constant indicating the first day of the week. If not supplied, Sunday is assumed to be the first day of the week. See **First Day of Week Constants** later in this section for recognized constants or numbers for this argument.

```
DayOfWeek(CurrentDate, crMonday)
```

returns 5 if the current date falls on a Friday.

Hour

Returns a numeric value indicating the hour of the supplied time or date-time in military time.

Hour (dt)

dt – a date-time or time value.

```
Hour(CurrentTime)
```

returns 17 if the current time is in the 5 P.M. hour.

IsDate

Returns a Boolean (true of false) value indicating whether or not the supplied number or string can be converted to a date value.

IsDate is helpful in determining if a supplied string or numeric value can be converted to a date with the DateValue (or similar) function. Because these other conversion functions will fail with a runtime error if an invalid value is supplied to them, using IsDate with an If-Then-Else statement can prevent runtime errors.

IsDate (s)

s – a string value to be evaluated for conversion to a date.

IsDate (n)

n – a numeric value to be evaluated as the number of days since December 30, 1899.

```
If IsDate({FromMainframe.OrderDateAsString}) Then
    DateValue({FromMainframe.OrderDateAsString})
Else
    DateValue(0,0,0)
```

returns a true order date if it can be converted, or 0/0/0 if it can't.

IsDateTime

Returns a Boolean (true of false) value indicating whether or not the supplied number or string can be converted to a date-time value.

IsDateTime is helpful in determining if a supplied string or numeric value can be converted to a date-time with the DateTimeValue (or similar) function. Because these other conversion functions will fail with a runtime error if an invalid value is supplied to them, using IsDateTime with an If-Then-Else statement can prevent runtime errors.

IsDateTime (s)

s – a string value to be evaluated for conversion to a date-time.

IsDateTime (n)

n – a numeric value to be evaluated as the number of days since December 30, 1899.

```
If IsDateTime({FromMainframe.IncidentDateTimeAsString}) Then
    DateTimeValue({FromMainframe.IncidentDateTimeAsString})
Else
    DateTimeValue(0,0,0,0,0,0)
```

returns a true incident date-time if it can be converted, or 0/0/0 at midnight if it can't.

IsTime

Returns a Boolean (true of false) value indicating whether or not the supplied number or string can be converted to a time value.

IsTime is helpful in determining if a supplied string or numeric value can be converted to a time with the TimeValue (or similar) function. Because these other conversion functions will fail with a runtime error if an invalid value is supplied to them, using IsTime with an If-Then-Else statement can prevent runtime errors.

IsTime (s)

s – a string value to be evaluated for conversion to a time.

IsTime (n)

n – a numeric value to be evaluated as the number of "24-hour units".

```
If IsTime({FromMainframe.IncidentTimeAsString}) Then
    TimeValue({FromMainframe.IncidentTimeAsString})
Else
    TimeValue(0,0,0)
```

returns a true incident time if it can be converted, or midnight if it can't.

Minute

Returns a numeric value indicating the minute of the supplied time or date-time.

Minute (dt)

dt – a date-time or time value.

```
Minute(CurrentTime)
```

returns 43 if the current time 5:43 P.M.

Month

Returns a numeric value indicating the month.

Month (dt)

dt – a date or date-time value.

```
Month(CurrentDate)
```

returns 5 if the current date is May 30, 2003.

MonthName

Returns a string value indicating the spelled-out month of the supplied numeric argument.

MonthName (n)

n – a numeric value between 1 and 12 indicating the number of the month.

MonthName (n, b)

n – a numeric value between 1 and 12 indicating the number of the month.
b – a Boolean (true or false) value, indicating whether to abbreviate the month.

```
MonthName (3, True)
```

returns "Mar".

Second

Returns a numeric value indicating the second of the supplied time or date-time.

Second (dt)

dt – a date-time or time value.

```
Second(CurrentTime)
```

returns 45 if the current time 5:43:45 P.M.

Time

Returns a time value when supplied with various other data types.
Time is functionally equivalent to TimeValue. See **TimeValue** for details.

Timer

Returns the number of seconds since midnight.

Timer may be useful as a "seed" for the Rnd (random number) function.

Timer

```
Timer
```

returns 64,917 at 6:01:57 P.M.

TimeSerial

Returns a time value based on hour, minute, and second arguments.

TimeSerial provides similar functionality to a specific usage of CTime, Time, and TimeValue. TimeSerial differs from these other functions in one significant way: the arguments supplied do not have to fall into a strict "hour between 0 and 24, minute between 0 and 59" requirement. By supplying other values, such as negative numbers, calculations, and so forth, arguments will be evaluated "relatively."

TimeSerial (n1, n2, n3)

n1 – a numeric value indicating the hour.

n2 – a numeric value indicating the minute.

n3 – a numeric value indicating the second.

```
TimeSerial(17,30,15)
```

returns 5:30:15PM.

```
TimeSerial(17,30-40,15+25)
```

returns 4:50:40PM.

TimeValue

Returns a time value based on one of several sets and types of arguments.

TimeValue can accept a wide variety of arguments that will be converted to a time. TimeValue comes in handy when you need to convert other data types to time, such as database fields from older systems that stored times as strings. TimeValue is functionally equivalent to Time and CTime.

TimeValue (dt)

dt – a date-time value that you wish to strip the time portion away from.

```
TimeValue(CurrentDateTime)
```

returns 6:23:19PM if the current time is 6:23 P.M., regardless of what day.

TimeValue (n)

n – a numeric value to be evaluated as the number of "24-hour units."

```
TimeValue(.25)
```

returns 6:00:00AM.

TimeValue (s)

s – a string value that will be evaluated for particular time equivalents.

```
TimeValue("17:15")
```

returns 5:15:00PM.

TimeValue (n1, n2, n3)

n1 – a numeric value between 0 and 23 indicating the hour.
n2 – a numeric value between 0 and 59 indicating the minute.
n3 – a numeric value between 0 and 59 indicating the second.

```
TimeValue(14,12,0)
```

returns 2:12:00PM.

WeekDay

Returns a numeric value indicating the day of the week.

WeekDay is functionally equivalent to DayOfWeek. See **DayOfWeek** for more information.

WeekdayName

Returns a string value containing a spelled-out name of the week.

WeekdayName will spell the name of the weekday ("Monday", etc.), based on a supplied numeric value.

WeekdayName (n)

n – numeric value between 1 and 7.

WeekdayName (n, b)

n – numeric value between 1 and 7.
b – a Boolean (true or false) value indicating whether to abbreviate the weekday name.

WeekdayName (n1, b, n2)

n1 – numeric value between 1 and 7.
b – Boolean (true or false) value indicating whether to abbreviate the weekday name.
n – numeric value or constant indicating the first day of the week. If not supplied, Sunday is assumed to be the first day of the week. See **First Day of Week Constants** later in this section for recognized constants or numbers for this argument.

```
WeekdayName (3, True, crMonday)
```

returns "Wed".

Year

Returns a numeric value indicating the year.

Year (dt)

dt – a date or date-time value.

```
Year(CurrentDate)
```

returns 2,003 if the current date is May 30, 2003.

Interval Types

The following interval types can be used with various date functions, such as DateAdd and DateDiff.

m	Month
d	Day (functionally equivalent to y)
yyyy	Year

y	Day of Year (functionally equivalent to d)
w	Weekday or Number of Weeks
ww	Week or Number of FirstDayOfWeeks
q	Quarter
h	Hour
m	Minute
s	Second

First Day of Week Constants

The following first-day-of-week values can be supplied to various functions that change output based on the first day of the week. Either the numeric value or the constant can be supplied.

crUseSystem	0 (default from Windows)
crSunday	1
crMonday	2
crTuesday	3
crWednesday	4
crThursday	5
crFriday	6
crSaturday	7

First Week of Year Constants

The following first-week-of-year values can be supplied to various functions that change output based on the first week of the year. Either the numeric value or the constant can be supplied.

crUseSystem	0 (default from Windows)
crFirstJan1	1
crFirstFourDays	2
crFirstFullWeek	3

Functions: Date Ranges

The following functions return date ranges based on the current date from the computer's clock. For point-in-time reporting purposes, you may change these ranges to be based on something other than the current date by using Report | Set Print Date/Time. All these functions return range values and must be used with a range operator, such as In.

Aged0To30Days

Returns a range in the last 30 days.

Aged0To30Days

```
If {AR.Due Date} In Aged0To30Days Then {AR.Amount Due}
```

returns the AR Amount due if the due date is in the past 30 days. Otherwise, 0 is returned.

Aged31To60Days

Returns a range between 31 and 60 days in the past.

Aged31To60Days

```
If {AR.Due Date} In Aged31To60Days Then {AR.Amount Due}
```

returns the AR Amount due if the due date is within 31 to 60 days past. Otherwise, 0 is returned.

Aged61To90Days

Returns a range between 61 and 90 days in the past.

Aged61To90Days

```
If {AR.Due Date} In Aged61To90Days Then {AR.Amount Due}
```

returns the AR Amount due if the due date is within 61 to 90 days past. Otherwise, 0 is returned.

AllDatesFromToday

Returns a range from today into the future (including today).

AllDatesFromToday

```
If {Shipments.Ship Date} In AllDatesFromToday Then
   "Product still needs to ship"
Else
   "Product has already shipped"
```

returns the appropriate string, depending on whether the ship date is in the future or the past.

AllDatesFromTomorrow

Returns a range from tomorrow into the future (including tomorrow).

AllDatesFromTomorrow

```
If {Shipments.Ship Date} In AllDatesFromTomorrow Then
   "Product ships tomorrow or thereafter"
Else
   "Product has already shipped"
```

returns the appropriate string, depending on whether the ship date is tomorrow or later.

AllDatesToToday

Returns a range up to, and including, today.

AllDatesToToday

```
If {Shipments.Ship Date} In AllDatesToToday Then
   "Product has been shipped"
Else
   "Product ships later"
```

returns the appropriate string, depending on whether the product shipped today or earlier.

AllDatesToYesterday

Returns a range up to, and including, yesterday.

AllDatesToYesterday

```
If {Shipments.Ship Date} In AllDatesToYesterday Then
    "Product yesterday or before"
Else
    "Product ships today or later"
```

returns the appropriate string, depending on whether the product shipped yesterday or earlier.

Calendar1stHalf

Returns a range including January 1 to June 30 of the current year.

Calendar1stHalf

```
If {Sales.Sale Date} In Calendar1stHalf Then
    "Group 1: Jan 1 - Jun 30"
Else
    "Group 2: Jul 1 - Dec 31"
```

returns one of two appropriate values, depending on whether the sale took place in the first or second half of the year.

Calendar2ndHalf

Returns a range including July 1 to December 31 of the current year.

Calendar2ndHalf

```
If {Sales.Sale Date} In Calendar2ndHalf Then
    "Group 1: Jul 1 - Dec 31"
Else
    "Group 2: Jan 1 - Jun 30"
```

returns one of two appropriate values, depending on whether the sale took place in the first or second half of the year.

Calendar1stQtr

Returns a range including January 1 to March 31 of the current year.

Calendar1stQtr

```
CurrencyVar Q1Total;
If {Sales.Sale Date} In Calendar1stQtr Then
    Q1Total := Q1Total + {Sales.Amount}
```

increments a variable with a sales amount only if the sale took place in the first calendar quarter.

Calendar2ndQtr

Returns a range including April 1 to June 30 of the current year.

Calendar2ndQtr

```
CurrencyVar Q2Total;
If {Sales.Sale Date} In Calendar2ndQtr Then
    Q2Total := Q2Total + {Sales.Amount}
```

increments a variable with a sales amount only if the sale took place in the second calendar quarter.

Calendar3rdQtr

Returns a range including July 1 to September 30 of the current year.

Calendar3rdQtr

```
CurrencyVar Q3Total;
If {Sales.Sale Date} In Calendar3rdQtr Then
    Q3Total := Q3Total + {Sales.Amount}
```

increments a variable with a sales amount only if the sale took place in the third calendar quarter.

Calendar4thQtr

Returns a range including October 1 to December 31 of the current year.

Calendar4thQtr

```
CurrencyVar Q4Total;
If {Sales.Sale Date} In Calendar4thQtr Then
    Q4Total := Q4Total + {Sales.Amount}
```

increments a variable with a sales amount only if the sale took place in the fourth calendar quarter.

Last4WeeksToSun

Returns a range including the four weeks prior to, and including, the most recent Sunday.

Last4WeeksToSun, unlike some other date and date range functions, considers a week to start on Monday and end on Sunday.

Last4WeeksToSun

```
If {AR.Invoice Date} In Last4WeeksToSun Then
    "Current"
Else
    "Past Due"
```

returns a string indicating the status of an account receivable based on the last four weeks.

Last7Days

Returns a range consisting of the last seven days, including today.

Last7Days

```
If {Sales.Sale Date} In Last7Days Then
    "Eligible for Price Protection"
Else
    "Not Eligible for Price Protection"
```

returns a string indicating if a sale is eligible for price protection because it took place within the last seven days.

LastFullMonth

Returns a range including the first day of last month to the last day of last month.

LastFullMonth

```
If {Sales.Sale Date} In LastFullMonth Then
    "Eligible for Price Protection"
Else
    "Not Eligible for Price Protection"
```

returns a string indicating if a sale is eligible for price protection because it took place within the last month.

LastFullWeek

Returns a range including Sunday through Saturday of the previous week.

LastFullWeek

```
If {Sales.Sale Date} In LastFullWeek Then
    "Eligible for Price Protection"
Else
    "Not Eligible for Price Protection"
```

returns a string indicating if a sale is eligible for price protection because it took place within the previous Sunday through Saturday.

LastYearMTD

Returns a range including the first day of this month last year through today's date last year.

LastYearMTD

```
CurrencyVar LastYearMTDSales;
If {Sales.Sale Date}In LastYearMTD Then
    LastYearMTDSales := LastYearMTDSales + {Sales.Amount}
```

accumulates a sales amount in a variable if the sale took place this month-to-date last year.

LastYearYTD
Returns a range including January 1 last year through today's date last year.

LastYearYTD

```
CurrencyVar LastYearYTDSales;
If {Sales.Sale Date}In LastYearYTD Then
    LastYearYTDSales := LastYearYTDSales + {Sales.Amount}
```

accumulates a sales amount in a variable if the sale took place this year-to-date last year.

MonthToDate
Returns a range including the first day of this month through today.

MonthToDate

```
CurrencyVar MTDSales;
If {Sales.Sale Date}In MonthToDate Then
    MTDSales := MTDSales + {Sales.Amount}
```

accumulates a sales amount in a variable if the sale took place from the first of this month through today.

Next30Days
Returns a range in the next 30 days.

Next30Days

```
If {Shipments.Ship Date} In Next30Days Then
"High Priority - shipping within the month"
```

returns the string value if the shipment date is in the next 30 days. Otherwise, an empty string is returned.

Next31To60Days
Returns a range between 31 and 60 days in the future.

Next31To60Days

```
If {Shipments.Ship Date} In Next31To60Days Then
"Medium Priority - shipping 2 months from now"
```

returns the string value if the shipment date is between 31 and 60 days in the future. Otherwise, an empty string is returned.

Next61To90Days

Returns a range between 61 and 90 days in the future.

Next61To90Days

```
If {Shipments.Ship Date} In Next61To90Days Then
"Low Priority - shipping 3 months from now"
```

returns the string value if the shipment date is between 61 and 90 days in the future. Otherwise, an empty string is returned.

Next91To365Days

Returns a range between 91 and 365 days in the future.

Next91To365Days

```
If {Shipments.Ship Date} In Next91To365Days Then
"No Concern - shipping over 3 months from now"
```

returns the string value if the shipment date is between 91 and 365 days in the future. Otherwise, an empty string is returned.

Over90Days

Returns a range from 90 days in the past and beyond.

Over90Days

```
If {AR.Due Date} In Over90Days Then {AR.Amount Due}
```

returns the AR Amount due if the due date is over 90 days past the current date. Otherwise, 0 is returned.

WeekToDateFromSun

Returns a range starting the previous Sunday through today.

WeekToDateFromSun

```
If {Sales.Sale Date} In WeekToDateFromSun Then
   "Eligible for Price Protection"
Else
   "Not Eligible for Price Protection"
```

returns a string indicating if a sale is eligible for price protection because it took place between this past Sunday and today.

YearToDate

Returns a range including January 1 through today's date.

YearToDate

```
CurrencyVar ThisYearYTDSales;
If {Sales.Sale Date}In YearToDate Then
    ThisYearYTDSales := ThisYearYTDSales + {Sales.Amount}
```

accumulates a sales amount in a variable if the sale took place this year-to-date.

Functions: Document Properties

This category of functions duplicates many of the Special Fields available from the Field Explorer. By making these values available to formulas, you may base formulas on various properties of the report, such as the page number that's currently printing, whether a group header is being repeated, and so forth.

DataDate

Returns a date value indicating the last date that data on the report was refreshed from the database.

DataDate will be the same date that appears to the left of the page navigation controls in the Preview tab. Click Report | Refresh Report Data (or use the appropriate toolbar button or keyboard shortcut) to refresh the database and update this value to the current date.

DataDate

```
"Data current as of " & ToText(DataDate)
```

returns the string "Data current as of 5/31/2003" if the report was refreshed on May 31, 2003.

DataTime

Returns a time value indicating the last time that data on the report was refreshed from the database.

DataTime will be the same time that appears to the left of the page navigation controls in the Preview tab. Click Report | Refresh Report Data (or use the appropriate toolbar button or keyboard shortcut) to refresh the database and update this value to the current time.

DataTime

```
"Data current as of " & ToText(DataTime)
```

returns the string "Data current as of 6:15:21PM" if the report was refreshed at 6:15 P.M.

FileAuthor

Returns a string value from the Author field in the File | Summary Info dialog box.

FileAuthor

```
"Report written by " & FileAuthor
```

returns "Report written by George Peck", if "George Peck" has been placed in the Author field in the Summary Info dialog box.

FileCreationDate

Returns a date value indicating the date that the report file was first created.

This value will not change if the report is later opened, modified, and resaved.

Functions: Document Properties

FileCreationDate

```
"Report first created " & ToText(FileCreationDate)
```

will return "Report first created 5/30/2003" if the report was initially created on May 30, 2003.

FileName

Returns a string value containing the file path and filename of the report stored on disk.

FileName

```
"Report location: " & FileName
```

returns "Report location: C:\Reports\Sales Analysis.rpt" if the report is stored as C:\Reports\Sales Analysis.rpt.

ModificationDate

Returns a date value indicating the date that the report file was last modified.
This value will change any time the report is opened, modified, and resaved.

ModificationDate

```
"Report last modified on " & ToText(ModificationDate)
```

will return "Report last modified on 5/31/2003" if the report was changed on May 31, 2003.

ModificationTime

Returns a time value indicating the time that the report file was last modified.
This value will change any time the report is opened, modified, and resaved.

ModificationTime

```
"Report last modified at " & ToText(ModificationTime)
```

will return "Report last modified at 6:33:20PM" if the report was saved at 6:33 P.M.

PrintDate

Returns a date value indicating the date that the report is formatted or printed.

By default, this value is taken from your computer's system clock. You may change it to another value by choosing Report | Set Print Date And Time from the pull-down menus.

PrintDate

```
"Report printed on " & ToText(PrintDate)
```

will return "Report printed on 5/31/2003" if the report is printed or formatted on May 31, 2003.

PrintTime

Returns a time value indicating the time that the report is formatted or printed.

By default, this value is taken from your computer's system clock. You may change it to another value by choosing Report | Set Print Date And Time from the pull-down menus.

PrintTime

```
"Report printed at " & ToText(PrintTime)
```

will return "Report printed at 6:38:33PM" if the report is printed or formatted at 6:38 P.M.

ReportComments

Returns a string value from the Comments field in the File | Summary Info dialog box.

ReportComments

```
"Report Information: " & ReportComments
```

returns "Report Information: Ablaze Group, Version 1, May 2003", taking the text from the Comments field in the Summary Info dialog box.

ReportTitle

Returns a string value from the Title field in the File | Summary Info dialog box.

ReportTitle

```
"Report Title: " & ReportTitle
```

returns "Report Title: Sales Analysis", taking the text from the Title field in the Summary Info dialog box.

Functions: Evaluation Time

This category of functions is used to force a formula to evaluate during one of Crystal Reports' three available report "passes."

By default, formulas evaluate during a certain pass based on their contents. For example, a formula that makes no reference to database fields, such as:

```
"Report printed on " & PrintDate
```

prints in the BeforeReadingRecords (or preread) pass by default.

A formula that makes reference to one or more database fields, such as:

```
{Orders.Order Amount} * 1.10
```

prints in the WhileReadingRecords (or first) pass by default.

And, any formula that makes reference to summary functions, report alerts, and various other "second-pass" functions, such as:

```
{Orders.Order Amount} %
Sum({Orders.Order Amount}, {Employee. Last Name})
```

prints in the WhilePrintingRecords (or second) pass by default.

While you cannot force a formula to an earlier report pass than its default, you can force it to a later pass. In particular, when using variables in formulas, you'll often need to force formulas that use the same variable to the same report pass to ensure consistent results.

BeforeReadingRecords

Forces a formula to evaluate in the "preread," BeforeReadingRecords, report pass.

BeforeReadingRecords

```
BeforeReadingRecords;
NumberVar Array RegionTotals := [0,0,0,0,0,0,0,0,0,0];
0
```

will create an array variable and fill it with zeros before the report reads records from the database.

EvaluateAfter (x)

Forces a formula to evaluate after another formula has been evaluated.

EvaluateAfter is required when you place two formulas in the same report section that evaluate in the same report pass. In this case, it's not predictable which formula will evaluate first. If both formulas, for example, refer to the same variable, you may get unintended results if one formula doesn't evaluate after the other formula.

EvaluateAfter (f)

f – the name of another report formula.

```
EvaluateAfter({@Show Count});
NumberVar BonusCount := 0
```

resets the BonusCount variable to zero after the @Show Count formula has already processed.

WhilePrintingRecords

Forces a formula to evaluate during the second, WhilePrintingRecords, pass.

WhilePrintingRecords

```
WhilePrintingRecords;
NumberVar GroupBonusCount := 0
```

resets the GroupBonusCount variable to zero during the WhilePrintingRecords pass (presumably because other WhilePrintingRecords formulas make use of GroupBonusCount).

WhileReadingRecords

Forces a formula to evaluate during the first, WhileReadingRecords, pass.

WhileReadingRecords

```
WhileReadingRecords;
StringVar GroupField
```

forces the contents of the GroupField variable to be displayed during the WhileReadingRecords pass. This may be helpful if you wish to create report groups based on this formula.

Functions: Financial

This category of functions supplies many standard financial calculations and algorithms. Many of these functions behave similarly to those available in Microsoft Excel.

ACCRINT

Returns a numeric value indicating total accrued interest for a security.

ACCRINT (d1, d2, d3, n1, n2, n3)

d1 – a date or date-time value indicating the issue date.
d2 – a date or date-time value indicating the date of first interest payment.
d3 – a date or date-time value indicating the date the security was purchased.
n1 – a numeric value indicating the annual interest rate.
n2 – a numeric value indicating the par value.
n3 – a numeric value indicating the number of payments per year: 1 = annual, 2 = semiannual, 4 = quarterly.

ACCRINT (d1, d2, d3, n1, n2, n3, n4)

d1 – a date or date-time value indicating the issue date.
d2 – a date or date-time value indicating the date of first interest payment.
d3 – a date or date-time value indicating the date the security was purchased.
n1 – a numeric value indicating the annual interest rate.
n2 – a numeric value indicating the par value.
n3 – a numeric value indicating the number of payments per year: 1 = annual, 2 = semiannual, 4 = quarterly.
n4 – a numeric value indicating the day basis system: 0 = US (NASD) 30/360, 1 = actual/actual, 2 = actual/360, 3 = actual/365, 4 = European 30/360.

```
ACCRINT(#1/1/1995#, #1/1/1996#, #6/1/1995#, .065, 100000, 4, 3)
```

returns 2,711.30.

ACCRINTM

Returns a numeric value indicating total accrued interest for a security that pays interest when it matures.

ACCRINTM (d1, d2, n1, n2)

d1 – a date or date-time value indicating the issue date.
d2 – a date or date-time value indicating the maturity date.
n1 – a numeric value indicating the annual interest rate.
n2 – a numeric value indicating the par value.

ACCRINTM (d1, d2, n1, n2, n3)

d1 – a date or date-time value indicating the issue date.
d2 – a date or date-time value indicating the maturity date.
n1 – a numeric value indicating the annual interest rate.
n2 – a numeric value indicating the par value.
n3 – a numeric value indicating the day basis system: 0 = US (NASD) 30/360, 1 = actual/actual, 2 = actual/360, 3 = actual/365, 4 = European 30/360.

```
ACCRINTM(#1/1/1995#, #1/1/2005#, .065, 100000, 3)
```

returns 65,053.42.

AmorDEGRC

Returns a numeric value indicating depreciation of an asset.

AmorDEGRC (n1, d1, d2, n2, n3, n4)

n1 – a numeric value indicating the asset's initial cost.
d1 – a date or date-time value indicating the asset's purchase date.
d2 – a date or date-time value indicating the end of the first period.
n2 – a numeric value indicating the asset's salvage value.
n3 – a numeric value indicating the period to calculate the depreciation for.
n4 – a numeric value indicating the depreciation rate.

AmorDEGRC (n1, d1, d2, n2, n3, n4, n5)

n1 – a numeric value indicating the asset's initial cost.
d1 – a date or date-time value indicating the asset's purchase date.
d2 – a date or date-time value indicating the end of the first period.
n2 – a numeric value indicating the asset's salvage value.
n3 – a numeric value indicating the period to calculate the depreciation for.

n4 – a numeric value indicating the depreciation rate.

n5 – a numeric value indicating the day basis system: 0 = US (NASD) 30/360, 1 = actual/actual, 2 = actual/360, 3 = actual/365, 4 = European 30/360.

```
AmorDEGRC (35000,#5/1/2000#,#1/1/2001#,15000,1,.1)
```

returns 7,292.00.

AmorLINC

Returns a numeric value indication linear depreciation of an asset.

AmorLINC (n1, d1, d2, n2, n3, n4)

n1 – a numeric value indicating the asset's initial cost.
d1 – a date or date-time value indicating the asset's purchase date.
d2 – a date or date-time value indicating the end of the first period.
n2 – a numeric value indicating the asset's salvage value.
n3 – a numeric value indicating the period to calculate the depreciation for.
n4 – a numeric value indicating the depreciation rate.

AmorLINC (n1, d1, d2, n2, n3, n4, n5)

n1 – a numeric value indicating the asset's initial cost.
d1 – a date or date-time value indicating the asset's purchase date.
d2 – a date or date-time value indicating the end of the first period.
n2 – a numeric value indicating the asset's salvage value.
n3 – a numeric value indicating the period to calculate the depreciation for.
n4 – a numeric value indicating the depreciation rate.
n5 – a numeric value indicating the day basis system: 0 = US (NASD) 30/360, 1 = actual/actual, 2 = actual/360, 3 = actual/365, 4 = European 30/360.

```
AmorLINC (35000,#5/1/2000#,#1/1/2001#,15000,1,.1)
```

returns 3,500.00.

CoupDayBS

Returns a numeric value indicating the days between the last coupon date and the settlement date.

CoupDayBS (d1, d2, n)

d1 – a date or date-time value indicating the purchase date.
d2 – a date or date-time value indicating the maturity date.

n – a numeric value indicating the number of payments (coupons) per year: 1 = annual, 2 = semiannual, 4 = quarterly.

CoupDayBS (d1, d2, n1, n2)

d1 – a date or date-time value indicating the purchase date.
d2 – a date or date-time value indicating the maturity date.
n1 – a numeric value indicating the number of payments (coupons) per year: 1 = annual, 2 = semiannual, 4 = quarterly.
n2 – a numeric value indicating the day basis system: 0 = US (NASD) 30/360, 1 = actual/actual, 2 = actual/360, 3 = actual/365, 4 = European 30/360.

```
CoupDayBS (#1/1/2000#, #5/31/2004#, 2, 3)
```

returns 32.

CoupDays

Returns a numeric value indicating the number of days in the coupon period that includes settlement.

CoupDays (d1, d2, n)

d1 – a date or date-time value indicating the purchase date.
d2 – a date or date-time value indicating the maturity date.
n – a numeric value indicating the number of payments (coupons) per year: 1 = annual, 2 = semiannual, 4 = quarterly.

CoupDays (d1, d2, n1, n2)

d1 – a date or date-time value indicating the purchase date.
d2 – a date or date-time value indicating the maturity date.
n1 – a numeric value indicating the number of payments (coupons) per year: 1 = annual, 2 = semiannual, 4 = quarterly.
n2 – a numeric value indicating the day basis system: 0 = US (NASD) 30/360, 1 = actual/actual, 2 = actual/360, 3 = actual/365, 4 = European 30/360.

```
CoupDays (#1/1/2000#, #5/31/2004#, 2, 3)
```

returns 182.5.

CoupDaysNC

Returns a numeric value indicating the number of days between the settlement date and the next coupon date.

Functions: Financial

CoupDaysNC (d1, d2, n)

d1 – a date or date-time value indicating the purchase date.
d2 – a date or date-time value indicating the maturity date.
n – a numeric value indicating the number of payments (coupons) per year: 1 = annual, 2 = semiannual, 4 = quarterly.

CoupDaysNC (d1, d2, n1, n2)

d1 – a date or date-time value indicating the purchase date.
d2 – a date or date-time value indicating the maturity date.
n1 – a numeric value indicating the number of payments (coupons) per year: 1 = annual, 2 = semiannual, 4 = quarterly.
n2 – a numeric value indicating the day basis system: 0 = US (NASD) 30/360, 1 = actual/actual, 2 = actual/360, 3 = actual/365, 4 = European 30/360.

```
CoupDaysNC (#1/1/2000#, #5/31/2004#, 2, 3)
```

returns 151.

CoupNCD

Returns a date value indicating the next coupon date after settlement.

CoupNCD (d1, d2, n)

d1 – a date or date-time value indicating the purchase date.
d2 – a date or date-time value indicating the maturity date.
n – a numeric value indicating the number of payments (coupons) per year: 1 = annual, 2 = semiannual, 4 = quarterly.

```
CoupNCD (#1/1/2000#, #5/31/2004#, 2)
```

returns 5/31/2000.

CoupNum

Returns a numeric value indicating the number of coupon periods between settlement and maturity.

CoupNum (d1, d2, n)

d1 – a date or date-time value indicating the purchase date.
d2 – a date or date-time value indicating the maturity date.

n – a numeric value indicating the number of payments (coupons) per year: 1 = annual, 2 = semiannual, 4 = quarterly.

```
CoupNum (#1/1/2000#, #5/31/2004#, 2)
```

returns 9.

CoupPCD

Returns a date value indicating the last coupon date before settlement.

CoupPCD (d1, d2, n)

d1 – a date or date-time value indicating the purchase date.
d2 – a date or date-time value indicating the maturity date.
n – a numeric value indicating the number of payments (coupons) per year: 1 = annual, 2 = semiannual, 4 = quarterly.

```
CoupPCD (#1/1/2000#, #5/31/2004#, 2)
```

returns 11/30/1999.

CumIPMT

Returns a numeric value indicating cumulative interest paid on a loan.

CumIPMT (n1, n2, n3, n4, n5, n6)

n1 – a numeric value indicating the interest rate, which must be provided on a per-period basis.
n2 – a numeric value indicating the total number of payment periods, which must be provided on a per-period basis.
n3 – a numeric value indicating the loan's total or "present" value of the loan.
n4 – a numeric value indicating the first period to include in the calculation.
n5 – a numeric value indicating the last period to include in the calculation.
n6 – a numeric value indicating the type of payment: 0 = end of payment period, 1 = beginning of payment period.

```
CumIPMT (.09/12, 60, 45000, 1, 30, 1)
```

returns –7,640.28.

CumPrinc

Returns a numeric value indicating cumulative principal paid on a loan.

Functions: Financial

CumPrinc (n1, n2, n3, n4, n5, n6)

n1 – a numeric value indicating the interest rate, which must be provided on a per-period basis.

n2 – a numeric value indicating the total number of payment periods, which must be provided on a per-period basis.

n3 – a numeric value indicating the loan's total or "present" value of the loan.

n4 – a numeric value indicating the first period to include in the calculation.

n5 – a numeric value indicating the last period to include in the calculation.

n6 – a numeric value indicating the type of payment: 0 = end of payment period, 1 = beginning of payment period.

```
CumPrinc (.09/12, 60, 45000, 1, 30, 1)
```

returns –20,174.89.

Days360

Returns a numeric value indicating the number of days between two dates using a 30-day-per-month/360-day-per-year financial calendar.

Days360 (d1, d2)

d1 – a date or date-time value indicating start date.
d2 – a date or date-time value indicating end date.

Days360 (d1, d2, b)

d1 – a date or date-time value indicating start date.
d2 – a date or date-time value indicating end date.
b – a Boolean (true or false) value indicating the basis for the calculation: False indicates US (NASD) 30/360; True indicates European 30/360.

```
Days360(#1/1/2003#, #12/31/2003#)
```

returns 360.

DB

Returns a numeric value indicating depreciation of an asset using the declining balance method.

DB (n1, n2, n3, n4)

n1 – a numeric value indicating the asset's initial cost.

n2 – a numeric value indicating the asset's salvage value.
n3 – a numeric value indicating the useful life of the asset.
n4 – a numeric value indicating the period to calculate the depreciation for.

DB (n1, n2, n3, n4, n5)

n1 – a numeric value indicating the asset's initial cost.
n2 – a numeric value indicating the asset's salvage value.
n3 – a numeric value indicating the useful life of the asset.
n4 – a numeric value indicating the period to calculate the depreciation for.
n5 – a numeric value indicating the number of months in the first year.

```
DB(35000,15000,7,5)
```

returns 2,458.71.

DDB

Returns a numeric value indicating depreciation of an asset using the double-declining balance method.

DDB (n1, n2, n3, n4)

n1 – a numeric value indicating the asset's initial cost.
n2 – a numeric value indicating the asset's salvage value.
n3 – a numeric value indicating the useful life of the asset.
n4 – a numeric value indicating the period to calculate the depreciation for.

DDB (n1, n2, n3, n4, n5)

n1 – a numeric value indicating the asset's initial cost.
n2 – a numeric value indicating the asset's salvage value.
n3 – a numeric value indicating the useful life of the asset.
n4 – a numeric value indicating the period to calculate the depreciation for.
n5 – a numeric value indicating the factor at which the rate declines; 2 indicates double-declining.

```
DDB(35000,5000,7,5)
```

returns 2,603.08.

DISC

Returns a numeric value indicating the discount rate for a security.

DISC (d1, d2, n1, n2)

d1 – a date or date-time value indicating the date the security was purchased.
d2 – a date or date-time value indicating the date of maturity.
n1 – a numeric value indicating the security's value when purchased.
n2 – a numeric value indicating the security's value at maturity.

DISC (d1, d2, n1, n2, n3)

d1 – a date or date-time value indicating the date the security was purchased.
d2 – a date or date-time value indicating the date of maturity.
n1 – a numeric value indicating the security's value when purchased.
n2 – a numeric value indicating the security's value at maturity.
n3 – a numeric value indicating the day basis system: 0 = US (NASD) 30/360, 1 = actual/actual, 2 = actual/360, 3 = actual/365, 4 = European 30/360.

```
DISC(#1/1/2000#,#12/31/2005#,10000,14000)
```

returns .05.

DollarDE

Returns a number indicating the true fractional value of a financial fractional "representation."

This function is helpful for calculating actual decimal values of such terms as "Five and seven eighths."

DollarDE (n1, n2)

n1 – a numeric value representing the number to be converted (such as 5.7 for "five and seven").
n2 – a numeric value representing the base of n1 (such as 8 for "eighths").

```
DollarDE (5.7, 8)
```

returns 5.88 (5.875 rounded to two decimal places).

DollarFR

Returns a number indicating the financial fractional "representation" of a true fractional value.

This function is helpful for converting actual decimal values into such terms as "Five and seven eighths."

DollarFR (n1, n2)

n1 – a numeric value representing the true fractional number to be converted (such as 5.875).

n2 – a numeric value representing the base of to convert n1 to (such as 8 for "eighths").

```
DollarFR (5.875, 8)
```

returns 5.70 (indicating "five and seven eighths").

Duration

Returns a number indicating the duration of a bond (sometimes known as the "Macauley duration").

Duration (d1, d2, n1, n2, n3)

d1 – a date or date-time value indicating the bond's purchase date.

d2 – a date or date-time value indicating the bond's maturity date.

n1 – a numeric value indicating the bond's interest rate.

n2 – a numeric value indicating the bond's yield.

n3 – a numeric value indicating the number of payments per year; 1 = annual, 2 = semiannual, 4 = quarterly.

Duration (d1, d2, n1, n2, n3, n4)

d1 – a date or date-time value indicating the bond's purchase date.

d2 – a date or date-time value indicating the bond's maturity date.

n1 – a numeric value indicating the bond's interest rate.

n2 – a numeric value indicating the bond's yield.

n3 – a numeric value indicating the number of payments per year: 1 = annual, 2 = semiannual, 4 = quarterly.

n4 – a numeric value indicating the day basis system: 0 = US (NASD) 30/360, 1 = actual/actual, 2 = actual/360, 3 = actual/365, 4 = European 30/360.

```
Duration(#1/1/2000#,#1/1/2030#,.08,.09,1)
```

returns 11.37 years.

Effect

Returns a numeric value indicating the effective annual interest rate.

Effect (n1, n2)

n1 – a numeric value indicating the annual interest rate.
n2 – a numeric value indicating the number of compounding periods.

```
Effect(.1,12)
```

returns 0.10471 (when formatted to show five decimal places).

FV

Returns a numeric value indicating the future value of an annuity.

FV (n1, n2, n3)

n1 – a numeric value indicating the interest rate (must be adjusted to a per-period rate).
n2 – a numeric value indicating the number of annuity payments.
n3 – a numeric value indicating the payment amount.

FV (n1, n2, n3, n4)

n1 – a numeric value indicating the interest rate (must be adjusted to a per-period rate).
n2 – a numeric value indicating the number of annuity payments.
n3 – a numeric value indicating the payment amount.
n4 – a numeric value indicating the present value (the total amount that a series of future payments is worth now).

FV (n1, n2, n3, n4, n5)

n1 – a numeric value indicating the interest rate (must be adjusted to a per-period rate).
n2 – a numeric value indicating the number of annuity payments.
n3 – a numeric value indicating the payment amount (a negative amount indicating paying money "out").
n4 – a numeric value indicating the present value (the total amount that a series of future payments is worth now).
n5 – a numeric value indicating the type of payment: 0 = end of payment period, 1 = beginning of payment period.

```
FV (.04/12, 60, -500)
```

returns 33,149.49.

FVSchedule

Returns a number indicating the future value of an annuity with several compounded interest rates.

FVSchedule (n, a)

n – a numeric value indicating the present value of the annuity.
a – a numeric array containing one or more interest rates.

```
FVSchedule (10000,[.04,.0475,.05])
```

returns 11,438.70.

IntRate

Returns a numeric value indicating the interest rate for a security.

IntRate (d1, d2, n1, n2)

d1 – a date or date-time value indicating the security purchase date.
d2 – a date or date-time value indicating the security maturity date.
n1 – a numeric value indicating the original security value.
n2 – a numeric value indicating the value at maturity.

IntRate (d1, d2, n1, n2, n3)

d1 – a date or date-time value indicating the security purchase date.
d2 – a date or date-time value indicating the security maturity date.
n1 – a numeric value indicating the original security value.
n2 – a numeric value indicating the value at maturity.
n3 – a numeric value indicating the day basis system: 0 = US (NASD) 30/360, 1 = actual/actual, 2 = actual/360, 3 = actual/365, 4 = European 30/360.

```
IntRate(#1/1/2000#,#1/1/2005#,10000,13000)
```

returns .06.

IPmt

Returns a numeric value indicating an interest payment based on fixed payments and interest rate.

Functions: Financial

IPmt (n1, n2, n3, n4)

n1 – a numeric value indicating the interest rate (must be adjusted to a per-period rate).
n2 – a numeric value indicating the payment period.
n3 – a numeric value indicating the total number of payments.
n4 – a numeric value indicating the present value.

IPmt (n1, n2, n3, n4, n5)

n1 – a numeric value indicating the interest rate (must be adjusted to a per-period rate).
n2 – a numeric value indicating the payment period.
n3 – a numeric value indicating the total number of payments.
n4 – a numeric value indicating the present value.
n5 – a numeric value indicating the future value after the last payment.

IPmt (n1, n2, n3, n4, n5, n6)

n1 – a numeric value indicating the interest rate (must be adjusted to a per-period rate).
n2 – a numeric value indicating the payment period.
n3 – a numeric value indicating the total number of payments.
n4 – a numeric value indicating the present value.
n5 – a numeric value indicating the future value after the last payment.
n6 – a numeric value indicating the type of payment: 0 = end of payment period, 1 = beginning of payment period.

```
IPmt(.09/12,30,60,30000)
```

returns –128.76.

IRR

Returns a numeric value indicating the internal rate of return for a series of payments and receipts.

IRR (a)

a – a numeric array indicating the series of payments and receipts (there must be at least one negative and one positive number in the array). An IRR of 10 percent (.1) is assumed.

IRR (a, n)

a – a numeric array indicating the series of payments and receipts (there must be at least one negative and one positive number in the array).

n – a numeric value indicating the "guess" of IRR.

```
IRR([-1000,-500,2000])
```

returns .19.

ISPMT

Returns a numeric value indicating interest paid during a period (assuming equal installments).

ISPMT (n1, n2, n3, n4)

n1 – a numeric value indicating the interest rate (must be adjusted to a per-period rate).
n2 – a numeric value indicating the period to calculate interest for.
n3 – a numeric value indicating the number of payment periods.
n4 – a numeric value indicating the present value.

```
ISPMT(.09/12,30,60,30000)
```

returns –112.50.

MDuration

Returns a number indicating the modified duration of a bond (sometimes known as the modified "Macauley duration").

MDuration (d1, d2, n1, n2, n3)

d1 – a date or date-time value indicating the bond's purchase date.
d2 – a date or date-time value indicating the bond's maturity date.
n1 – a numeric value indicating the bond's interest rate.
n2 – a numeric value indicating the bond's yield.
n3 – a numeric value indicating the number of payments per year; 1 = annual, 2 = semiannual, 4 = quarterly.

MDuration (d1, d2, n1, n2, n3, n4)

d1 – a date or date-time value indicating the bond's purchase date.
d2 – a date or date-time value indicating the bond's maturity date.
n1 – a numeric value indicating the bond's interest rate.
n2 – a numeric value indicating the bond's yield.
n3 – a numeric value indicating the number of payments per year: 1 = annual, 2 = semiannual, 4 = quarterly.

n4 – a numeric value indicating the day basis system: 0 = US (NASD) 30/360, 1 = actual/actual, 2 = actual/360, 3 = actual/365, 4 = European 30/360.

```
MDuration(#1/1/2000#,#1/1/2030#,.08,.09,1)
```

returns 10.43 years.

MIRR
Returns a numeric value indicating the modified internal rate of return for a series of payments and receipts.

MIRR (a, n1, n2)
a – a numeric array indicating the series of payments and receipts (there must be at least one negative and one positive number in the array).
n1 – a numeric value indicating interest rate cost.
n2 – a numeric value indicating interest rate return.

```
MIRR([-1000,-500,2000], .9, .6)
```

returns .26.

Nominal
Returns a numeric value indicating the nominal annual interest rate.

Nominal (n1, n2)
n1 – a numeric value indicating effective rate.
n2 – a numeric value indicating number of compounding periods.

```
Nominal(.08,12)
```

returns .07721 (when formatted with five decimal places).

NPer
Returns a numeric value indicating the number of payments, based on a fixed number of payments and interest rate.

NPer (n1, n2, n3)
n1 – a numeric value indicating the interest rate (must be adjusted to a per-period value).

n2 – a numeric value indicating the combined principal/interest payment.
n3 – a numeric value indicating the present value of the loan.

NPer (n1, n2, n3, n4)

n1 – a numeric value indicating the interest rate (must be adjusted to a per-period value).
n2 – a numeric value indicating the combined principal/interest payment.
n3 – a numeric value indicating the present value of the loan.
n4 – a numeric value indicating the future value of the loan after final payment.

NPer (n1, n2, n3, n4, n5)

n1 – a numeric value indicating the interest rate (must be adjusted to a per-period value).
n2 – a numeric value indicating the combined principal/interest payment.
n3 – a numeric value indicating the present value of the loan.
n4 – a numeric value indicating the future value of the loan after final payment.
n5 – a numeric value indicating the type of payment: 0 = end of payment period, 1 = beginning of payment period.

```
NPer(.09/12,-750,40000)
```

returns 68.37 (indicating months).

NPV

Returns a numeric value indicating the net present value of an inv`estment.

NPV (n, a)

n – a numeric value indicating the discount rate.
a – a numeric array indicating payments/receipts.

```
NPV(.05,[1000,2000,1500,1750])
```

returns 5,501.93.

OddFPrice

Returns a numeric value indicating the price of a security that pays interest with regularity, with the exception of a short or long (odd) first period.

OddFPrice (d1, d2, d3, d4, n1, n2, n3, n4)

d1 – a date or date-time value indicating the purchase date.
d2 – a date or date-time value indicating the date of maturity.
d3 – a date or date-time value indicating the issue date.
d4 – a date or date-time value indicating the date of first interest payment.
n1 – a numeric value indicating the interest rate.
n2 – a numeric value indicating the annual yield of the security.
n3 – a numeric value indicating the security redemption value (per $100 face value).
n4 – a numeric value indicating the number of payments per year: 1 = annual, 2 = semiannual, 4 = quarterly.

OddFPrice (d1, d2, d3, d4, n1, n2, n3, n4, n5)

d1 – a date or date-time value indicating the purchase date.
d2 – a date or date-time value indicating the date of maturity.
d3 – a date or date-time value indicating the issue date.
d4 – a date or date-time value indicating the date of first interest payment.
n1 – a numeric value indicating the interest rate.
n2 – a numeric value indicating the annual yield of the security.
n3 – a numeric value indicating the security redemption value (per $100 face value).
n4 – a numeric value indicating the number of payments per year: 1 = annual, 2 = semiannual, 4 = quarterly.
n5 – a numeric value indicating the day basis system: 0 = US (NASD) 30/360, 1 = actual/actual, 2 = actual/360, 3 = actual/365, 4 = European 30/360.

```
OddFPrice (#2/1/2000#,#1/1/2030#,#1/1/2000#,
   #1/1/2001#,.05,.055,75,1)
```

returns 87.69.

OddFYield

Returns a numeric value indicating the yield of a security that pays interest with regularity, with the exception of a short or long (odd) first period.

OddFYield (d1, d2, d3, d4, n1, n2, n3, n4)

d1 – a date or date-time value indicating the purchase date.
d2 – a date or date-time value indicating the date of maturity.
d3 – a date or date-time value indicating the issue date.
d4 – a date or date-time value indicating the date of first interest payment.
n1 – a numeric value indicating the interest rate.
n2 – a numeric value indicating the purchase price (per $100 face value).

n3 – a numeric value indicating the security redemption value (per $100 face value).
n4 – a numeric value indicating the number of payments per year: 1 = annual, 2 = semiannual, 4 = quarterly.

OddFYield (d1, d2, d3, d4, n1, n2, n3, n4, n5)

d1 – a date or date-time value indicating the purchase date.
d2 – a date or date-time value indicating the date of maturity.
d3 – a date or date-time value indicating the issue date.
d4 – a date or date-time value indicating the date of first interest payment.
n1 – a numeric value indicating the interest rate.
n2 – a numeric value indicating the purchase price (per $100 face value).
n3 – a numeric value indicating the security redemption value (per $100 face value).
n4 – a numeric value indicating the number of payments per year: 1 = annual, 2 = semiannual, 4 = quarterly.
n5 – a numeric value indicating the day basis system: 0 = US (NASD) 30/360, 1 = actual/actual, 2 = actual/360, 3 = actual/365, 4 = European 30/360.

```
OddFPrice (#2/1/2000#,#1/1/2030#,#1/1/2000#,
   #1/1/2001#,.05,13.23,75,1)
```

returns .0549 (formatted with four decimal places).

OddLPrice

Returns a numeric value indicating the price of a security that pays interest with regularity, with the exception of a short or long (odd) last period.

OddLPrice (d1, d2, d3, n1, n2, n3, n4)

d1 – a date or date-time value indicating the purchase date.
d2 – a date or date-time value indicating the date of maturity.
d3 – a date or date-time value indicating the security's last coupon date.
n1 – a numeric value indicating the interest rate.
n2 – a numeric value indicating the annual yield of the security.
n3 – a numeric value indicating the security redemption value (per $100 face value).
n4 – a numeric value indicating the number of payments per year: 1 = annual, 2 = semiannual, 4 = quarterly.

OddLPrice (d1, d2, d3, n1, n2, n3, n4, n5)

d1 – a date or date-time value indicating the purchase date.
d2 – a date or date-time value indicating the date of maturity.

d3 – a date or date-time value indicating the security's last coupon date.
n1 – a numeric value indicating the interest rate.
n2 – a numeric value indicating the annual yield of the security.
n3 – a numeric value indicating the security redemption value (per $100 face value).
n4 – a numeric value indicating the number of payments per year: 1 = annual, 2 = semiannual, 4 = quarterly.
n5 – a numeric value indicating the day basis system: 0 = US (NASD) 30/360, 1 = actual/actual, 2 = actual/360, 3 = actual/365, 4 = European 30/360.

```
OddLPrice(#2/1/2000#,#1/1/2030#,#1/1/2000#,.05,.055,75,1)
```

returns 84.64.

OddLYield

Returns a numeric value indicating the yield of a security that pays interest with regularity, with the exception of a short or long (odd) last period.

OddLYield (d1, d2, d3, n1, n2, n3, n4)

d1 – a date or date-time value indicating the purchase date.
d2 – a date or date-time value indicating the date of maturity.
d3 – a date or date-time value indicating the security's last coupon date.
n1 – a numeric value indicating the interest rate.
n2 – a numeric value indicating the purchase price (per $100 face value).
n3 – a numeric value indicating the security redemption value (per $100 face value).
n4 – a numeric value indicating the number of payments per year: 1 = annual, 2 = semiannual, 4 = quarterly.

OddLYield (d1, d2, d3, n1, n2, n3, n4, n5)

d1 – a date or date-time value indicating the purchase date.
d2 – a date or date-time value indicating the date of maturity.
d3 – a date or date-time value indicating the security's last coupon date.
n1 – a numeric value indicating the interest rate.
n2 – a numeric value indicating the purchase price (per $100 face value).
n3 – a numeric value indicating the security redemption value (per $100 face value).
n4 – a numeric value indicating the number of payments per year: 1 = annual, 2 = semiannual, 4 = quarterly.
n5 – a numeric value indicating the day basis system: 0 = US (NASD) 30/360, 1 = actual/actual, 2 = actual/360, 3 = actual/365, 4 = European 30/360.

```
OddLYield (#2/1/2000#,#1/1/2030#,#1/1/2000#,.05,84.64,75,1)
```

returns .055 (formatted with three decimal places).

Pmt

Returns a numeric value indicating the payment for an annuity with fixed payments and interest rate.

Pmt (n1, n2, n3)

n1 – a numeric value indicating the interest rate (must be adjusted to a per-period rate).
n2 – a numeric value indicating the number of payment periods.
n3 – a numeric value indicating the principal/present value of the annuity.

Pmt (n1, n2, n3, n4)

n1 – a numeric value indicating the interest rate (must be adjusted to a per-period rate).
n2 – a numeric value indicating the number of payment periods.
n3 – a numeric value indicating the principal/present value of the annuity.
n4 – a numeric value indicating the desired future value/balance after the final payment.

Pmt (n1, n2, n3, n4, n5)

n1 – a numeric value indicating the interest rate (must be adjusted to a per-period rate).
n2 – a numeric value indicating the number of payment periods.
n3 – a numeric value indicating the principal/present value of the annuity.
n4 – a numeric value indicating the desired future value/balance after the final payment.
n5 – a numeric value indicating the type of payment: 0 = end of payment period, 1 = beginning of payment period.

```
Pmt(.05/12,36,10000)
```

returns –299.71.

PPmt

Returns a numeric value indicating the principal payment for a specific period of an annuity with fixed payments and interest rate.

PPmt (n1, n2, n3, n4)

n1 – a numeric value indicating the interest rate (must be adjusted to a per-period rate).
n2 – a numeric value indicating the specific period to calculate the principal for.
n3 – a numeric value indicating the number of payment periods.
n4 – a numeric value indicating the present value.

PPmt (n1, n2, n3, n4, n5)

n1 – a numeric value indicating the interest rate (must be adjusted to a per-period rate).
n2 – a numeric value indicating the specific period to calculate the principal for.
n3 – a numeric value indicating the number of payment periods.
n4 – a numeric value indicating the present value.
n5 – a numeric value indicating the desired future value/balance after the final payment.

PPmt (n1, n2, n3, n4, n5, n6)

n1 – a numeric value indicating the interest rate (must be adjusted to a per-period rate).
n2 – a numeric value indicating the specific period to calculate the principal for.
n3 – a numeric value indicating the number of payment periods.
n4 – a numeric value indicating the present value.
n5 – a numeric value indicating the desired future value/balance after the final payment.
n6 – a numeric value indicating the type of payment: 0 = end of payment period, 1 = beginning of payment period.

```
PPmt(.09/12,24,60,35000)
```

returns –551.05.

Price

Returns a numeric value indicating the price of a security (per $100 face value) that pays periodic interest.

Price (d1, d2, n1, n2, n3, n4)

d1 – a date or date-time value indicating the purchase date.
d2 – a date or date-time value indicating the date of maturity.
n1 – a numeric value indicating the interest rate.
n2 – a numeric value indicating the annual yield of the security.
n3 – a numeric value indicating the security redemption value (per $100 face value).

n4 – a numeric value indicating the number of payments per year: 1 = annual, 2 = semiannual, 4 = quarterly.

Price (d1, d2, n1, n2, n3, n4, n5)

d1 – a date or date-time value indicating the purchase date.
d2 – a date or date-time value indicating the date of maturity.
n1 – a numeric value indicating the interest rate.
n2 – a numeric value indicating the annual yield of the security.
n3 – a numeric value indicating the security redemption value (per $100 face value).
n4 – a numeric value indicating the number of payments per year: 1 = annual,
2 = semiannual, 4 = quarterly.
n5 – a numeric value indicating the day basis system: 0 = US (NASD) 30/360,
1 = actual/actual, 2 = actual/360, 3 = actual/365, 4 = European 30/360.

```
Price (#1/1/2000#,#1/1/2005#,.055,.05,50,1)
```

returns 62.99.

PriceDisc

Returns a numeric value indicating the discounted price of a security (per $100 face value).

PriceDisc (d1, d2, n1, n2)

d1 – a date or date-time value indicating the purchase date.
d2 – a date or date-time value indicating the date of maturity.
n1 – a numeric value indicating the discount rate.
n2 – a numeric value indicating the security redemption value (per $100 face value).

PriceDisc (d1, d2, n1, n2, n3)

d1 – a date or date-time value indicating the purchase date.
d2 – a date or date-time value indicating the date of maturity.
n1 – a numeric value indicating the discount rate.
n2 – a numeric value indicating the security redemption value (per $100 face value).
n3 – a numeric value indicating the day basis system: 0 = US (NASD) 30/360,
1 = actual/actual, 2 = actual/360, 3 = actual/365, 4 = European 30/360.

```
PriceDisc (#1/1/2000#,#1/1/2005#,.055,50)
```

returns 36.25.

PriceMat

Returns a numeric value indicating the price of a security (per $100 face value) that pays interest only at maturity.

PriceMat (d1, d2, d3, n1, n2)

d1 – a date or date-time value indicating the purchase date.
d2 – a date or date-time value indicating the date of maturity.
d3 – a date or date-time value indicating the issue date.
n1 – a numeric value indicating the interest rate.
n2 – a numeric value indicating the security's yield.

PriceMat (d1, d2, d3, n1, n2, n3)

d1 – a date or date-time value indicating the purchase date.
d2 – a date or date-time value indicating the date of maturity.
d3 – a date or date-time value indicating the issue date.
n1 – a numeric value indicating the interest rate.
n2 – a numeric value indicating the security's yield.
n3 – a numeric value indicating the day basis system: 0 = US (NASD) 30/360, 1 = actual/actual, 2 = actual/360, 3 = actual/365, 4 = European 30/360.

```
PriceMat(#3/1/2000#,#3/1/2005#,#1/1/2000#,.055,.05)
```

returns 101.82.

PV

Returns a numeric value indicating the present value of an annuity.

PV (n1, n2, n3)

n1 – a numeric value indicating the interest rate (must be adjusted to a per-period rate).
n2 – a numeric value indicating the number of annuity payments.
n3 – a numeric value indicating the payment amount.

PV (n1, n2, n3, n4)

n1 – a numeric value indicating the interest rate (must be adjusted to a per-period rate).
n2 – a numeric value indicating the number of annuity payments.
n3 – a numeric value indicating the payment amount.
n4 – a numeric value indicating the future value/balance after final payment.

PV (n1, n2, n3, n4, n5)

n1 – a numeric value indicating the interest rate (must be adjusted to a per-period rate).
n2 – a numeric value indicating the number of annuity payments.
n3 – a numeric value indicating the payment amount.
n4 – a numeric value indicating the future value/balance after final payment.
n5 – a numeric value indicating the type of payment: 0 = end of payment period,
1 = beginning of payment period.

```
PV (.04/12, 60, -500)
```

returns 27,149.53.

Rate

Returns a numeric value indicating per-period interest for an annuity.

Rate (n1, n2, n3)

n1 – a numeric value indicating the number of annuity payments.
n2 – a numeric value indicating the payment amount.
n3 – a numeric value indicating the annuity's present value.

Rate (n1, n2, n3, n4)

n1 – a numeric value indicating the number of annuity payments.
n2 – a numeric value indicating the payment amount.
n3 – a numeric value indicating the annuity's present value.
n4 – a numeric value indicating the future value/balance after final payment.

Rate (n1, n2, n3, n4, n5)

n1 – a numeric value indicating the number of annuity payments.
n2 – a numeric value indicating the payment amount.
n3 – a numeric value indicating the annuity's present value.
n4 – a numeric value indicating the future value/balance after final payment.
n5 – a numeric value indicating the type of payment: 0 = end of payment period,
1 = beginning of payment period.

Rate (n1, n2, n3, n4, n5, n6)

n1 – a numeric value indicating the number of annuity payments.
n2 – a numeric value indicating the payment amount.

n3 – a numeric value indicating the annuity's present value.
n4 – a numeric value indicating the future value/balance after final payment.
n5 – a numeric value indicating the type of payment: 0 = end of payment period,
1 = beginning of payment period.
n6 – a numeric value indicating your "guess" of the return to use as a starting point
for the calculation. If you omit this argument, 10 percent (.1) is assumed.

```
Rate(36, -750, 35000)
```

returns .0134 (when formatted to four decimal places).

Received

**Returns a numeric value indicating the amount received at maturity for a
fully invested security.**

Received (d1, d2, n1, n2)

d1 – a date or date-time value indicating the purchase date.
d2 – a date or date-time value indicating the date of maturity.
n1 – a numeric value indicating the investment amount.
n2 – a numeric value indicating the discount rate.

Received (d1, d2, n1, n2, n3)

d1 – a date or date-time value indicating the purchase date.
d2 – a date or date-time value indicating the date of maturity.
n1 – a numeric value indicating the investment amount.
n2 – a numeric value indicating the discount rate.
n3 – a numeric value indicating the day basis system: 0 = US (NASD) 30/360,
1 = actual/actual, 2 = actual/360, 3 = actual/365, 4 = European 30/360.

```
Received(#1/1/2000#,#1/1/2005#,10000,.075)
```

returns 16,000.00.

SLN

Returns a numeric value indicating straight-line depreciation of an asset.

SLN (n1, n2, n3)

n1 – a numeric value indicating original cost of the asset.
n2 – a numeric value indicating the salvage of the asset at the end of its life.

n3 – a numeric value indicating the life of the asset.

```
SLN(35000,7500,7)
```

returns a per-year depreciation of 3,928.57.

SYD

Returns a numeric value indicating sum-of-years-digits depreciation of an asset.

SYD (n1, n2, n3, n4)

n1 – a numeric value indicating original cost of the asset.
n2 – a numeric value indicating the salvage of the asset at the end of its life.
n3 – a numeric value indicating the life of the asset.
n4 – a numeric value indicating the period to calculate depreciation for.

```
SYD(35000,7500,7,2)
```

returns a second-year depreciation of 5,892.86.

TBillEq

Returns a numeric value indicating the bond-equivalent yield for a Treasury bill.

TBillEq (d1, d2, n)

d1 – a date or date-time value indicating the purchase date.
d2 – a date or date-time value indicating the date of maturity.
n – a numeric value indicating the discount rate.

```
TBillEq(#1/1/2000#,#12/31/2000#,.08)
```

returns 0.0864 (8.64%) when formatted with four decimal places.

TBillPrice

Returns a numeric value indicating the price for a Treasury bill (per $100 face value).

TBillPrice (d1, d2, n)

d1 – a date or date-time value indicating the purchase date.
d2 – a date or date-time value indicating the date of maturity.

n – a numeric value indicating the discount rate.

```
TBillPrice(#1/1/2000#,#12/31/2000#,.08)
```

returns 91.89.

TBillYield

Returns a numeric value indicating the yield for a Treasury bill.

TBillYield (d1, d2, n)

d1 – a date or date-time value indicating the purchase date.
d2 – a date or date-time value indicating the date of maturity.
n – a numeric value indicating the price per $100 face value.

```
TBillYield(#1/1/2000#,#12/31/2000#,91.89)
```

returns .087 (8.7%) when formatted with three decimal places.

VDB

Returns the variable declining balance for an asset.

VDB supports various depreciation options, such as double-declining balance or other method and partial depreciation periods.

VDB (n1, n2, n3, n4, n5)

n1 – a numeric value indicating the asset's initial cost.
n2 – a numeric value indicating the asset's salvage value.
n3 – a numeric value indicating the useful life of the asset.
n4 – a numeric value indicating the start period to calculate depreciation for.
n5 – a numeric value indicating the end period to calculate depreciation for.

VDB (n1, n2, n3, n4, n5, n6)

n1 – a numeric value indicating the asset's initial cost.
n2 – a numeric value indicating the asset's salvage value.
n3 – a numeric value indicating the useful life of the asset.
n4 – a numeric value indicating the start period to calculate depreciation for.
n5 – a numeric value indicating the end period to calculate depreciation for.
n6 – a numeric value indicating the factor at which the rate declines – 2 indicates double-declining.

VDB (n1, n2, n3, n4, n5, n6)

n1 – a numeric value indicating the asset's initial cost.

n2 – a numeric value indicating the asset's salvage value.

n3 – a numeric value indicating the useful life of the asset.

n4 – a numeric value indicating the start period to calculate depreciation for.

n5 – a numeric value indicating the end period to calculate depreciation for.

n6 – a Boolean (true/false) value indicating whether to switch from declining-balance to straight-line if declining-balance is less. True will always use declining-balance. False will switch to straight-line if declining-balance is less.

VDB (n1, n2, n3, n4, n5, n6, n7)

n1 – a numeric value indicating the asset's initial cost.

n2 – a numeric value indicating the asset's salvage value.

n3 – a numeric value indicating the useful life of the asset.

n4 – a numeric value indicating the start period to calculate depreciation for.

n5 – a numeric value indicating the end period to calculate depreciation for.

n6 – a numeric value indicating the factor at which the rate declines – 2 indicates double-declining.

n7 – a Boolean (true/false) value indicating whether to switch from declining-balance to straight-line if declining-balance is less. True will always use declining-balance. False will switch to straight-line if declining-balance is less.

```
VDB(50000,15000,7,2,5)
```

returns 10,510.20 depreciation for years two through five.

XIRR

Returns a numeric value indicating the internal rate of return for a series of payments and receipts.

XIRR differs from IRR in that it calculates internal rate of return for payments/ receipts that aren't necessarily periodic.

XIRR (na, da)

na – a numeric array indicating the series of payments and receipts (there must be at least one negative and one positive number in the array).

da – an array of date or date-time values indicating the matching dates for the numeric array. There must be one entry in this array for each entry in the numeric array.

XIRR (na, da, n)

na – a numeric array indicating the series of payments and receipts (there must be at least one negative and one positive number in the array).
da – an array of date or date-time values indicating the matching dates for the numeric array. There must be one entry in this array for each entry in the numeric array.
n – a numeric value indicating the "guess" of IRR.

```
XIRR([-1000,-500,2000],[#1/1/2000#,#5/1/2000#,#6/30/2000#])
```

returns 1.08.

XNPV

Returns a numeric value indicating the net present value of an investment.

XNPV differs from NPV in that it calculates net present value for payments/receipts that aren't necessarily periodic.

XNPV (n, na, da)

n – a numeric value indicating the discount rate.
na – a numeric array indicating payments/receipts.
da – an array of date or date-time values that correspond to the numeric array. There must be one entry in the date array for each entry in the numeric array.

```
XNPV(.05,[1000,2000,1500,1750],
[#1/1/2000#,#5/1/2000#,#6/30/2000#,#12/31/2000#])
```

returns 6,098.72.

YearFrac

Returns a numeric value indicating what fraction of the year is represented by two dates.

YearFrac (d1, d2)

d1 – a date or date-time value indicating the first date in the year.
d2 – a date or date-time value indicating the second date in the year.

YearFrac (d1, d2, n)

d1 – a date or date-time value indicating the first date in the year.

d2 – a date or date-time value indicating the second date in the year.
n – a numeric value indicating the day basis system: 0 = US (NASD) 30/360,
1 = actual/actual, 2 = actual/360, 3 = actual/365, 4 = European 30/360.

```
YearFrac(#1/1/2003#,#3/31/2003#)
```

returns .25.

Yield

Returns a numeric value indicating the yield of a security that pays periodic interest.

Yield (d1, d2, n1, n2, n3, n4)

d1 – a date or date-time value indicating the purchase date.
d2 – a date or date-time value indicating the date of maturity.
n1 – a numeric value indicating the interest rate.
n2 – a numeric value indicating the purchase price of the security
(per $100 face value).
n3 – a numeric value indicating the security redemption value (per $100 face value).
n4 – a numeric value indicating the number of payments per year: 1 = annual,
2 = semiannual, 4 = quarterly.

Yield (d1, d2, n1, n2, n3, n4, n5)

d1 – a date or date-time value indicating the purchase date.
d2 – a date or date-time value indicating the date of maturity.
n1 – a numeric value indicating the interest rate.
n2 – a numeric value indicating the purchase price of the security
(per $100 face value).
n3 – a numeric value indicating the security redemption value (per $100 face value).
n4 – a numeric value indicating the number of payments per year: 1 = annual,
2 = semiannual, 4 = quarterly.
n5 – a numeric value indicating the day basis system: 0 = US (NASD) 30/360,
1 = actual/actual, 2 = actual/360, 3 = actual/365, 4 = European 30/360.

```
Yield (#1/1/2000#,#1/1/2005#,.055,62.99,50,1)
```

returns .087 (formatted with three decimal places).

Functions: Financial

YieldDisc

Returns a numeric value indicating the yield of a discounted security.

YieldDisc (d1, d2, n1, n2)

d1 – a date or date-time value indicating the purchase date.
d2 – a date or date-time value indicating the date of maturity.
n1 – a numeric value indicating purchase price (per $100 face value).
n2 – a numeric value indicating the security redemption value (per $100 face value).

YieldDisc (d1, d2, n1, n2, n3)

d1 – a date or date-time value indicating the purchase date.
d2 – a date or date-time value indicating the date of maturity.
n1 – a numeric value indicating purchase price (per $100 face value).
n2 – a numeric value indicating the security redemption value (per $100 face value).
n3 – a numeric value indicating the day basis system: 0 = US (NASD) 30/360,
1 = actual/actual, 2 = actual/360, 3 = actual/365, 4 = European 30/360.

```
YieldDisc(#1/1/2000#,#1/1/2005#,36.25,50)
```

returns .0759 (when formatted with four decimal places).

YieldMat

Returns a numeric value indicating the yield of a security that pays interest only at maturity.

YieldMat (d1, d2, d3, n1, n2)

d1 – a date or date-time value indicating the purchase date.
d2 – a date or date-time value indicating the date of maturity.
d3 – a date or date-time value indicating the issue date.
n1 – a numeric value indicating the interest rate.
n2 – a numeric value indicating purchase price (per $100 face value).

YieldMat (d1, d2, d3, n1, n2, n3)

d1 – a date or date-time value indicating the purchase date.
d2 – a date or date-time value indicating the date of maturity.
d3 – a date or date-time value indicating the issue date.

n1 – a numeric value indicating the interest rate.
n2 – a numeric value indicating purchase price (per $100 face value).
n3 – a numeric value indicating the day basis system: 0 = US (NASD) 30/360, 1 = actual/actual, 2 = actual/360, 3 = actual/365, 4 = European 30/360.

```
YieldMat(#3/1/2000#,#3/1/2005#,#1/1/2000#,.055,101.82)
```

returns .05.

Functions: Math

This set of functions performs standard math, algebraic, and geometrical calculations.

Abs

Returns a numeric value indicating the absolute value of a number.

Abs (n)

n – a numeric value to return the absolute value for.

```
Abs(-27.3)
```

returns 27.30.

Atn

Returns a numeric value (in radians) indicating the arctangent of the source number.

Atn (n)

n – a numeric value to return the arctangent of.

```
Atn(45)
```

returns 1.55.

Cos

Returns a numeric value indicating the cosine of the source number.

Cos (n)

n – a numeric value, in radians, to return the cosine of.

```
Cos(45)
```

returns .53.

Exp

Returns a numeric value indicating *e* (the base of the natural logarithm) raised to a power.

Exp (n)

n – a numeric value indicating the power to raise *e* to.

```
Exp(10)
```

returns 22,026.47 (*e* raised to the power of 10).

Fix

Returns a whole number with decimal places truncated.
Fix is functionally equivalent to Truncate. See **Truncate** for more information.

Int

Returns a numeric value indicating the integer portion of the supplied number.

Int (n)

n – a numeric value that you want to extract the integer portion of.

```
Int(3.574)
```

returns 3.00.

Log

Returns a numeric value indicating the logarithm of the supplied number.

Log (n)

n – a numeric value to return the logarithm of.

```
Log(22026.47)
```

returns 10.

Pi

Returns the value of Pi (approximately 3.142).

Although this function appears as "Pi" in the Function tree, "crPi" will appear when you double-click the function name. If you type in the function yourself, type it as "crPi".

crPi

```
crPi
```

returns 3.142 (when formatted to show three decimal places).

Remainder

Returns a numeric value indicating the remainder of a division operation (not the quotient).

The Remainder function operates similar to the Mod arithmetic operator. Among other things, Remainder can be used with the RecordNumber function to shade every other line of a report in alternating colors.

Remainder (n1, n2)

n1 – a numeric value indicating the numerator of the division.
n2 – a numeric value indicating the denominator of the division.

```
Remainder (10,3)
```

returns 1.00 (the remainder of dividing 10 by 3).

```
If Remainder (RecordNumber, 2) = 0 Then
   crSilver
Else
   crNoColor
```

will shade every other details section silver if used as a conditional formatting formula for the details sections background color.

Rnd

Returns a numeric value between 0 and 1 represented as a random number.

Rnd may be helpful in situations where you wish to add a certain "randomness" to portions of your report. By multiplying Rnd by a larger number (10, 100, and so forth), you may get larger numbers that may appropriate for other uses.

Rnd

Rnd (n)

n – a number to act as a "seed" to generate the random number.

```
Rnd
```

returns a different fractional number within each record and report refresh.

```
Rnd(Timer)
```

uses the Timer function to generate a "seed" number to increase "randomness" of the numbers returned.

Round

Returns a numeric value rounded to a specified number of decimal places.

Round (n)

n – a numeric value to be rounded to the nearest whole number.

Round (n1, n2)

n1 – a numeric value to be rounded.
n2 – a numeric value indicating the number of decimal places to round *n1* to.

```
Round (1.7821, 1)
```

returns 1.80.

Sgn

Returns a numeric value indicating the sign of the supplied number.

Sgn returns –1 if the source number is negative, 0 if the source number is zero, and 1 if the source number is positive.

Sgn (n)

n – a numeric value to determine the sign of.

```
Sgn (-25)
```

returns −1.00.

Sin

Returns a numeric value indicating the sine of the supplied angle.

Sin (n)

n – a numeric value indicating the angle to calculate the sine of (in radians).

```
Sin(45)
```

returns .85.

Sqr

Returns a numeric value indicating the square root of the source number.

Sqr (n)

n – a numeric value to return the square root of.

```
Sqr (25)
```

returns 5.00.

Tan

Returns a numeric value indicating the tangent of the supplied angle.

Tan (n)

n – a numeric value indicating an angle (in radians).

```
Tan(45)
```

returns 1.62.

Truncate

Returns a numeric value indicating the source number truncated to a specified number of decimal places.

Truncate is similar to Round in that it removes decimal places. However, Truncate doesn't round the source number in the process—it simply removes the decimal places.

Truncate (n)

n – a numeric value to be truncated to zero decimal places.

Truncate (n1, n2)

n1 – a numeric value to be truncated.
n2 – a numeric value indicating the number of decimal places to truncate.

```
Truncate (1.489,1)
```

returns 1.40.

Functions: Print State

This category of functions exposes a variety of functions that generally pertain to the current state of the report when being formatted or printed. Some of these functions duplicate items found in the Special Fields category of the Field Explorer.

DrillDownGroupLevel (version 9 only)

Returns a numeric value indicating how many group levels a viewer has drilled down into when viewing the report online (0 is returned if a viewer has not drilled down).

This function, new to Crystal Reports 9, is very helpful when you need to determine where a viewer is in a drill-down hierarchy. You may use this function, for example, to suppress a group header if a viewer has drilled down to the group's first level (showing the series of just group headers and footers for the group). You will see a different DrillDownGroupLevel result and be able to show the group header when the viewer drills down to the next level where they're seeing details sections and just a single group header and footer.

DrillDownGroupLevel

```
DrillDownGroupLevel
```

returns 2.00 if the viewer has drilled into the second group.

```
DrillDownGroupLevel = 1
```

will suppress Group Header #1 when a viewer first drills down when placed in a conditional suppression formula for Group Header #1.

GroupNumber

Returns a numeric value indicating the sequential number of the group that is currently being displayed.

GroupNumber is helpful in various conditional formatting situations, such as conditionally setting a New Page Before property, or shading every other group footer. This function returns the same value as the GroupNumber special field.

GroupNumber

```
GroupNumber > 1
```

when used as a conditional New Page Before formula for Group Header #1, will not start a new page before the report's first group.

GroupSelection

Returns a string value indicating the Group Selection Formula.

This function returns the same information as the Group Selection Formula special field.

GroupSelection

```
GroupSelection
```

returns "Sum ({Orders.Order Amount}, {Orders.Customer ID}) > $15000.00" if a group selection formula is limited groups on the report.

InRepeatedGroupHeader

Returns a Boolean (true/false) value indicating whether or not the report is currently exposing a repeated group header.

InRepeatedGroupHeader is helpful when you wish to avoid resetting variables in a repeated group header, when you want to add a "continued" message, or similar conditional behavior.

InRepeatedGroupHeader

```
If Not InRepeatedGroupHeader Then
    NumberVar GroupTotal := 0
```

will reset the GroupTotal variable to 0 only if this is the first group header for the group.

IsNull

Returns a Boolean (true/false) value indicating if the supplied field contains a null value.

Null database values may not appear with all databases. Also, the setting of the Convert Null Database Fields To Default option (from File | Report Options or File | Options) affects whether null database values will exist or not.

IsNull (f)

f – any field name from a database table.

```
If IsNull ({Sales.Cust}) Then
    "No customer for this sale"
Else
    {Sales.Cust}
```

returns the string "No customer for this sale" if the field is null. Otherwise, it returns the field's value.

Next (Crystal Syntax only)

Returns the contents of the supplied field for the next database record.

Next (f)

f – any field name from a database table.

```
If {Sales.Cust} = Next({Sales.Cust}) Then
    {Sales.Cust} & " continues on next page"
```

compares the current customer name to the next customer name. If they're the same, the formula returns a "continues on next page" message.

NextIsNull

Returns a Boolean (true/false) value indicating if the supplied field in the next record contains a null value.

Null database values may not appear with all databases. Also, the setting of the Convert Null Database Fields To Default option (from File | Report Options or File | Options) affects whether null database values will exist or not.

NextIsNull (f)

f – any field name from a database table.

```
If NextIsNull ({Sales.Cust}) Then
   "Last order for " & {Sales.Cust}
```

returns a "last order" string if the next record's customer field is null (this assumes that the report is sorted on {Sales.Cust}).

NextValue (Basic Syntax only)

Returns the contents of the supplied field for the next database record.

This function is equivalent to Next. See **Next** for more information.

OnFirstRecord

Returns a Boolean (true/false) value indicating if the current record is the first record on the report.

OnFirstRecord is helpful for some conditional formatting requirements.

OnFirstRecord

```
Not OnFirstRecord
```

when used as a conditional formula for Group Header #1's New Page Before property, avoids a page break before the first group header on the report.

OnLastRecord

Returns a Boolean (true/false) value indicating if the current record is the last record on the report.

OnLastRecord is helpful for some conditional formatting requirements.

Functions: Print State

OnLastRecord

```
Not OnLastRecord
```

when used as a conditional formula for Group Footer #1's New Page After property, avoids a page break after the last group footer on the report.

PageNofM

Returns a string value indicating the current page number, followed by " of ", followed by the total number of report pages.
    PageNofM returns the same string as the Page N of M special field.

PageNofM

```
PageNofM
```

returns "Page 3 of 20" if the current page being formatted is page 3 of a 20-page report.

PageNumber

Returns a numeric value indicating the current page being formatted or printed on the report.
    PageNumber returns the same value as the Page Number special field.

PageNumber

```
PageNumber = 1
```

when supplied as a conditional formula for the Page Header Suppress property, will prevent the Page Header from being printed on the first page of the report.

Previous (Crystal Syntax only)

Returns the contents of the supplied field for the previous database record.

Previous (f)

f – any field name from a database table.

```
If {Sales.Cust} = Previous({Sales.Cust}) Then
    {Sales.Cust} & " continued from previous page"
```

compares the current customer name to the previous customer name. If they're the same, the formula returns a "continued from previous page" message.

PreviousIsNull

Returns a Boolean (true/false) value indicating if the supplied field in the previous record contains a null value.

Null database values may not appear with all databases. Also, the setting of the Convert Null Database Fields To Default option (from File | Report Options or File | Options) affects whether null database values will exist or not.

PreviousIsNull (f)

f – any field name from a database table.

```
If PreviousIsNull ({Sales.Cust}) Then
    "First order for " & {Sales.Cust}
```

returns a "first order" string if the previous record's customer field is null (this assumes that the report is sorted on {Sales.Cust}).

PreviousValue (Basic Syntax only)

Returns the contents of the supplied field for the previous database record.

This function is equivalent to Previous. See **Previous** for more information.

RecordNumber

Returns a numeric value indicating the sequential number of the current record.

RecordNumber can be used for certain conditional formatting situations. RecordNumber returns the same value as the Record Number special field.

RecordNumber

```
If RecordNumber Mod 2 = 0 Then
    crSilver
Else
    crNoColor
```

when supplied as a conditional formula to the Details section background color property, shades every other details section silver.

RecordSelection

Returns a string value containing the report's record selection formula.
   RecordSelection returns the same value as the Record Selection Formula special field.

RecordSelection

```
RecordSelection
```

returns "{Sales.State} in ["MT", "ID", "WY", "CO"]" if a record selection formula has been created limiting the report to several states.

TotalPageCount

Returns a numeric value indicating the total number of pages on the report.
   TotalPageCount returns the same value as the Total Page Count special field.

TotalPageCount

```
If PageNumber < TotalPageCount Then "report continues on next page"
```

prints a "report continues on next page" message of the report is not printing the last page.

Functions: Programming Shortcuts

This category of functions supplies shortcuts for other, more involved programming constructs (such as If-Then-Else or Select-Case).

Choose (index, choice1, choice2, ..., choiceN)

Returns a value (the data type depends on function arguments) from the list of "choices."

Choose (n, c1, c2...)

n –a numeric value indicating which entry in the "choice" list to return.
$c1$ – the first entry in the choice list. $c1$ can be any data type or a range value (arrays, however, aren't allowed).
$c2$ – the next entry in the choice list. It must be the same data type as $c1$. Additional choice entries can follow $c2$, each separated by a comma.

```
Choose(5,"January","February","March","April","May","June")
```

returns "May".

IIF (expression, truePart, falsePart)

Returns a value (the data type depends on function arguments) based on the outcome of a conditional test.

IIF (e, v1, v2)

e – a Boolean expression using comparison operators or other Boolean logic. Returns True or False.

v1 – a value of any data type (excluding an array) indicating what the function returns if *e* is true.

v2 – a value of the same data type as *v1* indicating what the function returns if *e* is false.

```
IIF({Sales.Amount} > 5000,"Bonus Sale","Normal Sale")
```

returns the string "Bonus Sale" for sales over $5,000. Otherwise, returns the string "Normal Sale".

Switch (expr1, value1, expr2, value2, ..., exprN, valueN)

Returns a value (the data type depends on function arguments) based on the outcome of several conditional tests.

Switch (e1, v1, e2..., v2...)

e1 – a Boolean expression using comparison operators or other Boolean logic. Returns True or False.

v1 – a value of any data type (excluding an array) that's returned if *e1* evaluates to True.

e2 – a Boolean expression using comparison operators or other Boolean logic. Returns True or False.

v2 – a value of the same data type as *v1* that's returned if *e2* evaluates to True. Additional pairs of expressions and values may be supplied. An equal number of expressions and values must be supplied.

```
Switch ({Sales.Amount} < 100, "Needs Improvement",
        {Sales.Amount} < 5000, "OK Sale",
```

```
{Sales.Amount} < 7500, "Bonus Sale",
True, "Fantastic Sale!")
```

returns a string value relating to the comparisons of the amount field. If the first three tests fail, the formula returns "Fantastic Sale".

Functions: Ranges

This category of functions test range values to determine if they contain a fixed lower or upper bound.

HasLowerBound (version 9 only)

Returns a Boolean (true/false) value indicating whether the supplied range has a defined lower bound.

If you supply a range array to HasLowerBound, *every* element of the array must have a lower bound for HasLowerBound to return True.

HasLowerBound (r)

r – a range or range array.

```
If HasLowerBound ({?Order Amounts}) Then
    "Orders start at " & ToText(Minimum({?Order Amounts}))
```

returns "Orders start at 1,000.00" if the Order Amounts parameter field (defined as a range parameter field) has a lower bound of 1,000 specified.

HasUpperBound (version 9 only)

Returns a Boolean (true/false) value indicating whether the supplied range has a defined upper bound.

If you supply a range array to HasUpperBound, *every* element of the array must have an upper bound for HasUpperBound to return True.

HasUpperBound (r)

r – a range or range array.

```
If HasUpperBound ({?Order Amounts}) Then
    "Orders end at " & ToText(Maximum({?Order Amounts}))
```

returns "Orders end at 5,000.00" if the Order Amounts parameter field (defined as a range parameter field) has an upper bound of 5,000 specified.

IncludesLowerBound (version 9 only)

Returns a Boolean (true/false) value indicating whether the supplied range has a defined lower bound.

If you supply a range array to IncludesLowerBound, *any* element of the array may have a lower bound for IncludesLowerBound to return True.

IncludesLowerBound (r)

r – a range or range array.

```
If IncludesLowerBound ({?Order Amounts}) Then
    "Orders start at " & ToText(Minimum({?Order Amounts}))
```

returns "Orders start at 1,000.00" if the Order Amounts parameter field (defined as a range parameter field) has a lower bound of 1,000 specified.

IncludesUpperBound (version 9 only)

Returns a Boolean (true/false) value indicating whether the supplied range has a defined upper bound.

If you supply a range array to IncludesUpperBound, *any* element of the array may have an upper bound for IncludesUpperBound to return True.

IncludesUpperBound (r)

r – a range or range array.

```
If IncludesUpperBound ({?Order Amounts}) Then
    "Orders end at " & ToText(Maximum({?Order Amounts}))
```

returns "Orders end at 5,000.00" if the Order Amounts parameter field (defined as a range parameter field) has an upper bound of 5,000 specified.

Functions: Strings

This category of functions allows manipulation or testing of string values, database fields, and other string formulas.

Asc

Returns a numeric value indicating the ASCII (internal character coding) value of the first character of the supplied string.

Functions: Strings

Asc (s)

s – a string value.

```
Asc ("X")
```

returns 88.00 (the ASCII code for a capital X).

```
Asc(" ")
```

returns 32.00 (the ASCII code for a space).

AscW

Returns a numeric value indicating the Unicode value of the first character of the supplied string.

AscW (s)

s – a string value.

```
AscW ("X")
```

returns 88.00 (the Unicode code for a capital X).

Chr

Returns a string value indicating the ASCII representation (internal character coding) of the supplied number.

Chr (n)

n – a whole number.

```
Chr(88)
```

returns "X".

```
Chr(34)
```

returns quotation marks.

ChrW

Returns a string value indicating the Unicode representation of the supplied number.

ChrW (n)

n – a whole number.

```
ChrW(88)
```

returns "X".

Filter

Returns a string array containing only strings that match the search string.

Filter (sa, s)

sa – a string array containing one or more individual strings to search.
s – a string value to search *sa* for.

Filter (sa, s, b)

sa – a string array containing one or more individual strings to search.
s – a string value to search *sa* for.
b – a Boolean (true/false) value indicating whether the search should return partial matches. If True, partial string matches will be returned. If False, only complete matches will be returned.

Filter (sa, s, b, n)

sa – a string array containing one or more individual strings to search.
s – a string value to search *sa* for.
b – a Boolean (true/false) value indicating whether the search should return string matches or nonmatches. If True, strings that match *s* will be returned. If False, strings that *do not* match *s* will be returned.
n – a numeric value indicating whether the search is case-sensitive. 0 = case-sensitive search, 1 = non-case-sensitive search.

```
StringVar Array Beatles := ["John","Paul","George","Ringo"];
Join (Filter(Beatles,"o"))
```

returns "John George Ringo" (the Join function concatenates the three elements of the Beatles string array that contain the letter "o").

InStr

Returns a numeric value indicating the first position in the source string where the search string appears.

Functions: Strings

InStr (s1, s2)

s1 – a string value indicating the source string to search.
s2 – a string value indicating the string to search for in *s1*.

InStr (n, s1, s2)

n – a numeric value indicating the position in *s1* to start searching for *s2*.
s1 – a string value indicating the source string to search.
s2 – a string value indicating the string to search for in *s1*.

InStr (s1, s2, n) (version 9 only)

s1 – a string value indicating the source string to search.
s2 – a string value indicating the string to search for in *s1*.
n – a numeric value indicating whether the search is case-sensitive: 0 = case-sensitive,
1 = not case-sensitive.

InStr (n1, s1, s2, n2) (version 9 only)

n1 – a numeric value indicating the position in *s1* to start searching for *s2*.
s1 – a string value indicating the source string to search.
s2 – a string value indicating the string to search for in *s1*.
n2 – a numeric value indicating whether the search is case-sensitive: 0 = case-sensitive,
1 = not case-sensitive.

```
Instr("The rain in Spain falls on the plain","spain")
```

returns 0.00 (the search is case-sensitive).

```
Instr("The rain in Spain falls on the plain","spain",1)
```

returns 13.00 (the search is not case-sensitive).

InStrRev

**Returns a numeric value indicating the last position in the source string
where the search string appears.**

In essence, InStrRev starts searching for the substring from right to left.

InStrRev (s1, s2)

s1 – a string value indicating the source string to search.
s2 – a string value indicating the string to search for in *s1*.

InStrRev (s1, s2, n)

s1 – a string value indicating the source string to search.
s2 – a string value indicating the string to search for in *s1*.
n – a numeric value indicating the position from the right of *s1* to start searching for *s2*.

InStrRev (s1, s2, n1, n2)

s1 – a string value indicating the source string to search.
s2 – a string value indicating the string to search for in *s1*.
n1 – a numeric value indicating the position from the right of *s1* to start searching for *s2*.
n2 – a numeric value indicating whether the search is case-sensitive:
0 = case-sensitive, 1 = not case-sensitive.

```
InstrRev("The rain in Spain falls on the plain","a",25)
```

returns 20.00 (the search starts at position 25 and proceeds left—finding a lowercase "a" at position 20).

IsNumeric

Returns a Boolean (true/false) value indicating whether or not the source string contains only numeric characters.

IsNumeric is helpful for testing the contents of a string value before converting it with the ToNumber function, as ToNumber will fail if it encounters any nonnumeric characters.

IsNumeric (s)

s – a string value to test for numeric content.

```
If IsNumeric ({FromMainframe.SalesAmount}) Then
   ToNumber({FromMainframe.SalesAmount}) * 1.1
Else
   0
```

checks that the SalesAmount string field contains only numeric values before converting it to a number with the ToNumber function.

Join

Returns a string value consisting of all the elements of the source string array concatenated together.

Join is helpful for, among other things, displaying all the values entered into a multivalue string parameter field in a single formula.

Join (a)

a – a string array.

Join (a, s)

a – a string array.
s – a string value to act as a "delimiter"; it will be inserted between each array element in the output string.

```
Join({?States Chosen},", ")
```

returns "CO, WY, MT, UT" if the four states were supplied to the multivalue States Chosen parameter field.

Left

Returns a string value indicating a limited number of characters extracted from the left side of the source string.

Left (s, n)

s – a string value used as the source string.
n – a numeric value indicating how many characters to extract from *s*.

```
Left ("George", 3)
```

returns "Geo".

Length

Returns a numeric value indicating how many characters are contained in the source string.

Len is functionally equivalent to Length.

Length (s)

s – a string value.

```
Length ("George")
```

returns 6.00.

LowerCase

Returns a string value indicating a lowercase representation of the source string.

LCase is functionally equivalent to LowerCase.

LowerCase (s)

s – a string value to be converted to lowercase.

```
LowerCase ("George Peck")
```

returns "george peck".

Mid

Returns a string value indicating a substring extracted from the source string.

Mid (s, n)

s – a string value to extract characters from.
n – a numeric value indicating the position to begin the extraction from *s*.

Mid (s, n1, n2)

s – a string value to extract characters from.
n1 – a numeric value indicating the position to begin the extraction from *s*.
n2 – a numeric value indicating how many characters to extract.

```
Mid("George Peck",8,3)
```

returns "Pec".

NumericText

Returns a Boolean (true/false) value indicating whether or not the source string contains only numeric characters.

NumericText is functionally equivalent to IsNumeric. See **IsNumeric** for more information.

ProperCase (version 9 only)

Returns a string value converted so that the first character, and any character immediately appearing after a space or nonalphanumeric character, will appear in uppercase. The remaining characters will appear in lowercase.

This function is very helpful when encountering proper names, such as first and last names, that are stored in a database in all uppercase characters.

ProperCase (s)

s – a string value.

```
ProperCase("GEORGE PECK,JR.")
```

returns "George Peck,Jr."

Replace

Returns a string value where a certain set of characters have been replaced by another set of characters.

Replace (s1, s2, s3)

s1 – the source string to search.
s2 – the characters to search *s1* for.
s3 – the characters to replace *s2* with in *s1*.

Replace (s1, s2, s3, n)

s1 – the source string to search.
s2 – the characters to search *s1* for.
s3 – the characters to replace *s2* with in *s1*.
n – a numeric value indicating the position in *s1* to start searching for *s2*.

Replace (s1, s2, s3, n1, n2)

s1 – the source string to search.
s2 – the characters to search *s1* for.
s3 – the characters to replace *s2* with in *s1*.
n1 – a numeric value indicating the position in *s1* to start searching for *s2*.
n2 – a numeric value indicating the number of replacements to make.

Replace (s1, s2, s3, n1, n2, n3)

s1 – the source string to search.
s2 – the characters to search *s1* for.
s3 – the characters to replace *s2* with in *s1*.
n1 – a numeric value indicating the position in *s1* to start searching for *s2*.
n2 – a numeric value indicating the number of replacements to make.
n3 – a numeric value indicating whether the search is case-sensitive: 0 = case-sensitive, 1 = not case-sensitive.

```
Replace("George Peck","George","Gregory")
```

returns "Gregory Peck".

ReplicateString

Returns a string value consisting of multiple duplications of a source string.

ReplicateString (s, n)

s – the source string to duplicate.
n – a numeric value indicating how many duplications of *s* to make.

```
ReplicateString ("*", 15)
```

returns "***************".

Right

Returns a string value indicating a limited number of characters extracted from the right side of the source string.

Right (s, n)

s – a string value used as the source string.
n – a numeric value indicating how many characters to extract from *s*.

```
Right ("George", 3)
```

returns "rge".

Roman (version 9 only)

Returns a string value expressing the supplied numeric argument as a Roman numeral value.

Roman (n)

n – a numeric value to convert to Roman numerals.

Roman (n1, n2)

n1 – a numeric value to convert to Roman numerals.
n2 – a numeric value indicating the type of Roman numeral to return; 0 = Classic; 1, 2, or 3 = various levels of precision; 4 = simplified.

Roman (1998)

returns "MCMXCVIII".

Roman (1998, 2)

returns "MXMVIII".

NOTE   *The best way to explore the various precision choices is to simply try them.*

Space

Returns a string value consisting of a specified number of spaces.

Space (n)

n – the number of space characters to duplicate.

```
"George" & Space(10) & "Peck"
```

returns "George   Peck".

Split

Returns a string array consisting of elements built from the supplied individual strings.

Split (s)

s – a string containing one or more individual strings separated by spaces.

Split (s1, s2)

s1 – a string containing one or more individual strings separated by the delimiter specified in *s2*.
s2 – a string value indicating the delimiter that separates individual values in *s1*.

Split (s1, s2, n)

s1 – a string containing one or more individual strings separated by the delimiter specified in *s2*.
s2 – a string value indicating the delimiter that separates individual values in *s1*.
n – a numeric value indicating how many elements should be placed in the array.

Split (s1, s2, n1, n2)

s1 – a string containing one or more individual strings separated by the delimiter specified in *s2*.
s2 – a string value indicating the delimiter that separates individual values in *s1*.
n1 – a numeric value indicating how many elements should be placed in the array (–1 for all).
n2 – a numeric value indicating how to treat the search for the delimiter. 0 = search is case-sensitive, 1 = search is not case-sensitive.

```
Split("John Paul George Ringo")[2]
```

returns "Paul".

```
Split("John And Paul And George And Ringo","and",-1,0)[1]
```

returns "John And Paul And George And Ringo", as only one element was added the array—the delimiter search is case-sensitive and "And" is not found.

```
Split("John And Paul And George And Ringo","and",-1,1)[1]
```

returns "John"—the delimiter search is not case-sensitive.

StrCmp

Returns a numeric value indicating how two strings compare alphabetically.

StrCmp returns –1 if the first string is less than the second string, 0 if the strings are equal, and 1 if the first string is greater than the second string.

Functions: Strings

StrCmp (s1, s2)

s1 – the first string to compare.
s2 – the string to compare to *s1*.

StrCmp (s1, s2, n)

s1 – the first string to compare.
s2 – the string to compare to *s1*.
n – a numeric value indicating how to treat the search for the delimiter. 0 = search is case-sensitive, 1 = search is not case-sensitive.

```
StrCmp ("abc","xyz")
```

returns –1.00.

StrReverse

Returns a string value consisting of the source string in reverse order.

StrReverse (s)

s – a string value to be reversed.

```
StrReverse ("George Peck")
```

returns "kceP egroeG".

ToNumber

Returns a numeric value indicating a numeric conversion of another nonnumeric value.

   ToNumber converts other numeric and Boolean values, as well as string values, to numbers. ToNumber is functionally equivalent to CDbl and Val.

ToNumber (v)

v – a numeric, string, or Boolean value to be converted to a number.

```
ToNumber ("5642.15")
```

returns 5,642.15 as a number.

NOTE *You may wish to test the value to convert with NumericText before you supply it to ToNumber, as ToNumber will fail if a string is supplied that doesn't contain all numeric values. If you wish to avoid the test, you may use Val, which will always return a result (perhaps 0), even if the supplied argument isn't numeric.*

ToText

Converts any nonstring data type to a string value.

ToText is an immensely valuable function used to convert any nonstring data type to a string. You'll often use ToText within a string formula to concatenate various types of data items into a single string result.

ToText (b)

b – a Boolean (true/false) value to be converted to a string.

```
ToText({Orders.Shipped})
```

returns the string "True" if the Boolean Shipped field holds a true value or "False" if the field is false.

ToText (n1, n2, s1, s2)

n1 – a numeric value to be converted to a string.
n2 – a numeric value indicating the number of decimal places to use when converting *n1*. This argument is optional.
s1 – a string value indicating the character or characters to use as a thousands separator when converting *n1*. This argument is optional.
s2 – a string value indicating the character or characters to use as a decimal separator when converting *n1*. This argument is optional.

```
ToText(21256.1255, 2, ",", "-")
```

returns the string "21,256-13" (showing two decimal places, a comma thousands separator, and a dash decimal separator).

ToText (n1, n2, s1, s2, s3)

n1 – a numeric value to be converted to a string.
s1 – a string value used to format the number. This argument is optional.

Functions: Strings

n2 – a numeric value indicating the number of decimal places to use when converting *n1*. This argument is optional.

s2 – a string value indicating the character or characters to use as a thousands separator when converting *n*. This argument is optional.

s3 – a string value indicating the character or characters to use as a decimal separator when converting *n*. This argument is optional.

```
ToText(21256.1255, "#,###,###.00000",2)
```

returns " 21,256.13000" (with leading spaces for extra # characters).

Numeric Formatting Strings

Character	Usage
#	Numeric placeholder. A single numeric character will be placed in each occurrence of #. If there are more # characters than numeric digits, leading or trailing spaces will be added for extra # characters.
0 (zero)	Numeric placeholder. A single numeric character will be placed in each occurrence of 0. If there are more 0 characters than numeric digits, leading or trailing zeros will be added for extra 0 characters.
, (comma)	Thousands separator. Indicates where the thousands separator should be placed in the resulting string. The thousands separator used is taken from a Windows default or the *s2* argument.
. (period)	Decimal separator. Indicates where the decimal separator should be placed in the resulting string. The decimal separator used is taken from a Windows default or the *s2* argument.

ToText (d, s1, s2, s3)

d – a date, time, or date/time value.

s1 – a string value used to format the date, time, or date/time value. This argument is optional.

s2 – a string value used to as a replacement label for "a.m." for morning hours. This argument is optional.

s3 – a string value used to as a replacement label for "p.m." for afternoon/evening hours. This argument is optional.

```
ToText(CurrentDate, "dddd M d, yyyy")
```

returns "Friday May 9, 2003" if CurrentDate contains May 9, 2003.

```
ToText(CurrentTime, "h:mm tt",
"in the morning", "in the afternoon")
```

returns the string " 4:27 in the afternoon" if CurrentTime is 4:27 P.M.

NOTE	*Any nonrecognized characters in the format string will be returned as a literal character. For example, a slash (/) or comma (,) in the format string will simply display within the resulting date string.*

Date/Time Formatting Strings

Character	Usage
M	month number without a leading zero for single-character month
MM	month number with a leading zero for single-character month
MMM	month name as a three-letter abbreviation
MMMM	month name fully spelled
d	day of month without a leading zero for single-character day
dd	day of month with a leading zero for single-character day
ddd	day of week name spelled as a three-letter abbreviation
dddd	day of week name fully spelled
yy	last two characters of year
yyyy	full four-character year
h	hours without a leading zero for a single-character hour (12-hour nonmilitary format)
hh	hours with a leading zero for a single-character hour (12-hour nonmilitary format)
H	hours without a leading zero for a single-character hour (24-hour military format)
HH	hours with a leading zero for a single-character hour (24-hour military format)
m	minutes without a leading zero for a single-character minute
mm	minutes with a leading zero for a single-character minute
s	seconds without a leading zero for a single-character second
ss	seconds with a leading zero for a single-character second
t	single-character uppercase A or P (for A.M. or P.M.)
tt	multiple-character uppercase AM or PM (for A.M. or P.M.)

NOTE	*CStr is functionally equivalent to ToText. It is provided to maintain compatibility with Basic syntax.*

Functions: Strings

ToWords

Returns a string value indicating the "spelled out" version of the numeric argument.

ToWords is often used to print checks.

ToWords (n)

n – a numeric value to spell as words.

```
ToWords (1145.31)
```

returns the string "one thousand one hundred forty-five and 31 / 100".

Trim

Returns a string value consisting of the source string with all leading and trailing spaces removed.

Trim (s)

s – a string value.

```
Trim ("    Leading and trailing spaces    ")
```

returns the string "Leading and trailing spaces" with no extra spaces before or after the string.

TrimLeft

Returns a string value consisting of the source string with all leading spaces removed.

LTrim is functionally equivalent to TrimLeft.

TrimLeft (s)

s – a string value.

```
TrimLeft ("    Leading and trailing spaces    ")
```

returns the string "Leading and trailing spaces   " with no extra spaces before the string, but with any trailing spaces remaining.

TrimRight

Returns a string value consisting of the source string with all trailing spaces removed.

RTrim is functionally equivalent to TrimRight.

TrimRight (s)

s – a string value.

```
TrimRight ("    Leading and trailing spaces    ")
```

returns the string "   Leading and trailing spaces" with no extra spaces after the string, but with any leading spaces remaining.

UpperCase

Returns a string value indicating an uppercase representation of the source string.

UCase is functionally equivalent to UpperCase.

UpperCase (s)

s – a string value to be converted to uppercase.

```
UpperCase ("George Peck")
```

returns "GEORGE PECK".

Val

Returns a numeric value indicating the numeric portion of the supplied string.

Val is helpful for converting string database fields that contain numeric data to actual numeric values. In particular, Val will not return an error if it encounters a nonnumeric character in the string—it will simply stop the conversion at that point.

Val (s)

s – a string value to be converted to a number.

```
Val ("12500.1a31")
```

returns 12,500.10 as a numeric value.

Functions: Summary

This category of functions largely duplicates summary functions available via the Insert | Summary option from the Crystal Reports pull-down menus. By using these summary functions, you may include the same summary calculations available from the Insert | Summary option in formulas. In fact, if you add a report summary to a report with Insert | Summary and then double-click it in the Fields tree of the Formula Editor, the following summary functions will be inserted into your formula automatically.

Average

Returns a numeric value indicating the average of the supplied database field or formula.

Average (f)

f – the database or formula field to summarize for the entire report. This must be a numeric field.

Average (f1, f2)

f1 – the database or formula field to summarize for a report group. This must be a numeric field.

f2 – the database or formula field indicating the group you wish to summarize for. An existing group on the report must be based on this field.

Average (f1, f2, s)

f1 – the database or formula field to summarize for a report group. This must be a numeric field.

f2 – the database or formula field indicating the group you wish to summarize for. An existing group on the report must be based on this field.

s – a string value indicating how often to "change" the summary for Boolean, date, or date-time grouping. See **Boolean Conditions**, **Date Conditions**, and **Time Conditions** later in this appendix for available choices.

```
Average({Sales.Amount})
```

returns the average of sales amounts for the entire report.

```
Average({Sales.Amount}, {Sales.Date}, "monthly")
```

returns the average of sales amounts for the sales date group, summarized for each month.

Correlation

Returns a numeric value indicating the correlation between the supplied database fields or formulas.

Correlation (f1, f2)

f1– the first database or formula field to summarize for the entire report. This must be a numeric field.

f2 – the second database or formula field to summarize for the entire report. This must be a numeric field.

Correlation (f1, f2, f3)

f1– the first database or formula field to summarize for the entire report. This must be a numeric field.

f2 – the second database or formula field to summarize for the entire report. This must be a numeric field.

f3 – the database or formula field indicating the group you wish to summarize for. An existing group on the report must be based on this field.

Correlation (f1, f2, f3, s)

f1– the first database or formula field to summarize for the entire report. This must be a numeric field.

f2 – the second database or formula field to summarize for the entire report. This must be a numeric field.

f3 – the database or formula field indicating the group you wish to summarize for. An existing group on the report must be based on this field.

s – a string value indicating how often to "change" the summary for Boolean, date, or date-time grouping. See **Boolean Conditions**, **Date Conditions**, and **Time Conditions** later in this appendix for available choices.

```
Correlation({Sales.Amount}, {Sales.Goal})
```

returns the correlation between sales amount and sales goal for the entire report.

```
Correlation({Sales.Amount}, {Sales.Goal}, {Sales.Date}, "monthly")
```

returns the correlation between sales amount and sales goal for the sales date group, summarized for each month.

Count

Returns a numeric value indicating the number of occurrences (count) of the supplied database field or formula.

Count (f)

f – the database or formula field to summarize for the entire report.

Count (f1, f2)

f1 – the database or formula field to summarize for a report group.
f2 – the database or formula field indicating the group you wish to summarize for. An existing group on the report must be based on this field.

Count (f1, f2, s)

f1 – the database or formula field to summarize for a report group.
f2 – the database or formula field indicating the group you wish to summarize for. An existing group on the report must be based on this field.
s – a string value indicating how often to "change" the summary for Boolean, date, or date-time grouping. See **Boolean Conditions**, **Date Conditions**, and **Time Conditions** later in this appendix for available choices.

```
Count({Sales.Amount})
```

returns the count of sales amounts for the entire report (in essence, this is the number of records on the report).

```
Count({Sales.Amount}, {Sales.Date}, "monthly")
```

returns the count of sales amounts for the sales date group, summarized for each month (in essence, this is the number of records in the group).

 NOTE

The Count function will count every record where the supplied field contains a nonnull value. If any occurrences of the supplied field contain null values, those records won't increment the count.

Covariance

Returns a numeric value indicating the covariance between the supplied database fields or formulas.

Covariance (f1, f2)

f1– the first database or formula field to summarize for the entire report. This must be a numeric field.

f2 – the second database or formula field to summarize for the entire report. This must be a numeric field.

Covariance (f1, f2, f3)

f1– the first database or formula field to summarize for the entire report. This must be a numeric field.

f2 – the second database or formula field to summarize for the entire report. This must be a numeric field.

f3 – the database or formula field indicating the group you wish to summarize for. An existing group on the report must be based on this field.

Covariance (f1, f2, f3, s)

f1– the first database or formula field to summarize for the entire report. This must be a numeric field.

f2 – the second database or formula field to summarize for the entire report. This must be a numeric field.

f3 – the database or formula field indicating the group you wish to summarize for. An existing group on the report must be based on this field.

s – a string value indicating how often to "change" the summary for Boolean, date, or date-time grouping. See **Boolean Conditions**, **Date Conditions**, and **Time Conditions** later in this appendix for available choices.

```
Covariance({Sales.Amount}, {Sales.Goal})
```

returns the covariance between sales amount and sales goal for the entire report.

```
Covariance({Sales.Amount}, {Sales.Goal}, {Sales.Date}, "monthly")
```

returns the covariance between sales amount and sales goal for the sales date group, summarized for each month.

DistinctCount

Returns a numeric value indicating the unique number of occurrences (distinct count) of the supplied database field or formula.

DistinctCount (f)

f – the database or formula field to summarize for the entire report.

DistinctCount (f1, f2)

f1 – the database or formula field to summarize for a report group.
f2 – the database or formula field indicating the group you wish to summarize for. An existing group on the report must be based on this field.

DistinctCount (f1, f2, s)

f1 – the database or formula field to summarize for a report group.
f2 – the database or formula field indicating the group you wish to summarize for. An existing group on the report must be based on this field.
s – a string value indicating how often to "change" the summary for Boolean, date, or date-time grouping. See **Boolean Conditions**, **Date Conditions**, and **Time Conditions** later in this appendix for available choices.

```
Distinctcount({Sales.Acct#})
```

returns the number of unique accounts for the entire report.

```
Distinctcount({Sales.Acct#}, {Sales.Date}, "monthly")
```

returns the number of unique accounts for the sales date group, summarized for each month.

Maximum

Returns a numeric value indicating the maximum of the supplied database field or formula.

Maximum returns the largest number, the latest date, or the string value last in the alphabet.

Maximum (f)

f – the database or formula field to summarize for the entire report.

Maximum (f1, f2)

f1 – the database or formula field to summarize for a report group.
f2 – the database or formula field indicating the group you wish to summarize for. An existing group on the report must be based on this field.

Maximum (f1, f2, s)

f1 – the database or formula field to summarize for a report group.
f2 – the database or formula field indicating the group you wish to summarize for. An existing group on the report must be based on this field.
s – a string value indicating how often to "change" the summary for Boolean, date, or date-time grouping. See **Boolean Conditions**, **Date Conditions**, and **Time Conditions** later in this appendix for available choices.

```
Maximum({Sales.Amount})
```

returns the highest sales amount for the entire report.

```
Maximum({Sales.Amount}, {Sales.Date}, "monthly")
```

returns the highest sales amount for the sales date group, summarized for each month.

Median

Returns a numeric value indicating the median of the supplied database field or formula.

Median (f)

f – the database or formula field to summarize for the entire report. This must be a numeric field.

Median (f1, f2)

f1 – the database or formula field to summarize for a report group. This must be a numeric field.
f2 – the database or formula field indicating the group you wish to summarize for. An existing group on the report must be based on this field.

Median (f1, f2, s)

f1 – the database or formula field to summarize for a report group. This must be a numeric field.
f2 – the database or formula field indicating the group you wish to summarize for. An existing group on the report must be based on this field.
s – a string value indicating how often to "change" the summary for Boolean, date, or date-time grouping. See **Boolean Conditions**, **Date Conditions**, and **Time Conditions** later in this appendix for available choices.

```
Median({Sales.Amount})
```

returns the median of sales amounts for the entire report.

```
Median({Sales.Amount}, {Sales.Date}, "monthly")
```

returns the median of sales amounts for the sales date group, summarized for each month.

Minimum

Returns a numeric value indicating the minimum of the supplied database field or formula.

Minimum returns the smallest number, the earliest date, or the string value first in the alphabet.

Minimum (f)

f – the database or formula field to summarize for the entire report.

Minimum (f1, f2)

f1 – the database or formula field to summarize for a report group.
f2 – the database or formula field indicating the group you wish to summarize for. An existing group on the report must be based on this field.

Minimum (f1, f2, s)

f1 – the database or formula field to summarize for a report group.
f2 – the database or formula field indicating the group you wish to summarize for. An existing group on the report must be based on this field.
s – a string value indicating how often to "change" the summary for Boolean, date, or date-time grouping. See **Boolean Conditions**, **Date Conditions**, and **Time Conditions** later in this appendix for available choices.

```
Minimum({Sales.Amount})
```

returns the lowest sales amount for the entire report.

```
Minimum({Sales.Amount}, {Sales.Date}, "monthly")
```

returns the lowest sales amount for the sales date group, summarized for each month.

Mode

Returns a numeric value indicating the mode (the most frequently occurring value) of the supplied database field or formula.

Mode (f)

f – the database or formula field to summarize for the entire report.

Mode (f1, f2)

f1 – the database or formula field to summarize for a report group.
f2 – the database or formula field indicating the group you wish to summarize for. An existing group on the report must be based on this field.

Mode (f1, f2, s)

f1 – the database or formula field to summarize for a report group.
f2 – the database or formula field indicating the group you wish to summarize for. An existing group on the report must be based on this field.
s – a string value indicating how often to "change" the summary for Boolean, date, or date-time grouping. See **Boolean Conditions**, **Date Conditions**, and **Time Conditions** later in this appendix for available choices.

```
Mode({Sales.Acct#})
```

returns the most frequently appearing account number for the entire report.

```
Mode({Sales.Acct#}, {Sales.Date}, "monthly")
```

returns the most frequently appearing account number for the sales date group, summarized for each month.

NthLargest

Returns a numeric value indicating the nth largest occurrence of the supplied database field or formula.

NthLargest returns the "nth" largest number, the "nth" latest date, or the "nth" string value last in the ASCII sort order.

NthLargest (n, f)

n – a numeric value (between 1 and 100). 5 returns the fifth largest, 2 the second largest, and so forth.
f – the database or formula field to summarize for the entire report.

NthLargest (n, f1, f2)

n – a numeric value (between 1 and 100). 5 returns the fifth largest, 2 the second largest, and so forth.
f1 – the database or formula field to summarize for a report group.
f2 – the database or formula field indicating the group you wish to summarize for. An existing group on the report must be based on this field.

NthLargest (n, f1, f2, s)

n – a numeric value (between 1 and 100). 5 returns the fifth largest, 2 the second largest, and so forth.
f1 – the database or formula field to summarize for a report group.
f2 – the database or formula field indicating the group you wish to summarize for. An existing group on the report must be based on this field.
s – a string value indicating how often to "change" the summary for Boolean, date, or date-time grouping. See **Boolean Conditions**, **Date Conditions**, and **Time Conditions** later in this appendix for available choices.

```
NthLargest(5, {Sales.Amount})
```

returns the fifth largest sales amount for the entire report.

```
NthLargest(5, {Sales.Amount}, {Sales.Date}, "monthly")
```

returns the fifth largest sales amount for the sales date group, summarized for each month.

NthMostFrequent

Returns a numeric value indicating the nth most frequent occurrence of the supplied database field or formula.

NthMostFrequent (n, f)

n – a numeric value (between 1 and 100). 5 returns the fifth most frequent, 2 the second most frequent, and so forth.
f – the database or formula field to summarize for the entire report.

NthMostFrequent (n, f1, f2)

n – a numeric value (between 1 and 100). 5 returns the fifth most frequent, 2 the second most frequent, and so forth.

f1 – the database or formula field to summarize for a report group.

f2 – the database or formula field indicating the group you wish to summarize for. An existing group on the report must be based on this field.

NthMostFrequent (n, f1, f2, s)

n – a numeric value (between 1 and 100). 5 returns the fifth most frequent, 2 the second most frequent, and so forth.

f1 – the database or formula field to summarize for a report group.

f2 – the database or formula field indicating the group you wish to summarize for. An existing group on the report must be based on this field.

s – a string value indicating how often to "change" the summary for Boolean, date, or date-time grouping. See **Boolean Conditions**, **Date Conditions**, and **Time Conditions** later in this appendix for available choices.

```
NthMostFrequent(5, {Sales.Acct#})
```

returns the fifth most frequently occurring account number for the entire report.

```
NthMostFrequent(5, {Sales.Acct#}, {Sales.Date}, "monthly")
```

returns the fifth most frequently occurring account number for the sales date group, summarized for each month.

NthSmallest

Returns a numeric value indicating the nth smallest occurrence of the supplied database field or formula.

NthSmallest returns the "nth" smallest number, the "nth" earliest date, or the "nth" string value first in the ASCII sort order.

NthSmallest (n, f)

n – a numeric value (between 1 and 100). 5 returns the fifth smallest, 2 the second smallest, and so forth.

f – the database or formula field to summarize for the entire report.

NthSmallest (n, f1, f2)

n – a numeric value (between 1 and 100). 5 returns the fifth smallest, 2 the second smallest, and so forth.

f1 – the database or formula field to summarize for a report group.

f2 – the database or formula field indicating the group you wish to summarize for. An existing group on the report must be based on this field.

NthSmallest (n, f1, f2, s)

n – a numeric value (between 1 and 100). 5 returns the fifth smallest, 2 the second smallest, and so forth.

f1 – the database or formula field to summarize for a report group.

f2 – the database or formula field indicating the group you wish to summarize for. An existing group on the report must be based on this field.

s – a string value indicating how often to "change" the summary for Boolean, date, or date-time grouping. See **Boolean Conditions**, **Date Conditions**, and **Time Conditions** later in this appendix for available choices.

```
NthSmallest (5, {Sales.Amount})
```

returns the fifth smallest sales amount for the entire report.

```
NthSmallest (5, {Sales.Amount}, {Sales.Date}, "monthly")
```

returns the fifth smallest sales amount for the sales date group, summarized for each month.

PercentOfAverage

Returns a numeric value indicating what percentage an average calculation in one group is of another average calculation in a later group or the entire report.

This function duplicates a Percentage Summary Field created with the Insert | Summary menu option.

PercentOfAverage (f1, f2, s)

This will show the percentage of the group value compared to the value for the entire report.

f1 – the database or formula field to summarize for the entire report. This must be a numeric field.

f2 – the database or formula field indicating the group you wish to summarize for. An existing group on the report must be based on this field.

s – a string value indicating how often to "change" the summary for Boolean, date, or date-time grouping. See **Boolean Conditions**, **Date Conditions**, and **Time**

Conditions later in this appendix for available choices. This argument is required only if *f2* is a date, date-time, time, or Boolean field.

PercentOfAverage (f1, f2, s1, f3, s2)

This will show the percentage of the group value compared to the value for a later group.

f1 – the database or formula field to summarize for the entire report. This must be a numeric field.

f2 – the database or formula field indicating the group you wish to summarize for. An existing group on the report must be based on this field.

s1 – a string value indicating how often to "change" the summary for Boolean, date, or date-time grouping. See **Boolean Conditions**, **Date Conditions**, and **Time Conditions** later in this appendix for available choices. This argument (and the comma that precedes it) is required only if *f2* is a date, date-time, time, or Boolean field.

f3 – the database or formula field indicating the later group field to use for the summary. An existing group on the report must be based on this field.

s2 – a string value indicating how often to "change" the summary for Boolean, date, or date-time grouping. See **Boolean Conditions**, **Date Conditions**, and **Time Conditions** later in this appendix for available choices. This argument (and the comma that precedes it) is required only if *f3* is a date, date-time, time, or Boolean field.

```
PercentOfAverage ({Sales.Amount}, {Sales.CustName})
```

returns the percentage that the average sales amount for each customer group makes up of the average sales amount for the entire report.

```
PercentOfAverage ({Sales.Amount}, {Sales.Date},
"monthly", {Sales.CustName})
```

returns the percentage that the average sales amount for each month makes up of the average sales amount for the higher-level customer name group.

PercentOfCount

Returns a numeric value indicating what percentage a count calculation in one group is of another count calculation in a later group or the entire report.

This function duplicates a Percentage Summary Field created with the Insert | Summary menu option.

Functions: Summary

PercentOfCount (f1, f2, s)

This will show the percentage of the group value compared to the value for the entire report.

f1– the database or formula field to summarize for the entire report.

f2 – the database or formula field indicating the group you wish to summarize for. An existing group on the report must be based on this field.

s – a string value indicating how often to "change" the summary for Boolean, date, or date-time grouping. See **Boolean Conditions**, **Date Conditions**, and **Time Conditions** later in this appendix for available choices. This argument is required only if *f2* is a date, date-time, time, or Boolean field.

PercentOfCount (f1, f2, s1, f3, s2)

This will show the percentage of the group value compared to the value for a later group.

f1– the database or formula field to summarize for the entire report.

f2 – the database or formula field indicating the group you wish to summarize for. An existing group on the report must be based on this field.

s1 – a string value indicating how often to "change" the summary for Boolean, date, or date-time grouping. See **Boolean Conditions**, **Date Conditions**, and **Time Conditions** later in this appendix for available choices. This argument (and the comma that precedes it) is required only if *f2* is a date, date-time, time, or Boolean field.

f3 – the database or formula field indicating the later group field to use for the summary. An existing group on the report must be based on this field.

s2 – a string value indicating how often to "change" the summary for Boolean, date, or date-time grouping. See **Boolean Conditions**, **Date Conditions**, and **Time Conditions** later in this appendix for available choices. This argument (and the comma that precedes it) is required only if *f3* is a date, date-time, time, or Boolean field.

```
PercentOfCount ({Sales.Amount}, {Sales.CustName})
```

returns the percentage that the number of records for each customer group makes up of the total number of records for the entire report.

```
PercentOfCount ({Sales.Amount}, {Sales.Date},
"monthly", {Sales.CustName})
```

returns the percentage that the number of records for each month makes up of the number of records for the higher-level customer name group.

NOTE   *PercentOfCount calculations will exclude records that contain an null value in the field being counted.*

PercentOfDistinctCount

Returns a numeric value indicating what percentage a distinct count calculation in one group is of another distinct count calculation in a later group or the entire report.

This function duplicates a Percentage Summary Field created with the Insert | Summary menu option.

PercentOfDistinctCount (f1, f2, s)

This will show the percentage of the group value compared to the value for the entire report.

f1– the database or formula field to summarize for the entire report.

f2 – the database or formula field indicating the group you wish to summarize for. An existing group on the report must be based on this field.

s – a string value indicating how often to "change" the summary for Boolean, date, or date-time grouping. See **Boolean Conditions**, **Date Conditions**, and **Time Conditions** later in this appendix for available choices. This argument is required only if *f2* is a date, date-time, time, or Boolean field.

PercentOfDistinctCount (f1, f2, s1, f3, s2)

This will show the percentage of the group value compared to the value for a later group.

f1– the database or formula field to summarize for the entire report.

f2 – the database or formula field indicating the group you wish to summarize for. An existing group on the report must be based on this field.

s1 – a string value indicating how often to "change" the summary for Boolean, date, or date-time grouping. See **Boolean Conditions**, **Date Conditions**, and **Time Conditions** later in this appendix for available choices. This argument (and the comma that precedes it) is required only if *f2* is a date, date-time, time, or Boolean field.

f3 – the database or formula field indicating the later group field to use for the summary. An existing group on the report must be based on this field.

s2 – a string value indicating how often to "change" the summary for Boolean, date, or date-time grouping. See **Boolean Conditions**, **Date Conditions**, and **Time Conditions** later in this appendix for available choices. This argument (and the comma that precedes it) is required only if *f3* is a date, date-time, time, or Boolean field.

```
PercentOfDistinctCount ({Sales.Acct#}, {Sales.CustName})
```

returns the percentage that the unique number of account numbers for each customer group makes up of the unique number of account numbers for the entire report.

```
PercentOfDistinctCount ({Sales.Acct#}, {Sales.Date},
"monthly", {Sales.CustName})
```

returns the percentage that the unique number of account numbers for each month makes up of the unique number of account numbers for the higher-level customer name group.

PercentOfMaximum

Returns a numeric value indicating what percentage a maximum calculation in one group is of another maximum calculation in a later group or the entire report.

This function duplicates a Percentage Summary Field created with the Insert | Summary menu option.

PercentOfMaximum (f1, f2, s)

This will show the percentage of the group value compared to the value for the entire report.

f1– the database or formula field to summarize for the entire report.
f2 – the database or formula field indicating the group you wish to summarize for. An existing group on the report must be based on this field.
s – a string value indicating how often to "change" the summary for Boolean, date, or date-time grouping. See **Boolean Conditions**, **Date Conditions**, and **Time Conditions** later in this appendix for available choices. This argument is required only if *f2* is a date, date-time, time, or Boolean field.

PercentOfMaximum (f1, f2, s1, f3, s2)

This will show the percentage of the group value compared to the value for a later group.

f1– the database or formula field to summarize for the entire report.
f2 – the database or formula field indicating the group you wish to summarize for. An existing group on the report must be based on this field.
s1 – a string value indicating how often to "change" the summary for Boolean, date, or date-time grouping. See **Boolean Conditions**, **Date Conditions**, and **Time Conditions** later in this appendix for available choices. This argument (and the comma that precedes it) is required only if *f2* is a date, date-time, time, or Boolean field.
f3 – the database or formula field indicating the later group field to use for the summary. An existing group on the report must be based on this field.

s2 – a string value indicating how often to "change" the summary for Boolean, date, or date-time grouping. See **Boolean Conditions**, **Date Conditions**, and **Time Conditions** later in this appendix for available choices. This argument (and the comma that precedes it) is required only if *f3* is a date, date-time, time, or Boolean field.

```
PercentOfMaximum ({Sales.Amount}, {Sales.CustName})
```

returns the percentage that the highest sales amount for each customer group makes up of the highest sales amount for the entire report.

```
PercentOfMaximum ({Sales.Amount}, {Sales.Date},
"monthly", {Sales.CustName})
```

returns the percentage that the highest sales amount for each month makes up of the highest sales amount for the higher-level customer name group.

PercentOfMinimum

Returns a numeric value indicating what percentage an minimum calculation in one group is of another minimum calculation in a later group or the entire report.

This function duplicates a Percentage Summary Field created with the Insert | Summary menu option.

PercentOfMinimum (f1, f2, s)

This will show the percentage of the group value compared to the value for the entire report.

f1 – the database or formula field to summarize for the entire report.

f2 – the database or formula field indicating the group you wish to summarize for. An existing group on the report must be based on this field.

s – a string value indicating how often to "change" the summary for Boolean, date, or date-time grouping. See **Boolean Conditions**, **Date Conditions**, and **Time Conditions** later in this appendix for available choices. This argument is required only if *f2* is a date, date-time, time, or Boolean field.

PercentOfMinimum (f1, f2, s1, f3, s2)

This will show the percentage of the group value compared to the value for a later group.

f1 – the database or formula field to summarize for the entire report.

f2 – the database or formula field indicating the group you wish to summarize for. An existing group on the report must be based on this field.

s1 – a string value indicating how often to "change" the summary for Boolean, date, or date-time grouping. See **Boolean Conditions**, **Date Conditions**, and **Time Conditions** later in this appendix for available choices. This argument (and the comma that precedes it) is required only if *f2* is a date, date-time, time, or Boolean field.

f3 – the database or formula field indicating the later group field to use for the summary. An existing group on the report must be based on this field.

s2 – a string value indicating how often to "change" the summary for Boolean, date, or date-time grouping. See **Boolean Conditions**, **Date Conditions**, and **Time Conditions** later in this appendix for available choices. This argument (and the comma that precedes it) is required only if *f3* is a date, date-time, time, or Boolean field.

```
PercentOfMinimum ({Sales.Amount}, {Sales.CustName})
```

returns the percentage that the lowest sales amount for each customer group makes up of the lowest sales amount for the entire report.

```
PercentOfMinimum ({Sales.Amount}, {Sales.Date},
"monthly", {Sales.CustName})
```

returns the percentage that the lowest sales amount for each month makes up of the lowest sales amount for the higher-level customer name group.

PercentOfSum

Returns a numeric value indicating what percentage a sum calculation in one group is of another sum calculation in a later group or the entire report.

This function duplicates a Percentage Summary Field created with the Insert | Summary menu option.

PercentOfSum (f1, f2, s)

This will show the percentage of the group value compared to the value for the entire report.

f1 – the database or formula field to summarize for the entire report. This must be a numeric field.

f2 – the database or formula field indicating the group you wish to summarize for. An existing group on the report must be based on this field.

s – a string value indicating how often to "change" the summary for Boolean, date, or date-time grouping. See **Boolean Conditions**, **Date Conditions**, and **Time Conditions** later in this appendix for available choices. This argument is required only if *f2* is a date, date-time, time, or Boolean field.

PercentOfSum (f1, f2, s1, f3, s2)

This will show the percentage of the group value compared to the value for a later group.

f1– the database or formula field to summarize for the entire report. This must be a numeric field.

f2 – the database or formula field indicating the group you wish to summarize for. An existing group on the report must be based on this field.

s1 – a string value indicating how often to "change" the summary for Boolean, date, or date-time grouping. See **Boolean Conditions**, **Date Conditions**, and **Time Conditions** later in this appendix for available choices. This argument (and the comma that precedes it) is required only if *f2* is a date, date-time, time, or Boolean field.

f3 – the database or formula field indicating the later group field to use for the summary. An existing group on the report must be based on this field.

s2 – a string value indicating how often to "change" the summary for Boolean, date, or date-time grouping. See **Boolean Conditions**, **Date Conditions**, and **Time Conditions** later in this appendix for available choices. This argument (and the comma that precedes it) is required only if *f3* is a date, date-time, time, or Boolean field.

```
PercentOfSum ({Sales.Amount}, {Sales.CustName})
```

returns the percentage that the total sales amount for each customer group makes up of the total sales amount for the entire report.

```
PercentOfSum ({Sales.Amount}, {Sales.Date},
"monthly", {Sales.CustName})
```

returns the percentage that the total sales amount for each month makes up of the total sales amount for the higher-level customer name group.

PopulationStdDev

Returns a numeric value indicating the population standard deviation of the supplied database field or formula.

PopulationStdDev (f)

f – the database or formula field to summarize for the entire report. This must be a numeric field.

PopulationStdDev (f1, f2)

f1 – the database or formula field to summarize for a report group. This must be a numeric field.

f2 – the database or formula field indicating the group you wish to summarize for. An existing group on the report must be based on this field.

PopulationStdDev (f1, f2, s)

f1 – the database or formula field to summarize for a report group. This must be a numeric field.

f2 – the database or formula field indicating the group you wish to summarize for. An existing group on the report must be based on this field.

s – a string value indicating how often to "change" the summary for Boolean, date, or date-time grouping. See **Boolean Conditions**, **Date Conditions**, and **Time Conditions** later in this appendix for available choices.

```
PopulationStdDev({Sales.Amount})
```

returns the population standard deviation of sales amounts for the entire report.

```
PopulationStdDev({Sales.Amount}, {Sales.Date}, "monthly")
```

returns the population standard deviation of sales amounts for the sales date group, summarized for each month.

PopulationVariance

Returns a numeric value indicating the population variance of the supplied database field or formula.

PopulationVariance (f)

f – the database or formula field to summarize for the entire report. This must be a numeric field.

PopulationVariance (f1, f2)

f1 – the database or formula field to summarize for a report group. This must be a numeric field.

f2 – the database or formula field indicating the group you wish to summarize for. An existing group on the report must be based on this field.

PopulationVariance (f1, f2, s)

f1 – the database or formula field to summarize for a report group. This must be a numeric field.

f2 – the database or formula field indicating the group you wish to summarize for. An existing group on the report must be based on this field.

s – a string value indicating how often to "change" the summary for Boolean, date, or date-time grouping. See **Boolean Conditions**, **Date Conditions**, and **Time Conditions** later in this appendix for available choices.

```
PopulationVariance({Sales.Amount})
```

returns the population variance of sales amounts for the entire report.

```
PopulationVariance({Sales.Amount}, {Sales.Date}, "monthly")
```

returns the population variance of sales amounts for the sales date group, summarized for each month.

PthPercentile

Returns a numeric value indicating the pth percentile of the supplied database field or formula.

PthPercentile returns the "pth" percentile value, such as the value that equates to the tenth percentile of the report or group.

PthPercentile (n, f)

n – a numeric value (between 0 and 100). 5 returns the fifth percentile, 2 the second percentile, and so forth.

f – the database or formula field to summarize for the entire report. This must be a numeric field.

PthPercentile (n, f1, f2)

n – a numeric value (between 0 and 100). 5 returns the fifth percentile, 2 the second percentile, and so forth.

f1 – the database or formula field to summarize for the entire report. This must be a numeric field.

f2 – the database or formula field indicating the group you wish to summarize for. An existing group on the report must be based on this field.

PthPercentile (n, f1, f2, s)

n – a numeric value (between 0 and 100). 5 returns the fifth percentile, 2 the second percentile, and so forth.

f1 – the database or formula field to summarize for the entire report. This must be a numeric field.

f2 – the database or formula field indicating the group you wish to summarize for. An existing group on the report must be based on this field.

s – a string value indicating how often to "change" the summary for Boolean, date, or date-time grouping. See **Boolean Conditions**, **Date Conditions**, and **Time Conditions** later in this appendix for available choices.

```
PthPercentile (5, {Sales.Amount})
```

returns the sales amount equating to the fifth percentile for the entire report.

```
PthPercentile (5, {Sales.Amount}, {Sales.Date}, "monthly")
```

returns the sales amount equating to the fifth percentile for the sales date group, summarized for each month.

StdDev

Returns a numeric value indicating the standard deviation of the supplied database field or formula.

StdDev (f)

f – the database or formula field to summarize for the entire report. This must be a numeric field.

StdDev (f1, f2)

f1 – the database or formula field to summarize for a report group. This must be a numeric field.

f2 – the database or formula field indicating the group you wish to summarize for. An existing group on the report must be based on this field.

StdDev (f1, f2, s)

f1 – the database or formula field to summarize for a report group. This must be a numeric field.

f2 – the database or formula field indicating the group you wish to summarize for. An existing group on the report must be based on this field.

s – a string value indicating how often to "change" the summary for Boolean, date, or date-time grouping. See **Boolean Conditions**, **Date Conditions**, and **Time Conditions** later in this appendix for available choices.

```
StdDev({Sales.Amount})
```

returns the standard deviation of sales amounts for the entire report.

```
StdDev({Sales.Amount}, {Sales.Date}, "monthly")
```

returns the standard deviation of sales amounts for the sales date group, summarized for each month.

Sum

Returns a numeric value indicating the sum of the supplied database field or formula.

Sum (f)

f – the database or formula field to summarize for the entire report. This must be a numeric field.

Sum (f1, f2)

f1 – the database or formula field to summarize for a report group. This must be a numeric field.
f2 – the database or formula field indicating the group you wish to summarize for. An existing group on the report must be based on this field.

Sum (f1, f2, s)

f1 – the database or formula field to summarize for a report group. This must be a numeric field.
f2 – the database or formula field indicating the group you wish to summarize for. An existing group on the report must be based on this field.
s – a string value indicating how often to "change" the summary for Boolean, date, or date-time grouping. See **Boolean Conditions**, **Date Conditions**, and **Time Conditions** later in this appendix for available choices.

```
Sum({Sales.Amount})
```

returns the sum of sales amounts for the entire report.

```
Sum({Sales.Amount}, {Sales.Date}, "monthly")
```

returns the sum of sales amounts for the sales date group, summarized for each month.

Variance

Returns a numeric value indicating the variance of the supplied database field or formula.

Variance (f)

f – the database or formula field to summarize for the entire report. This must be a numeric field.

Variance (f1, f2)

f1 – the database or formula field to summarize for a report group. This must be a numeric field.

f2 – the database or formula field indicating the group you wish to summarize for. An existing group on the report must be based on this field.

Variance (f1, f2, s)

f1 – the database or formula field to summarize for a report group. This must be a numeric field.

f2 – the database or formula field indicating the group you wish to summarize for. An existing group on the report must be based on this field.

s – a string value indicating how often to "change" the summary for Boolean, date, or date-time grouping. See **Boolean Conditions**, **Date Conditions**, and **Time Conditions** later in this appendix for available choices.

```
Variance({Sales.Amount})
```

returns the variance of sales amounts for the entire report.

```
Variance({Sales.Amount}, {Sales.Date}, "monthly")
```

returns the variance of sales amounts for the sales date group, summarized for each month.

WeightedAverage

Returns a numeric value indicating the average of the supplied database field or formula, given a weight by another field or formula.

WeightedAverage (f1, f2)

f1 – the database or formula field to summarize for the entire report. This must be a numeric field.

f2 – the database or formula field to use as the weight.

WeightedAverage (f1, f2, f3)

f1 – the database or formula field to summarize for a report group. This must be a numeric field.
f2 – the database or formula field to use as the weight.
f3 – the database or formula field indicating the group you wish to summarize for. An existing group on the report must be based on this field.

WeightedAverage (f1, f2, f3, s)

f1 – the database or formula field to summarize for a report group. This must be a numeric field.
f2 – the database or formula field to use as the weight.
f3 – the database or formula field indicating the group you wish to summarize for. An existing group on the report must be based on this field.
s – a string value indicating how often to "change" the summary for Boolean, date, or date-time grouping. See **Boolean Conditions**, **Date Conditions**, and **Time Conditions** later in this appendix for available choices.

```
WeightedAverage({Sales.Amount},{Sales.Goal})
```

returns the average of sales amounts weighted by goal for the entire report.

```
WeightedAverage({Sales.Amount}, {Sales.Date}, "monthly")
```

returns the average of sales amounts weighted by goal for the sales date group, summarized for each month.

Boolean Conditions

The following string values can be used in a summary function when using a Boolean group field.

- "any change"

- "change to No"

- "change to Yes"

- "every No"

- "every Yes"

- "next is No"

- "next is Yes"

Date Conditions

The following string values can be used in a summary function when using a date or date-time group field.

- ■ "daily"
- ■ "semimonthly"
- ■ "semiannually"
- ■ "monthly"
- ■ "quarterly"
- ■ "biweekly"
- ■ "weekly"
- ■ "annually"

Time Conditions

The following string values can be used in a summary function when using a time or date-time group field.

- ■ "by AMPM"
- ■ "by hour"
- ■ "by minute"
- ■ "by second"

Functions: Type Conversion

This category of functions is used to convert from one data type to another. These functions are modeled after functions of the same name found in Visual Basic and Visual Basic for Applications.

CBool

Returns a Boolean (true/false) conversion of the source field.

CBool will return False for a value of 0 (zero). Otherwise, CBool returns True.

CBool (n)

n – a numeric value.

```
CBool(-1)
```

returns True.

CCur

Returns a currency value.

CCur (v)

v – a value of number, currency, or string data type.

```
CCur ("1125.13894")
```

returns $1,125.14 as a currency value.

CDate

Returns a date value.

CDate is functionally equivalent to Date and DateValue. See **DateValue** for details.

CDateTime

Returns a date-time value.

CDateTime is functionally equivalent to DateTime and DateTimeValue. See **DateTimeValue** for details.

CDbl

Returns a numeric value.

CDbl is functionally equivalent to ToNumber. See **ToNumber** for details.

CStr

Converts any nonstring data type to a string value.

CStr is functionally equivalent to ToText, including returning the same result and accepting the same arguments. See **ToText** for complete information.

CTime

Returns a time value.

CTime is functionally equivalent to Time and TimeValue. See **TimeValue** for details.

Operators: Arithmetic

This category of operators performs standard arithmetic functions, such as addition, subtraction, and so forth.

Add (+)

Adds two numbers.

n1 + n2

n1 – a numeric value.
n2 – a numeric value.

```
2 + 2
```

returns 4.00.

Divide (/)

Divides two numbers.

n1 / n2

n1 – a numeric value.
n2 – a numeric value.

```
10 / 5
```

returns 2.00.

Exponentiate (^)

Raises a number to a power.

n1 ^ n2

n1 – a numeric value.

n2 – a numeric value to raise *n1* to the power of.

```
5 ^ 2
```

returns 25.00.

Integer Divide (\)

Divides two numbers, returning an integer result.

n1 \ n2

n1 – a numeric value.
n2 – a numeric value.

```
10 \ 3
```

returns 3.00, contrasted with:

```
10 / 3
```

which returns 3.33.

Modulus

Performs division on two numeric values and returns the remainder of the division rather than the result of the division.

    Use the Mod function for particular situations where the remainder of numeric division is required, rather than the actual result. For example, this operator can be used with the RecordNumber function in a conditional formatting formula to shade every other details section.

n1 Mod n2

n1 – a numeric value
n2 – a numeric value

```
If RecordNumber Mod 2 = 0 Then crSilver Else crNoColor
```

when supplied as a conditional formula for the Details section background color, shades every other details section silver.

NOTE *Crystal Reports also includes the Remainder function, which performs a similar operation.*

Multiply (*)

Multiplies two numbers.

n1 * n2

n1 – a numeric value.
n2 – a numeric value.

```
5 * 4
```

returns 20.00.

Negate (–)

Returns the negative equivalent of a number.

–n

n – a numeric value.

```
-14
```

returns –14.00.

```
-{GLDetails.DRAmount}
```

returns a positive debit amount if the DRAmount field is coded as a negative number in the database.

Percent (%)

Calculates the percentage one number is of another number.

n1 % n2

n1 – a numeric value.
n2 – a numeric value.

```
5 % 20
```

returns 25.00.

```
{Sales.Amount} % Sum({Sales.Amount},{Sales.Rep})
```

returns the percentage each individual sale is of a sales rep's total sales.

Subtract (−)

Subtracts one number from another.

n1 − n2

n1 − a numeric value.
n2 − a numeric value.

```
25 - 10
```

returns 15.00.

Operators: Array

This set of operators pertain to arrays. An *array* is a collection of data items stored in a single "bucket," such as a single variable. If an array contains 15 items, it is said to have 15 *elements*. Arrays can contain any supported Crystal Reports data type, such as number, string, date-time, and so forth.

In

Returns a Boolean (true/false) value indicating whether a single value is in an array.

v In a

v − a value of the same data type as the *a* array.
a − an array.

```
5 In [1,3,5,7,9]
```

returns True.

```
If {Customer.Region} In ["CO","MT","UT","WY"] Then
    "Rocky Mountain Region"
Else
    "Rest of Country"
```

returns one of two strings based on the existence of a database field in the supplied string literal array.

Make Array

Creates an array of values.

This is functionally equivalent to the MakeArray function. See **MakeArray** in the Functions – Arrays section for details.

Redim

"Resets" an existing array variable to an empty state with a specified number of elements.

Redim a (n)

a – an existing array variable.
n – a positive number.

```
WhilePrintingRecords;
StringVar Array Beatles;
Redim Beatles [4];
Beatles[1]
```

declares an existing string array and resets it to a string array with four elements, each containing an empty string. The formula returns an empty string to the report (the first element of the reset array).

Redim Preserve

"Resizes" an existing array variable with a specified number of elements, retaining existing contents of the array variable.

Redim Preserve a (n)

a – an existing array variable.
n – a positive number.

```
WhilePrintingRecords;
StringVar Array Beatles;
Redim Preserve Beatles [8];
Beatles[1]
```

declares an existing string array and expands it to contain eight elements, retaining any existing data in the array. The formula returns "John" to the report (the existing data in the first element of the array).

Subscript ([])
Extracts an individual element of an array.

a[n]
a – an array value.
n – a numeric value or range indicating the element or elements to extract.

```
WhilePrintingRecords;
StringVar Array Beatles;
Beatles[3]
```

returns "George", the third element of the Beatles array.

Operators: Boolean

This set of operators pertain to Boolean (true/false) values, functions, and expressions.

And
Returns true if both associated Boolean values are true.

b1 And b2
b1 – a Boolean value or expression.
b2 – a Boolean value or expression.

```
2 + 2 = 4 And 10 / 2 = 5
```

returns True.

```
If {Customer.Region} = "CA" And
    {Customer.Last Year's Sales} > 50000 Then
    "California Bonus Customer"
Else
    "Other Customer"
```

returns "California Bonus Customer" if both Boolean expressions in the If test are true.

Eqv (Logical equivalence)

Returns true if both associated Boolean values are the same.

b1 Eqv b2

b1 – a Boolean value or expression.
b2 – a Boolean value or expression.

```
2 + 2 = 4 Eqv 10 / 2 = 5
```

returns True.

```
2 + 2 = 8 Eqv 10 / 2 = 5
```

returns False.

```
2 + 2 = 8 Eqv 10 / 2 = 1
```

returns True.

Imp (Logical implication)

Returns true if both associated Boolean values are the same, or if the second value is true while the first value is false.

b1 Imp b2

b1 – a Boolean value or expression.
b2 – a Boolean value or expression.

```
2 + 2 = 4 Imp 10 / 2 = 5
```

returns True.

```
2 + 2 = 8 Imp 10 / 2 = 1
```

returns True.

```
2 + 2 = 4 Imp 10 / 2 = 1
```

returns False.

```
2 + 2 = 8 Imp 10 / 2 = 5
```

returns True.

Not

Reverses the Boolean value (true becomes false and false becomes true).

Not requires a Boolean value or expression to follow it. As such, you may need to enclose a Boolean expression in parentheses for Not to evaluate properly.

Not b

b – a Boolean value or expression.

```
Not (2 + 2 = 4)
```

returns False.

```
Not 2 + 2 = 4
```

results in an error, as Not expects the first occurrence of the number 2 to be Boolean.

```
If Not InRepeatedGroupHeader Then "New Group Starts Here"
```

returns the "new group" string if InRepeatedGroupHeader is false.

Or

Returns true if either or both associated Boolean values are true.

b1 Or b2

b1 – a Boolean value or expression.
b2 – a Boolean value or expression.

```
2 + 2 = 4 Or 10 / 2 = 1
```

returns True.

```
If {Customer.Last Year's Sales} > 50000 Or
   {Customer.Last Year's Sales} < 0 Then
    "Customer needs attention"
```

Operators: Boolean

```
Else
    "Normal customer"
```

returns "Customer needs attention" if either Boolean expression in the If test is true.

Xor (Logical exclusion)

Returns true if the associated Boolean values return opposite values (one true, the other false).

b1 Xor b2

b1 – a Boolean value or expression.
b2 – a Boolean value or expression.

```
2 + 2 = 4 Xor 10 / 2 = 6
```

returns True.

```
2 + 2 = 5 Xor 10 / 2 = 5
```

returns True.

```
2 + 2 = 4 Xor 10 / 2 = 5
```

returns False.

Operators: Comparisons

This category of operators compares values to each other. You may combine comparison operators together with other Boolean operators, such as And, Or, and Not.

Equal (=)

Returns a Boolean (true/false) value indicating whether the two supplied values are equal to each other.

v1 = v2

v1 – a value of any supported data type.
v2 – a value of the same data type as *v1*.

```
10 = 10
```

returns True.

```
If {Sales.State} = "CO" Then "Colorado"
```

returns "Colorado" if the state field is equal to "CO".

Greater or Equal (>=)

Returns a Boolean (true/false) value indicating whether the first supplied value is greater than or equal to the second value.

This operator compares strings from the perspective of sort order.

v1 >= v2

v1 – a value of any supported data type.
v2 – a value of the same data type as *v1*.

```
"abc" >= "wyz"
```

returns False, based on string sort order.

```
If {Sales.Amount} >= 5000 Then "Great Order"
```

returns "Great Order" if the sale amount is exactly $5,000, or anything greater than $5,000.

Greater Than (>)

Returns a Boolean (true/false) value indicating whether the first supplied value is greater than the second value.

This operator compares strings from the perspective of sort order.

v1 > v2

v1 – a value of any supported data type.
v2 – a value of the same data type as *v1*.

```
#1/1/2000# > #1/1/1999#
```

returns True.

```
If {Sales.Amount} > 10000 Then "Eligible for Bonus"
```

returns "Eligible for Bonus" if the sale amount is greater than $10,000. If the amount is exactly $10,000 or less, an empty string is returned.

Less or Equal (<=)

Returns a Boolean (true/false) value indicating whether the first supplied value is less than or equal to the second value.

This operator compares strings from the perspective of sort order.

v1 <= v2

v1 – a value of any supported data type.
v2 – a value of the same data type as *v1*.

```
100 <= 100
```

returns True.

```
If {Sales.Amount} <= 100 Then "Small Order"
```

returns "Small Order" if the sale amount is exactly $100, or anything less than $100.

Less Than (<)

Returns a Boolean (true/false) value indicating whether the first supplied value is less than the second value.

This operator compares strings from the perspective of sort order.

v1 < v2

v1 – a value of any supported data type.
v2 – a value of the same data type as *v1*.

```
#1/1/2000# < #1/1/1999#
```

returns False.

```
If {Sales.Amount} < 100 Then "Improved Performance Required"
```

returns "Improved Performance Required" if the sale amount is less than $100. If the amount is exactly $100 or greater, an empty string is returned.

Not Equal (<>)

Returns a Boolean (true/false) value indicating whether the two supplied values are not equal to each other.

v1 <> v2

v1 – a value of any supported data type.
v2 – a value of the same data type as *v1*.

```
10 <> 15
```

returns True.

```
If {Sales.State} <> "CO" Then "Out-Of-State Sale"
```

returns "Out-Of-State Sale" if the state field is something other than "CO".

> NOTE   *Case sensitivity of string comparisons is based on the database case sensitivity setting in File | Report Options (applies to the current report only) and File | Options (applies to all new reports in the future).*

Operators: Control Structures

This category of operators might well exist in a separate section of the Formula Editor called "programming constructs." However, as they don't take "arguments" per se, they've been placed in the Operator tree. These operators are most familiar to computer programmers, as they duplicate typical programming logic and flow within a single Crystal Reports formula.

Do While

Loops through formula logic while a condition is true.

Do While differs from While Do in regards to when the loop condition is evaluated. Do While evaluates the loop condition *after* a loop iteration (so that at least one loop will always occur). While Do evaluates the condition *before* a loop iteration (the logic within the loop may not occur at all if the condition is immediately false).

Do <formula logic> While b

b – a Boolean value or expression.

```
NumberVar Counter := 1;
StringVar Accum;
do
(   Accum := Accum + "-";
    Counter := Counter + 1)
while Counter < 100;
Accum
```

returns a string containing 99 dash characters (the loop iterated while the counter was less than 100—once it reached 100, the loop did not repeat).

> **NOTE** *If you wish to include more than one Crystal Reports statement within the loop, separate statements with a semicolon and surround all statements (between the Do and While) with parentheses.*

Exit For

Exits a For loop before its normal conclusion.

Exit For

```
NumberVar Counter;
StringVar Accum;
for Counter := 1 to 1000 step 2 do
(
    Accum := Accum & ToText(Counter);
    If Len(Accum) > 245 Then Exit For;
);
Accum
```

returns the string in the Accum variable consisting of "1.003.005.007.009.00" and so forth. Within the loop, the Accum variable is tested for a length exceeding 245 characters and the loop is exited if this occurs.

Exit While

Exits a Do or While loop before its normal conclusion.

Exit While

```
NumberVar Counter := 1;
StringVar Accum;
do
(    Accum := Accum + "-";
     Counter := Counter + 1;
     If Length(Accum) = 100 Then Exit While)
while True;
Accum
```

returns a string containing 100 dash characters (the loop iterates until the length of the Accum variable reaches 100 characters and the Exit While statement executes).

For

Loops through formula logic a specified number of times.

For v := n1 To n2 Step n3 Do

v – a numeric variable that the loop will increment as it progresses.

n1 – a numeric value indicating the beginning value that will be assigned to *v* when the loop starts.

n2 – a numeric value indicating the ending value in *v* that will stop the loop.

n3 – a numeric value indicating the amount to increment *v* every time the loop iterates. This value, as well as the Step keyword that precedes it, are optional. If omitted, *v* is incremented by 1 with each loop iteration.

```
NumberVar Counter;
StringVar Accum;
for Counter := 1 to 100 step 2 do
(
     Accum := Accum & ToText(Counter);
);
Accum
```

returns contents of the Accum variable, consisting of the string "13579111315" and so forth, through "99". The Counter variable increments from 1 to 100, incrementing by 2 every time the loop iterates.

> NOTE
>
> *If you wish to include more than one Crystal Reports statement within the loop, separate statements with a semicolon and surround all statements (after the Do keyword) with parentheses.*

If Then Else

Performs a Boolean test, returning one value if the test is true and an alternate value if the test is false.

If b Then v1 Else v2

b – a Boolean expression (typically using comparison operators discussed earlier in this section).
v1 – a value of any supported data type that is returned if *b* evaluates to True.
v1 – a value of the same data type as *v1* that is returned if *b* evaluates to False. This value, and the Else keyword that precedes it, is optional.

```
If {Sales.State} = "CO" Then
    "Sales Tax Required"
Else
    "No Tax"
```

returns the string "Sales Tax Required" if the Boolean expression after If evaluates to true. Otherwise, the formula returns "No Tax".

```
If {Sales.Amount} > 5000 Then "Bonus Order"
```

returns "Bonus Order" if the sales amount exceeds $5,000. Otherwise, an empty string is returned.

Option Loop

Specifies how many iterations a loop should go through before an error is returned.

By default, Crystal Reports stops loop processing and returns an error if a loop iterates 100,000 times. This behavior prevents infinite loops from occurring. If you wish to lower the maximum number of iterations, use Option Loop.

Option Loop n

n – a numeric value indicating the number of loop iterations that will occur before an error is returned.

Option Loop must be the first statement in the formula.

```
NumberVar Counter;
Do
    Counter := Counter + 1
While True
```

will iterate 100,000 time before returning an error.

```
Option Loop 100;
NumberVar Counter;
Do
    Counter := Counter + 1
While True
```

will iterate 100 times before returning an error.

Select Case

Returns one of several available values based on a series of conditions.

Select Case duplicates the capabilities of sophisticated If-Then-Else logic. However, Select Case is often easier to understand and maintain than complex If-Then-Else formulas.

Select e Case v1: <formula logic> Case v2 <formula logic>…: Default: <formula logic>

e – a value or expression of any data type to test.
v1 – a value or "list" of values (separated by commas) matching in data type to *e* to test against *e*.
v2 – an additional value or "list" of values (separated by commas) matching in data type to *e* to test against *e*.

Additional pairs of Case/<formula logic> combinations may be added. The Default keyword and colon are optional. Formula logic after each Case statement must return the same data type as all other formula logic.

```
Select {Sales.State}
    Case "OR","ID","MT","WA":
        "Northwest"
    Case "CA","AZ","TX","NM":
        "Southwest"
```

```
Case "ME","MA","NH","NY":
    "Northeast"
Case "FL","NC","GA","SC":
    "Southeast"
Default:
    "Rest of Country"
```

examines the state field and begins testing it against each Case statement. Once it finds a match, it returns the value following the case statement. If no matches are found, the value following the default statement is returned. Were the Default keyword, colon, and "Rest of Country" string literal to be left out, the formula would return an empty string if no matches were found.

```
Select {Sales.LastYearRevenue}
    Case Is < 100:
        "Improved Performance Needed"
    Case 100 To 1000:
        "Average Year"
    Case Is > 1000:
        "Excellent Year"
```

examines the Last Year Revenue field and begins testing against the ranges specified in each Case statement, returning the appropriate string following the Case statement that matches. No Default keyword is provided, as any number will fall into one of the three Case statements. Were a number to somehow not fall into one of the existing Case statements, a zero would be returned.

While Do

Loops through formula logic while a condition is true.

While Do differs from Do While in regards to when the loop condition is evaluated. Do While evaluates the loop condition *after* a loop iteration (so that at least one loop will always occur). While Do evaluates the condition *before* a loop iteration (the logic within the loop may not occur at all if the condition is immediately false).

While b <formula logic> Do

b – a Boolean value or expression.

```
NumberVar Counter := 1;
StringVar Accum;
While Counter < 100 Do
```

```
(   Accum := Accum + "-";
    Counter := Counter + 1
);
Accum
```

returns a string containing 99 dash characters (the loop iterated while the counter was less than 100—once it reached 100, the loop did not repeat).

> **NOTE**   *If you wish to include more than one Crystal Reports statement within the loop, separate statements with a semicolon and surround all statements (between the Do and While) with parentheses.*

Operators: Conversion

A single operator exists to convert to one data type from another.

Currency ($)

Converts a numeric value to a currency value.
The CCur function can also be used to convert from another data type to currency.

$

```
$100
```

returns $100.00.

```
${Sales.Amount} * 1.1
```

returns 10 percent above the sales amount as a currency value.

> **NOTE**   *Crystal Reports prohibits both values in a multiplication formula from being currency—one or the other can be, but not both. If necessary, you'll need to convert one currency value to a numeric value with ToNumber or CDbl.*

Operators: Other

This category of operators contains, in essence, operators that don't fit in any other category and perform miscellaneous functions.

Assignment (:=)

Assigns a value to a variable.

In Crystal syntax, don't confuse the assignment operator (:=) with the equals comparison operator (=). In Basic syntax, equals (=) acts as both assignment and equals comparison.

var := v

var – a previously declared variable name.
v – a value or expression of the same data type as *var*.

```
SalesRepBonus := SalesRepBonus + 1
```

adds 1 to the value already in the SalesRepBonus variable and places the result back into the SalesRepBonus variable.

```
NumberVar SalesRepBonus := 0
```

declares a number variable named SalesRepBonus and assigns it a value of zero in a single statement.

Comment (//)

Treats any text following the two slashes as a comment.

Basic Syntax uses the apostrophe (') or the word Rem to indicate a comment. Crystal Report 9 allows you to add comment slashes to multiple formula lines at once by highlighting them and clicking the Comment/Uncomment button in the Formula Workshop toolbar.

//

```
//The following formula calculates
//commission based on sale amount
Select {Orders.Order Amount}
    Case Is < 100:
        .01
    Case 100 to 1000:
        .05
    Case Is > 1000:
        .1
```

The first two lines of the formula are ignored by the Formula Editor when evaluating the formula logic.

> **NOTE**
>
> *If you are troubleshooting a formula, you may prefer to simply "comment out" certain formula lines that you wish to later use again. For example, you may be working on five different methods of calculating a result. By adding or removing two slashes in front of the various formula lines, you may try various methods of calculations without having to delete and retype each line.*

Date-time literal (#)

Returns a date-time value from the supplied string.

#s#

s – a string that can be interpreted as a date, time, or date-time combination.

```
#1/1/2000 10:15 am#
```

returns a date-time value of 1/1/2000 10:15:00AM.

```
#Sep 10, 02#
```

returns a date-time value of 9/10/2002 12:00:00AM.

> **NOTE**
>
> *Crystal Reports is fairly creative in what it will interpret as date or time material between the # characters. If the string can't be understood, an error will occur.*

Parentheses

Used to force evaluation of formula expressions in a certain order.

Parentheses allow you to force calculations to occur in other than the default *order of precedence* (exponentiation, then multiplication/division left to right, then addition/subtraction left to right). In Basic syntax, parentheses are also used to delimit array subscripts.

(<expression>)

```
10 + 10 * 2
```

returns 30.00. The order of precedence causes the multiplication to be done first, then the addition.

```
(10 + 10) * 2
```

returns 40.00. The parentheses force the addition to be performed first, then the multiplication.

Operators: Pattern

This set of operators allow partial string matches to be evaluated.

Like

Returns a Boolean (true/false) value based on a partial string match.

Like uses DOS-style "wildcards" (the asterisk and question mark) to determine if the source string contains the characters specified in the wildcard-based mask. This is helpful for checking for partial text matches. This operator is similar to the LooksLike function.

s1 Like s2

s1 – the source string to be searched.
s2 – the mask string to search against. The mask can include a question mark wildcard to indicate a single-character substitution and/or an asterisk to indicate a multiple-character substitution.

```
"George Peck" Like "G?orge*"
```

returns True.

StartsWith

Returns a Boolean (true/false) value if leading characters match the source string.

s1 StartsWith s2

s1 – the source string to be searched.
s2 – the characters to search for as the first characters of *s1*.

```
"George Peck" StartsWith "Ge"
```

returns True.

NOTE *Case sensitivity of string comparisons is based on the database case sensitivity setting in File | Report Options (applies to the current report only) and File | Options (applies to all new reports in the future).*

Operators: Ranges

These operators either create various ranges of values or test existing ranges. A *range* of values consists of beginning and ending values, and every value in between (some ranges can have no beginning and/or ending value—in other words, the range can be "everything above x" or "everything below y").

Both End Points Excluded Range

Creates a range of values between the two endpoints, not including the endpoints.

v1 _To_ v2

v1 – a value of any data type to act as the lower endpoint.
v2 – a value of the same data type as *v1* to act as the upper endpoint.

```
1 In (1 _to_ 100)
```

returns False, as the lower endpoint (1) is not included in the range.

```
99 In (1 _to_ 100)
```

returns True.

In Range

Returns a Boolean (true/false) value indicating whether the single value is in the range.

v In r

v – a single value of any supported data type.
r – a range value or variable of the same data type as *v*.

```
5 In (1 To 100)
```

returns True.

```
If {Parts.PartNo} In (1000 to 5000) Then
   "Taxable"
Else
   "Non-taxable"
```

returns the string "Taxable" if the part number is in the range of 1000 to 5000 inclusive.

Left End Point Excluded Range

Creates a range of values between the two endpoints, not including the first endpoint.

v1 _To v2

v1 – a value of any data type to act as the lower endpoint.
v2 – a value of the same data type as *v1* to act as the upper endpoint.

```
1 In (1 _to 100)
```

returns False, as the lower endpoint (1) is not included in the range.

```
100 In (1 _to 100)
```

returns True, as the upper endpoint (100) is included in the range.

Make Range

Creates a range of values between, and including, the two endpoints.

v1 To v2

v1 – a value of any data type to act as the lower endpoint.
v2 – a value of the same data type as *v1* to act as the upper endpoint.

```
1 In (1 to 100)
```

returns True.

```
100 In (1 to 100)
```

returns True.

Right End Point Excluded Range

Creates a range of values between the two endpoints, not including the second endpoint.

v1 To_ v2

v1 – a value of any data type to act as the lower endpoint.

v2 – a value of the same data type as *v1* to act as the upper endpoint.

```
1 In (1 to_ 100)
```

returns True, as the lower endpoint (1) is included in the range.

```
100 In (1 to_ 100)
```

returns False, as the upper endpoint (100) is not included in the range.

UpFrom

Creates a range of values including a lower endpoint upward, with no upper endpoint.
　　Is >= v is functionally equivalent to UpFrom.

upFrom v

v – a value of any data type to act as the lower endpoint.

```
99999999 In UpFrom 100
```

returns True.

```
HasUpperBound (UpFrom 100)
```

returns False (the HasUpperBound function evaluates whether the supplied range has an upper endpoint).

Up From But Not Including

Creates a range of values from a lower endpoint upward (the lower endpoint not being included), with no upper endpoint.
　　Is > v is functionally equivalent to UpFrom_.

upFrom_ v

v – a value of any data type to act as the lower endpoint.

```
100 In UpFrom_ 100
```

returns False (the lower endpoint is not included in the range).

```
HasUpperBound (UpFrom_ 100)
```

returns False (the HasUpperBound function evaluates whether the supplied range has an upper endpoint).

UpTo

Creates a range of values from an upper endpoint downward (including the upper endpoint) with no lower endpoint.
Is <= v is functionally equivalent to UpTo.

upTo v

v – a value of any data type to act as the lower endpoint.

```
-9999999 In UpTo 100
```

returns True.

```
HasLowerBound (UpTo 100)
```

returns False (the HasLowerBound function evaluates whether the supplied range has a lower endpoint).

Up To But Not Including

Creates a range of values from an upper endpoint downward (not including the upper endpoint) with no lower endpoint.
Is < v is functionally equivalent to UpTo_.

upTo_ v

v – a value of any data type to act as the lower endpoint.

```
100 In UpTo_ 100
```

returns False (the upper endpoint is not included in the range).

```
HasLowerBound (UpTo_ 100)
```

returns False (the HasLowerBound function evaluates whether the supplied range has a lower endpoint).

Operators: Scope

This set of operators is used when declaring variables (see "Operators: Variable Declaration" later in this appendix). These operators determine how long a variable retains its value during report processing.

Global

Forces a variable to retain its value in this formula, and all other formulas in the current report (but not subreports).

In Crystal Syntax, this is the default scope for variable declarations that do not include a scope keyword.

Global t v

t – a variable declaration statement.
v – a valid variable name.

```
Global NumberVar BonusCount
```

declares a numeric variable called BonusCount that will retain its value throughout the entire report, but not in any subreports.

```
NumberVar BonusCount
```

is functionally equivalent to the previous declaration, as Global is the default variable scope.

Local

Forces a variable to retain its value in this formula only.

In Basic Syntax, this is the default scope for variable declarations that do not include a scope keyword.

Local t v

t – a variable declaration statement.
v – a valid variable name.

```
Local NumberVar BonusCount
```

Operators: Scope

declares a numeric variable called BonusCount that will retain its value only during the calculation of this formula. If BonusCount is declared in any other formulas, it will contain zero.

Shared

Forces a variable to retain its value in this formula, in all other formulas in the current report, and in all subreports.

Shared t v

t – a variable declaration statement.
v – a valid variable name.

```
Shared NumberVar BonusCount
```

declares a numeric variable called BonusCount that will retain its value throughout the entire report and in all subreports.

Operators: Strings

This set of operators applies to string manipulation, such as string "concatenation" (the process of combining two or more strings into a single string).

Concatenate (& or +)

Concatenates (combines) strings into a single string.
The + operator requires that surrounding values be strings, while the & operator performs an implicit conversion to string of all surrounding values.

s1 + s2

s1 – a string value.
s2 – a string value.

```
"Page Number: " + PageNumber
```

returns an error, as the PageNumber function returns a numeric value.

```
"Page Number: " + ToText(PageNumber,0)
```

returns "Page Number: 1" if the first page of the report is printing.

v1 & v2

v1 – a value of any data type.
v2 – a value of any data type.

```
"Page Number: " & PageNumber
```

returns "Page Number: 1.00" if the first page of the report is printing, performing an implicit conversion of PageNumber to a string data type.

```
"Page Number: " & ToText(PageNumber,0)
```

returns "Page Number: 1" if the first page of the report is printing.

NOTE *When using the & operator to concatenate strings, you may still need to use ToText or CStr to control how values are formatted when they are concatenated.*

In String

Returns a Boolean value (true/false) based on if the first string is contained in the second string.

s1 In s2

s1 – a string value to search for in *s2*.
s2 – the source string to search.

```
"eor" in "George"
```

returns True.

```
If "(303)" In {Customer.Phone} Then "Denver Area Code"
```

returns the string "Denver Area Code" if the characters "(303)" are contained anywhere in the customer phone database field. Otherwise, the formula returns an empty string.

Insert Empty String ("") (version 9 Function Tree only)

Inserts a pair of quotation marks in the formula.

In Crystal Reports versions prior to 9 (as well as in 9), you may simply type quotation mark pairs in directly.

""

```
StringVar BonusCustomer := ""
```

declares a string variable called BonusCustomer and sets it to contain an empty string.

Subscript []
Extracts a substring from a larger string.

s[n]
s – a string value.
n – a numeric value or range indicating the character or characters to extract.

```
"George Peck"[2 to 4]
```

returns "eor".

Operators: Variable Declarations

This category of operators is used to declare variables within formulas. Whenever a variable is used in any formula, it must first be declared using one of the following operators.

BooleanVar
Declares a Boolean (true/false) variable to contain an array or single value.

BooleanVar Array varname

BooleanVar varname

varname – a variable name that is not the same as any other Crystal Reports formula keyword, does not contain a space, and does not start with a number or certain special characters.

```
BooleanVar Array Workdays :=
   [False, True, True, True, True, True, False];
Workdays[DayOfWeek(CurrentDate)]
```

returns True if the CurrentDate is Monday through Friday. The formula declares a Boolean array variable containing seven elements and then extracts the element associated with the day of the week.

```
BooleanVar BonusReached;
If {Sales.Amount} > 5000 Then BonusReached := True
```

declares a Boolean variable and assigns it a value of True if a sales amount is exceeded.

CurrencyVar

Declares a currency variable to contain an array, array of ranges, range, or single value.

CurrencyVar Array varname

CurrencyVar Range Array varname

CurrencyVar Range varname

CurrencyVar varname

varname – a variable name that is not the same as any other Crystal Reports formula keyword, does not contain a space, and does not start with a number or certain special characters.

```
CurrencyVar Range GoodSales := upFrom 5000;
If {Sales.Amount} In GoodSales Then "Good Job"
```

declares a currency range variable and assigns it all values including and above $5,000. If a sale amount is included in the variable, "Good Job" is returned by the formula.

```
CurrencyVar HighAmount;
If {Sales.Amount} > HighAmount Then
    HighAmount := {Sales.Amount}
```

declares a currency variable. If the sales amount is higher than what's retained in the variable from previous records, the variable is assigned the value of the higher sales amount.

Operators: Variable Declarations

DateTimeVar

Declares a date-time variable to contain an array, array of ranges, range, or single value.

DateTimeVar Array varname

DateTimeVar Range Array varname

DateTimeVar Range varname

DateTimeVar varname

varname – a variable name that is not the same as any other Crystal Reports formula keyword, does not contain a space, and does not start with a number or certain special characters.

```
DateTimeVar Range WorkDays :=
     #6/2/2003 8:00am# To #6/6/2003 5:00pm#;
If Not ({Salary.WorkDate} In WorkDays) Then
    {Salary.DailyPay} + {Salary.OvertimePay}
Else
    {Salary.DailyPay}
```

declares a date-time range variable and assigns it a value of Monday at 8 A.M. through Friday at 5 P.M. The variable is then checked against a work date to determine if overtime should be added to an employee's pay.

```
DateTimeVar OutOfTolerance;
If {Meas.Sample Value} > {Standards.Sample} Then
   OutOfTolerance := {Meas.Sample Date Time}
```

declares a date-time variable and tests to see if a sample reading was out of tolerance. If so, the date-time that the exception occurred is assigned to the variable.

DateVar

Declares a date variable to contain an array, array of ranges, range, or single value.

DateVar Array varname

DateVar Range Array varname

DateVar Range varname

DateVar varname

varname – a variable name that is not the same as any other Crystal Reports formula keyword, does not contain a space, and does not start with a number or certain special characters.

```
DateVar Range Array CompanyHolidays :=
   [DateValue("1/1/2003") to DateValue("1/2/2003"),
    DateValue("2/17/2003"),DateValue("5/26/2003"),
    DateValue("7/4/2003"),DateValue("9/1/2003"),
    DateValue("11/27/2003") to DateValue("11/28/2003"),
    DateValue("12/25/2003") to DateValue("12/31/2003")];
If {Salary.WorkDate} In CompanyHolidays Then
    "Bonus Pay Required"
```

declares a date range array and sets it to the individual dates and date ranges that make up company holidays. The variable is then checked to see if a work day qualifies for bonus pay.

NumberVar

Declares a number variable to contain an array, array of ranges, range, or single value.

NumberVar Array varname

NumberVar Range Array varname

NumberVar Range varname

NumberVar varname

varname – a variable name that is not the same as any other Crystal Reports formula keyword, does not contain a space, and does not start with a number or certain special characters.

```
NumberVar SalesRepTotal;
If {Sales.Amount} > {SalesRep.BonusLevel} Then
    SalesRepTotal :=
        SalesRepTotal + {Sales.Amount}
```

declares a number variable and tests to see if a sales amount exceeded a bonus
level. If so, the variable is incremented by the amount of the sale.

```
NumberVar SalesRepTotal := 0
```

declares a number variable and resets it to zero in the same formula statement.

StringVar

**Declares a string variable to contain an array, array of ranges, range, or
single value.**

StringVar Array varname

StringVar Range Array varname

StringVar Range varname

StringVar varname

varname – a variable name that is not the same as any other Crystal Reports
formula keyword, does not contain a space, and does not start with a number
or certain special characters.

```
StringVar ShippersUsed;
If Not ({Orders.Ship Via} In ShippersUsed) Then
    ShippersUsed := ShippersUsed & {Orders.Ship Via} & ", "
```

declares a string variable. A test is performed to see if the shipper database field
is already contained in the variable. If not, the shipper database field is added to
what's already in the variable, concatenated with a comma and space.

```
StringVar Shippers;
Left(Shippers, Length(Shippers)-2)
```

declares a string variable and returns all but the right two characters of the variable to the report.

TimeVar

Declares a time variable to contain an array, array of ranges, range, or single value.

TimeVar Array varname

TimeVar Range Array varname

TimeVar Range varname

TimeVar varname

varname – a variable name that is not the same as any other Crystal Reports formula keyword, does not contain a space, and does not start with a number or certain special characters.

```
TimeVar Range WorkHours;
If DayOfWeek({Sales.Date}) In 2 to 6 Then
    WorkHours := TimeValue("9:00 am") To TimeValue("7:00 pm")
Else
    WorkHours := TimeValue("10:00 am") To TimeValue("5:00 pm");
"Store Hours: " & Minimum(WorkHours) &
             " to " & Maximum(WorkHours)
```

declares a time range variable. The day of the week is checked and the variable is given an hour range for weekdays or weekends. The formula returns a string extracting the lower bound and upper bound of the range.

NOTE   *Some of the previous examples illustrate the capability of declaring a variable and assigning it a value in the same formula statement.*

Index

INTERNATIONAL CONTACT INFORMATION

AUSTRALIA
McGraw-Hill Book Company Australia Pty. Ltd.
TEL +61-2-9900-1800
FAX +61-2-9878-8881
http://www.mcgraw-hill.com.au
books-it_sydney@mcgraw-hill.com

CANADA
McGraw-Hill Ryerson Ltd.
TEL +905-430-5000
FAX +905-430-5020
http://www.mcgraw-hill.ca

GREECE, MIDDLE EAST, & AFRICA
(Excluding South Africa)
McGraw-Hill Hellas
TEL +30-210-6560-990
TEL +30-210-6560-993
TEL +30-210-6560-994
FAX +30-210-6545-525

MEXICO (Also serving Latin America)
McGraw-Hill Interamericana Editores S.A. de C.V.
TEL +525-117-1583
FAX +525-117-1589
http://www.mcgraw-hill.com.mx
fernando_castellanos@mcgraw-hill.com

SINGAPORE (Serving Asia)
McGraw-Hill Book Company
TEL +65-6863-1580
FAX +65-6862-3354
http://www.mcgraw-hill.com.sg
mghasia@mcgraw-hill.com

SOUTH AFRICA
McGraw-Hill South Africa
TEL +27-11-622-7512
FAX +27-11-622-9045
robyn_swanepoel@mcgraw-hill.com

SPAIN
McGraw-Hill/Interamericana de España, S.A.U.
TEL +34-91-180-3000
FAX +34-91-372-8513
http://www.mcgraw-hill.es
professional@mcgraw-hill.es

UNITED KINGDOM, NORTHERN, EASTERN, & CENTRAL EUROPE
McGraw-Hill Education Europe
TEL +44-1-628-502500
FAX +44-1-628-770224
http://www.mcgraw-hill.co.uk
computing_europe@mcgraw-hill.com

ALL OTHER INQUIRIES Contact:
McGraw-Hill/Osborne
TEL +1-510-420-7700
FAX +1-510-420-7703
http://www.osborne.com
omg_international@mcgraw-hill.com